FORGIVENESS, RECONCILIATION,
AND MORAL COURAGE

STUDIES IN PRACTICAL THEOLOGY

Series Editors

Don S. Browning

James W. Fowler

Friedrich Schweitzer

Johannes A. van der Ven

FORGIVENESS, RECONCILIATION, AND MORAL COURAGE

*Motives and Designs for Ministry
in a Troubled World*

Robert L. Browning and Roy A. Reed

WILLIAM B. EERDMANS PUBLISHING COMPANY
GRAND RAPIDS, MICHIGAN / CAMBRIDGE, U.K.

Wm. B. Eerdmans Publishing Co.

255 Jefferson Ave. S.E., Grand Rapids, Michigan 49503 /
P.O. Box 163, Cambridge CB3 9PU U.K.

Printed in the United States of America

08 07 06 05 04   7 6 5 4 3 2 1

Library of Congress Cataloging-in-Publication Data

Browning, Robert L.
    Forgiveness, reconciliation, and moral courage: motives and designs
    for ministry in a troubled world / Robert L. Browning and Roy A. Reed.
       p.   cm.
    Includes bibliographical references and index.
    ISBN 0-8028-2774-8 (pbk.: alk. paper)
  1. Reconciliation — Religious aspects — Christianity. 2. Forgiveness —
Religious aspects — Christianity.   I. Reed, Roy A.   II. Title.

BT738.27.B76   2004
234'.5 — dc22

                                        2004043326

www.eerdmans.com

Contents

Acknowledgments

In our study we have sought to bring together biblical, theological, and historical understandings with recent scientific research concerning the dynamics and results of specific expressions of forgiveness, reconciliation, and moral courage. In this process we have researched the literature but also have listened to laity and pastors concerning their perceptions of the real issues of ministry at the personal/interpersonal, social/political, and religious/interreligious levels.

In making our study we have received the assistance of many selfless people. Listening to laity from four representative congregations would not have been possible without the help of pastors David and Suzanne Hill, James Hickman, Lafayette Scales, Joseph Fete, and many willing and lively laity. We cannot thank them enough.

We are especially grateful to Dr. James Fowler, Candler Professor at Emory University and one of the four editors of the Studies in Practical Theology series. As our editor, Dr. Fowler was a warm and engaging guide and a source of sound recommendations.

We were given additional help in the form of honest feedback and suggestions from several friends who read the manuscript: Dr. Norma Cook Everist, Professor of Educational Ministries at Wartburg Theological Seminary, Dubuque, Iowa; The Rev. Richard Burnett, Rector of Trinity Episcopal Church, Columbus, Ohio; The Rev. Mark Trotter, Pastor Emeritus, First United Methodist Church, San Diego, California; Dr. Walter Dickhaut, former Dean, Bangor Theological School, Bangor, Maine; Dr. Richard Deats, past Executive Director and current magazine editor for the Fellowship of Reconciliation, Nyack, New York; Dr. Peter Browning, Chaplain and Associate Professor of Religion and Philosophy, Drury University, Springfield, Missouri.

One of the most exciting parts of our book is the case study of the creative approach to the Sacrament of Reconciliation developed by Mary Fran Cassidy, Director of Religious Education for St. Brigid of Kildare parish, Dublin, Ohio. Mary Fran's honest and cooperative spirit pointed us in fresh directions in the transfer of insights from Catholic to Protestant patterns.

Also, we thank Sister Rita Jane Radecki, Consultant for the Department of Religious Education, Catholic Diocese, Columbus, Ohio, for her kind assistance in identifying and making available Roman Catholic curriculum resources for the Sacrament of Reconciliation. She and her colleagues also gave us permission to use the Facilitator's Guide for the Reconciliation Workshop employed by St. Brigid of Kildare church, to be found in Appendix B.

We have been stimulated and challenged by the pioneering research on forgiveness and reconciliation of Dr. Robert Enright, Professor of Psychology, the University of Wisconsin, Madison. We are grateful to him for sharing with us early findings and for helping us get permission to use his research in our book.

As Emeritus faculty we have received strong support from our colleagues at The Methodist Theological School in Ohio. This is especially true of Ms. Datha Myers, Faculty Secretary, whose generous cooperation, on an over-time basis, made possible a manuscript we could present with confidence. Moreover, our dear friend, Dr. Joanmarie Smith, Emeritus Professor of Christian Education, gave us encouraging affirmation and thoughtful suggestions.

Of course, our book would not have been published without the acceptance and guidance of Jon Pott, Editor-in-Chief of Eerdmans, and his fine staff. We are pleased to have had this opportunity to work with all of them.

Finally, how can we express our gratitude for the love and patience we have received from our spouses, Jackie and Nancy? There is no adequate way; but we shall keep on trying!

ROBERT L. BROWNING
ROY A. REED

Introduction

"Forgive and you will be forgiven."

Luke 6:37

". . . and forgive us our trespasses as we forgive those who trespass against us."

Luke 11:4

"Love your enemies, do good to those who hate you, bless those who curse you. Pray for those who abuse you. . . . Do to others as you would have them do to you."

Luke 6:27-31

"All this is from God, who reconciled us to himself through Christ and has given us the ministry of reconciliation."

2 Corinthians 5:18

The purpose of this book is to bring alive the above and other biblical teachings concerning the power of forgiveness and the ministries of reconciliation and righteousness — both personal and social — in our contemporary life. It is our belief that the Christian church has a profound message

1

of forgiveness and reconciliation for a world suffering from many conflicts and divisions. These conflicts range from the unimaginable loss of life caused by the events of September 11, 2001, and the resulting worldwide war on terrorism to those found in our marriages and families, and to the conflicts between groups, nations, and religious communities — all crying for healing and unity of spirit and action. While it is true that God's loving, forgiving, reconciling spirit has broken through to hurting peoples well beyond the church's ministries of reconciliation, as will be highlighted below, we propose to identify and celebrate specific ways the church can be true to her calling. Especially, we shall focus on ways Christians can heal divisions by confessing their own unloving attitudes and actions, genuinely repent, request and receive forgiveness, sow the seeds of reconciliation, and work with others to bring justice and peace to our relationships in the world. In addition, we shall discuss ways the church can enter the circle early in life to build moral fiber in our children and youth and in all of the facets of their lives. We shall seek to clarify the church's role in building moral character, on the one hand, and in helping persons and groups deal with sin and moral failure through a spirit of contrition, repentance, forgiveness, reconciliation, and peace, on the other hand.

Theologian Karl Barth has been quoted often concerning how to proclaim the good news of the gospel for our world. He asserted that we should take the Bible in one hand and the local newspaper in the other in order to relate the story of God's love, forgiveness, and reconciliation to the specific life issues of people. Barth's picture of the correlation of the gospel and the lives of people was pre-Internet. Today, in order to be in touch with the issues of our time we must be open to the incredible information coming from the World Wide Web, the 150 plus channels of television, the videos, books, magazines, newsletters, commercials, music, art, theater, and cinema, and the interfacing almost instantly of all of the above. Also, we will be greatly helped in our assessment if we listen, face to face, to people in their varying settings to discern and clarify the differing ways they perceive their life concerns and the answers they are seeking.

When we look at the amazing mass of messages coming to us from these sources concerning forgiveness, reconciliation, and the quest for moral and spiritual renewal, we perceive a deep longing for a clear path to follow toward the reconciliation and healing of divided persons, families, political and religious groups, societies, and nations. We also perceive God's indwelling presence calling us into a future of love strong enough to get us through the valleys of mistrust, anxiety, hate, retaliation, and fear to an honest desire and commitment to move toward forgiveness and creative ministries of reconciliation.

As a way of introducing this book we shall present: (1) pictures of the explosion of stories about the power of forgiveness and reconciliation and the need for moral and spiritual strength seen in the multimedia of our day — at the personal/interpersonal, social/political, religious/interreligious, and research/study levels. (2) An outline of the result of our own research and reflection, including our effort to listen to the way members of the faith community in four representative denominations see the issues of forgiveness and reconciliation and the church's role in strengthening moral fiber of persons in our society. We shall then describe in some detail the chapters that follow and our rationale for addressing the issues we do. The latter is done in order for readers to be proactive in deciding how to get the most meaning out of our time together.

Pictures of the Explosion of Apologies, the Power of Forgiveness and Reconciliation, and the Need for Moral Renewal

Personal/Interpersonal

One of the most revealing phenomena concerning the human need for confession, repentance, and the quest for a clear conscience is to be found on the World Wide Web. Type in www.theconfessor.co.uk and up come blue-sky panels with a series of biblical passages about sin and the redemptive value of confession. Visitors are invited to type in their wrongdoings and their need for forgiveness. There is no cost, no request for money, no promise of forgiveness from God or others. Over 16,000 visitors a day unload their guilt and pain anonymously.[1] There are countless reports of individuals confessing publicly their sins of commission or omission and requesting forgiveness. The most visible, of course, was the belated confession of sin by President Clinton and his public request for forgiveness from his family, staff, cabinet, Monica Lewinsky and her family, and the American people. The story was carried in every form of media possible. On September 12, 1999, *The New York Times* quoted President Clinton as saying, "I have asked all for their forgiveness. More than sorrow is required, at least two more things. First, genuine repentance: a determination to change and to repair breaches of my own making. I have repented. Second, what my Bible calls a broken spirit: an understanding that I must have God's help to be the person that I want to be,

---

1. George Myers, Jr., "E-confessions: Good for Our Cybersouls?" *The Columbus Dispatch,* April 16, 2000, p. H3.

a willingness to give the forgiveness I seek. . . ." Regardless of the varying responses that are evoked by Clinton's actions, his confession, profession of repentance, and request for forgiveness became an international drama of the
importance of confession, contrition, repentance, forgiveness, and reconciliation. Most of all, the episode became a lightning rod, calling for moral recti-
tude most centrally in our personal and interpersonal lives and what that
quality can mean for our family, social, political, and religious lives as well.

The spontaneous movement toward public confession and the request
for forgiveness is widespread. One of the most unexpected illustrations comes
from Japanese elementary schools. Children are full participants in the maintenance of their school. They clean the halls and toilets of their schools and do
other tasks to help keep their environment positive. After working together they
have a period of evaluation, during which they are invited to confess their mistakes and omissions, followed by a discussion about how to improve. Schools in
the U.S. have experienced a spate of gun violence resulting in the death of several students and teachers. Columbine High School in Littleton, Colorado, the
high school in Paducah, Kentucky, and several others were in the news for
months. Accounts of the student killers and the students and teachers who were
killed or injured were often accompanied by fellow students' request for forgiveness of the perpetrators. On the other hand, considerable controversy resulted from the call for forgiveness of Timothy McVeigh, the convicted bomber,
by some family members of the 168 victims in the destruction of the federal
building in Oklahoma City, especially in the days before his execution.

While there were many reports of personal confession, requests for forgiveness, and stories of reconciliation, those coming from Murder Victims'
Families for Reconciliation are quite significant and arresting. The case of
Walter Everett is one of the most convincing in respect to the power of forgiveness. Walter Everett's son was murdered by one of his friends in a night of
partying. Everett was the pastor of a United Methodist church in Hartford,
Connecticut, at the time. He sought to understand how such a murder could
have occurred. In the process of his quest he wrote and finally visited the
young man who had committed the murder. Over time his Christian faith
strengthened him to the point that he forgave his son's friend who had committed the murder. Later, he agreed to stand by the young man at his parole
hearing. Finally, staying in touch with the young man after he was paroled, he
agreed to officiate at the offender's wedding in November 1994. Since then he
has taken a strong stand against capital punishment.[2]

---

2. Barbara Hood, ed., *Not in Our Name: Murder Victims' Families Speak Out against the
Death Penalty* (Atlantic, Va.: Murder Victims' Families for Reconciliation), p. 20.

Wanda Suber, an African American woman, is the head of an innovative rehabilitation program for prisoners in the state of Ohio. She is motivated in her work by the fact that she is a victim of a life-threatening gunshot wound inflicted on her by her father. In an explosion of rage her father killed her mother and a sister as well. Wanda Suber told her story to one of the authors, a story of how her Christian faith led her to be able to forgive her father and to commit herself to the process of forgiveness and reconciliation of prisoners who had committed murder. She leads the Bureau of Community Service. In her program, offenders offer service to others by building houses, landscaping and beautifying communities, constructing classroom aids, etc. Suber shared her story in print, saying,

> I am still learning to truly survive. I know that I want to do all I can to help break the cycle of violence. I also know that helping each side to heal will help society in the process. Hate is an awful burden, for either side — the offenders and the survivors and their families — to carry. Like anyone else, criminals must be allowed to embrace their own cycle of recovery. More important, like anyone else, when offenders feel that forgiveness is an option they become inspired to behave like productive citizens.[3]

Later, we shall explore both human nature and the essentials of the Christian faith that apparently made it possible for the people we have cited to forgive, move toward reconciliation, and be genuinely concerned about strengthening the moral fiber of persons in our global society.

Social/Political Apologies and Calls for Repentance, Forgiveness, Reconciliation, and Moral Courage

We agree with Don Irish when he identified the years 1990 to 2000 as the decade of apologies on a worldwide scale. Irish stated, "Nowadays contrition in all its shadings seems routine as leaders everywhere engage in a kind of premillennial washing of the spears. . . . Countries no less than people feel a need for a moral reckoning!"[4] Irish maintains that over one hundred national leaders have issued public apologies for various civil rights violations. Then, he

---

3. Wanda Suber, "A Survivor's Path Toward Healing," *The Voice* (Columbus, Ohio: Memorial to Our Lost Children, vol. 2, issue 1, 1997), p. 1.

4. Don Irish, "An Era of Apologies," *Fellowship* (Nyack, N.Y.: Fellowship of Reconciliation, vol. 64, March-April 1998), p. 4.

ticks off a list of twenty-one apologies, starting with former President Mikhail Gorbachev (April 1990). Gorbachev confessed that the Katyn Forest massacre of Polish officers and the execution of Poles held in Soviet prison camps were acts committed by Stalin's secret police in 1940 rather than by the Nazis as had been maintained. Since then there have been many other apologies: the French government's apology for complicity with Nazis during the Vichy regime (July 17, 1995), President de Klerk's apology for the pain and suffering caused by apartheid in South Africa (Aug. 22, 1996), Canada's apology to indigenous tribes for 150 years of paternalistic assistance programs and racial residential schools that devastated aboriginal communities (Jan. 8, 1998), and on and on.

Of course, one of the greatest efforts to bring about national healing through confession, forgiveness, and reconciliation is the work of the South African Truth and Reconciliation Commission with Archbishop Tutu as chairperson. After the election of Nelson Mandela as president of South Africa there was a cry for justice and a recognition that so many were guilty of oppression and murder on both sides at times, that there could never be a day when all would step forward and confess without a process that would lead to amnesty and a new start as a nation. President Mandela appointed the members of the Truth and Reconciliation Commission with the intent to make amnesty a possibility for all who confess. Bishop Tutu opened the Commission process with this prayer. "We pray that all those people who have been injured in either body or spirit may receive healing. . . . We pray, too, for all those who may be found to have committed these crimes against their fellow human beings, that they come to repentance and confess their guilt to Almighty God and that they too might become the recipients of your divine mercy and forgiveness."[5]

The process of seeking forgiveness and reconciliation in South Africa was very difficult and often painful. A Gross Human Rights Violation Committee went out to the hinterlands to the people to hear stories of victims. The suffering and pain of the victims were "heard, recognized, and reverenced by the nation." The stories came largely from apartheid victims but also included persons who had been hurt by ANC counterattacks. The Amnesty Committee then heard requests for amnesty. The requirements were: Only individuals, not groups, can apply. Full disclosure is essential. Abuses must have been politically motivated. The principle of "proportionality" applies. The degree of violation must bear some relation to the individual's political goals in the context of that particular era. Methodist bishop Peter Story, who helped organize the Commission, stated that a carrot-and-stick balance had

---

5. Desmond Tutu, *No Future without Forgiveness* (New York: Doubleday, 1999), p. 113.

to be attained. He said, "If amnesty is granted, the slate is wiped clean. If not, the disclosures before the Commission are not to be used in any subsequent court prosecution. Evidence would have to be independently sought by the attorney general. If the perpetrators didn't come forward by the cutoff date of May, 1997, they would live the rest of their lives in fear of being hunted down or fingered by the evidence of a former colleague."[6] Some in South Africa and in the wider world decry that repentance was not required. Only truth was required. Peter Story concludes that the Commission had to steer a delicate course between persons who wanted to "prosecute and punish" and those who wanted to "forgive and forget." The Commission chose the biblical paradigm of reconciliation: ". . . it is necessary to both remember and judge — and forgive," said Story.[7] Bishop Tutu reminds us, moreover, that reparations are also often needed in order for reconciliation to be a real possibility. He wants those forgiven to replace hovels and shacks, give access to water, electricity, health care, good education, and jobs for all those who have suffered from apartheid. Serious steps toward genuine reconciliation must follow forgiveness and amnesty. Bishop Tutu concludes, "It is ultimately in our best self-interest that we become forgiving, repentant, reconciling, and reconciled people because without forgiveness and reconciliation we have no future."[8]

Again, there are innumerable stories of the quest for truth and reconciliation, forgiveness and reconciliation all over the world — in Bosnia, Kosovo, Ireland, Indonesia/East Timor, India/Pakistan, China/Tibet, the United States/Cuba, Israel/Palestine, United States/Afghanistan/Iraq — and of the trying path toward forgiveness and reconciliation and the moral courage needed in the struggle to eliminate terrorism. In all of these situations religious and ethnic factors are often interrelated with economic and political to the degree that it becomes very difficult to find the sources of the problems or the processes whereby truth, forgiveness, and reconciliation can find their way into reality. The United Nations General Assembly, recognizing the depth of the problems of peace and reconciliation among people, responded positively to an appeal from every living Nobel Peace laureate by proclaiming the years 2001-2010 to be "The International Decade for a Culture of Peace and Nonviolence for the Children of the World."[9] It is so true that children are the

---

6. Peter Story, "A Different Kind of Justice: Truth and Reconciliation in South Africa," *Christian Century*, September 10-17, 1997, p. 790. See also the video of the March 30, 1999, PBS broadcast of "Facing the Truth with Bill Moyers."

7. Story, "A Different Kind of Justice," p. 789.

8. Tutu, *No Future without Forgiveness*, p. 165.

9. Decade for a Culture of Peace and Nonviolence for the Children of the World (Nyack, N.Y.: Fellowship of Reconciliation, 2000), or www.nonviolence.org/for.

ones most injured in mind, body, and spirit by our inhumanity and oppression. And now, after the undeclared war on terrorism, how can we move beyond the unfortunate military phases to a nonviolent strategy that will include a quest for a deep understanding of why the violence and terrorism erupted, or discover ways to find peace and justice? We return to these issues of the social and political quest for forgiveness, reconciliation, and the development of moral courage at several places in this book.

Religious/Interreligious Calls for Forgiveness, Reconciliation, and Moral Courage

There have been many individuals who have identified their religious motivations for personal/interpersonal, social/political initiatives for forgiveness and reconciliation, and their desire for a strong moral and ethical foundation for society. In addition, many religious bodies have recently taken seriously their own need to confess past sins of commission and omission, have publicly repented, apologized, asked for forgiveness, and sought reconciliation. The media pictures of these confessions and requests for forgiveness have been dramatic.

Probably the most visible and far-reaching has been the confession and request for forgiveness of the Roman Catholic Church. In celebration of the Great Jubilee of the year 2000, the Catholic Church announced on November 29, 1999, that she intended to purify the memory of the church by confessing past sins, repenting, and calling for reconciliation. The purification sought to liberate the church's conscience from ". . . all forms of resentment and violence that are the legacy of past faults. . . . This should lead — if done correctly — to a corresponding recognition of guilt and contribute to the path of reconciliation."[10] The document, *Memory and Reconciliation,* lists the sins having to do with ethical failures, the divisions among Christians, the use of force in evangelization and in seeking to serve the truth, the sins against the Jews, etc. Pope John Paul II conducted a Day of Pardon liturgy on Sunday, March 12, 2000, where he preached a sermon inviting a "profound examination of conscience," led a liturgy of confession of sins that have harmed the unity of the body of Christ, sins against the people of Israel, sins against love, peace, the rights of people, and respect for cultures and religions, sins against

10. *Memory and Reconciliation: The Church and the Faults of the Past* (Rome: International Theological Commission, found at www.vatican.va/roman-curia.../rc-cfaith-doc-20000307-Memory.reconc-itc-enhtm), p. 2.

the dignity of women and the unity of the human race, sins against the fundamental rights of the person. The Pope ends each confession with ". . . we ask your forgiveness, have mercy on us and accept our repentance. We ask through Christ our Lord."[11] The Curia's decision to take such a major step has been both praised and criticized widely. It has been praised as a bold effort to cleanse the church from past sins and to establish a fresh sense of honesty and integrity in the contemporary world. It has been criticized for not being explicit enough about the specific sins admitted. For instance, there was not enough specificity about the church's failures during the Holocaust.

Several other churches have confessed and asked for forgiveness. The Southern Baptist Church apologized to African Americans for condoning racism for most of its history (June 21, 1995). The Episcopal Church confessed her sins against Native Americans. The church asked for forgiveness for colonists who referred to them as ". . . infidels and savages who lived in darkness and miserable ignorance of the true knowledge and worship of God." The church held a reconciliation service on November 1, 1997, at Jamestown Island in Virginia, the site of the first permanent English settlement in America. The United Methodist Church celebrated the Act of Repentance and Reconciliation regarding the past sins of racism and the racial divisions that resulted within Methodism. The celebration took place at the General Conference in Cleveland, Ohio, in May 2000. An effort is now under way to seek unity among several denominations that exist within what is being called Pan-Methodism. Of course, the ongoing work of the Consultation on Church Union (COCU) is very important, as are efforts between the Roman Catholic Church and the Eastern Orthodox churches, between Roman Catholic and various Protestant bodies, and the successful negotiations between the Episcopal Church and the Evangelical Lutheran Church of America, etc. All of these are promising dialogues pointing to reconciliation, often starting with admissions of past sins of pride and arrogance and the request for forgiveness.

Greatly needed are efforts to bring understanding and reconciliation between the various world religions. The violence in India between Hindus and Christians, the violence in East Timor between Muslims and Christians, the continuing clashes between Catholics and Protestants in Ireland, and more recently the splits between the Christian, Muslim, Jewish, Hindu, and Sikh communities in the effort to deal with terrorism in the Middle East, Afghanistan, Pakistan, and India, and the split between the Shiites and Sunnis in Iraq — all confused by political and economic factors — are illustrations of

---

11. *Universal Prayer-Day for Pardon* (www.vatican.va/news_services/liturgy/documents/ ns_lit_doc_20000312_prayer-day-pardon_en.html), p. 6.

the need for forgiveness and reconciliation within the religious community. We agree with Hans Küng that a global ethic is essential if we are to solve many of our international problems. Küng has marshaled solid evidence that there can be no world peace and justice unless there is unity and cooperation between the world's religions.[12] We shall return to this urgent matter later in the book.

The bringing of interreligious harmony and cooperation will take much patience and honest dialogue over a long period of time. It also will be profoundly deepened if the parties start with a spirit of confession and genuine requests for forgiveness. One of the most powerful pictures of walking the walk toward understanding comes from the Internet. Click on www.reconciliationwalk.org/1980729.htm and you will discover a group of dedicated Christians who are asking for forgiveness for the damage done to Muslims, Jews, and Orthodox Christians by the Crusades. This group of Western Christians traveled to the Middle East "with God's humility in their hearts and words of apology on their lips." They retraced the route of the first Crusaders, roughly keeping the timeline of the three-year march to Jerusalem. They apologized and asked for forgiveness as they dialogued with Muslims, Jews, and Eastern Christians whose ancestors were slaughtered. The walk started in Cologne, Germany, where the first Crusaders started, and it ended in Jerusalem. Twenty-five hundred people walked long miles, visited thousands of towns and cities, and collected remarkable stories. The apology was received officially in July 1999 by senior Christian clergy, the Greek Orthodox Patriarch, the Chief Rabbi of Israel, and the Grand Mufti of Jerusalem. According to the participants, the process ". . . communicated a humility and repentance that Middle Easterners have never before seen in Western Christianity. And it is this message that will change our future together."[13]

Research on the Factors That Lead to Forgiveness and Reconciliation and the Increase of Moral Fiber

Much research and writing, of course, have already been done concerning the dynamics of forgiveness, reconciliation, and moral development. What is now emerging is the quest for the systematic, scientific study of the dynamics

12. Hans Küng, *Global Responsibility: In Search of a New World Ethic* (New York: Continuum, 1991).

13. The Reconciliation Walk, www.reconciliationwalk.org/1980729.htm, p. 4.

of change essential for forgiveness and reconciliation to become realities between persons, in marriage and family groups, between ethnic and religious groups, and between nations. One of the most visible initiatives is the Campaign for Forgiveness Research, co-chaired by former President Jimmy Carter, Archbishop Desmond Tutu, Dr. Robert Coles, Ruby Bridges Hall, and Elizabeth Elliott. The group is seeking several million dollars to fund scientific research on forgiveness and reconciliation in various settings. Dr. Everett Worthington, executive director of the group, states that ". . . the qualities of the human spirit that could promote forgiveness in the face of great loss and horror, and the difference between victims and perpetrators will be scientifically studied . . ." in order to discern if there is a path toward forgiveness and reconciliation for humankind to follow.[14]

Interestingly enough the above program will not be totally new. Dr. Robert Enright of the University of Wisconsin–Madison has led a strong team of researchers at the International Forgiveness Institute, which he and others founded. Enright and his team have identified twenty steps involved in genuine forgiveness at whatever levels — personal, social, and political.[15] We will discuss Enright's findings in relation to the questions of our human capacity to forgive, how forgiveness and reconciliation are two very different things, and specific ways to teach persons to forgive and seek reconciliation. Enright also is working on the relationship of moral development theories to forgiveness and reconciliation.

Other academic institutions are conducting related research as well. One illustration is a Reconciliation Symposium at Emory University. The Symposium has followed up with several workshops aimed at implementation. Top leaders have discussed and made recommendations concerning reconciliation between races and ethnic groups, international peace and justice, sexual and gender issues, environmental policy, social justice, commercialization of the academy, conflicts between science and religion, and others. The symposium and workshops were led by a Year of Reconciliation (2001) team. For more information, call the office of Institutional Planning and Research (404-727-0765). Forgiveness and reconciliation research is expanding rapidly. The Campaign for Forgiveness Research, with the help of the John Templeton Foundation, has funded fifty-eight research proposals. Dr. Everett Worthing-

14. A Campaign for Forgiveness Research, www.templeton.org/forgiveness/forgiveresearch.asp.

15. Robert D. Enright and Joanna North, eds., *Exploring Forgiveness* (Madison: University of Wisconsin Press, 1998); Robert D. Enright, *Forgiveness Is a Choice: A Step-by-Step Process for Resolving Anger and Restoring Hope* (Washington, D.C.: American Psychological Association, 2001).

ton, chair, on his own has been researching forgiveness at the Virginia Commonwealth University for several years. He has created teams of researchers working out of several other colleges and universities (www.has.vcu.edu/psy/faculty/Worthington.html).[16] Other notable centers of research are Stanford University in its Forgiveness Project, which focuses on training persons to forgive as a way to ameliorate anger and distress with implications for the prevention and treatment of cardiovascular and other chronic diseases (www.Stanford.edu/alexsox/forgiveness-article.htm); Case Western Reserve University, which is bringing together all major research findings on forgiveness with support of the John Templeton Foundation (www.templeton.org/grantopp/introduction.asp); Coventry University (U.K.) and its Centre for Forgiveness and Reconciliation, which is focusing on issues of forgiveness, reconciliation, and the pursuit of justice in the struggling international scene (www.Coventry-isl.org.UK/forgive/about/backgrd.htm). It is important that religious leaders be in full communication with these and many other centers studying and developing training and counseling models for forgiveness, reconciliation, and moral courage.

Listening to the Perceptions of Members of Four Congregations

It was our belief that a book dealing with forgiveness, reconciliation, and the development of moral fiber would not be relevant unless we listened to people face to face. We chose four congregations — Roman Catholic, United Methodist, Southern Baptist, and an independent Pentecostal church. These four churches represented varying theological, sociological, racial, and cultural perspectives. We spoke with the pastors of each congregation about the possibility of recruiting a focus group of laity, from fifteen to twenty-five persons, who would be willing to complete our survey instrument and then have a full discussion of their responses and their honest reasons for saying what they did. We wanted to hear persons of varying life situations and ages share their views about the nature of God, human nature, sin, the importance of confession, repentance, contrition, forgiveness, and reconciliation; the moral failures causing guilt and pain; the liturgical and educational approaches that are most highly valued or omitted and why. By entering into dialogue with

16. Everett L. Worthington, Jr., ed., *Dimensions of Forgiveness: Psychological and Theological Perspectives* (Radnor, Pa.: Templeton Foundation, 1998); Michael E. McCullough, Kenneth Pargament, Carl E. Thoresen, *Forgiveness: Theory, Research, and Practice* (New York: Guilford, 2000). See these publications for annotated listings of many research projects being conducted at cooperating colleges, universities, and research agencies.

these representative persons we could more nearly identify the life issues they were experiencing and address those in our writing. Our great appreciation goes to all who gave of their energy and time to help us in our desire to make this study much more significant and genuinely helpful. We agreed to respect the confidentiality of each participant and of the congregations involved. The report and analysis of the findings from the four focus groups is found in Chapter 1.

Before you read Chapter 1 we invite you to turn to Appendix A and complete the survey instrument so that you will know firsthand what the questions were. Then, you can compare your responses to those of the participants in our four focus groups.

Also, we invite you to read the book in any way that will engage you the most. The outline of the chapters in the book that follows will assist you in knowing in advance what issues will be presented and discussed. In this way you may want to go to a later chapter rather than read sequentially in order to stimulate your interest. Then, you can go to earlier chapters in order to understand the assumptions that led us to later conclusions. You may wish to read Chapter 1, "What People Are Really Thinking: A Survey of Four Churches," in order to enter into dialogue with the participants in the four focus groups and to discover why we planned the book in the way we did.

The Rationale for and an Outline of the Chapters to Follow

By starting with our perceptions of the concerns most alive and vibrant coming from our multimedia world and from the persons in the four live congregational settings, we invite you to continue the dialogical pattern throughout the book. You can have an internal dialogue with yourself or an external dialogue with others within your family, work, school, or congregational settings. Having already responded to the survey in Appendix A and read Chapter 1, you are prepared to move forward as you wish.

Chapter 2. Are Forgiveness, Reconciliation, and Moral Courage Really Possible? (The Nature of Human Nature)

Is it possible for human beings to forgive others or themselves? Are we free to decide our destiny or are we caught in original sin or a pit of collective evil? Are we in possession of a basic moral sense, given us at birth by our Creator? Do we have to identify and face our sins of commission and omission before

God, receive God's forgiveness through Christ in order to be free to forgive others or ourselves? How can we become responsible, moral, loving persons and create an affirming, reconciling society? Is God loving and forgiving by nature? How do forgiveness and reconciliation relate to our desire for a righteous, just, and peaceful world?

We look at the concept of Imago Dei and the possibility of being born with a moral sense in dialogue with Martin Buber and James A. Wilson. We assess how and if we "fall" into sin in conversation with the scriptures, with Søren Kierkegaard, Reinhold Niebuhr, L. Gregory Jones, and others. We discuss the human capacity for justice and mercy (forgiveness), and reconciliation in dialogue with moral development thinkers Lawrence Kohlberg, Carol Gilligan, Robert Enright, Joanna North, and Everett Worthington.

Chapter 3. Forgiveness and Reconciliation in the Bible: The Relation of Justice and Mercy

The story of forgiveness and reconciliation in the Bible is a story of grace, or, more accurately, it is the story of a paradoxical relation of justice and mercy as attributes of God and as integral parts of human relations. We eventually discover in the story that mercy, in God and in humanity, is an attribute even deeper than justice.

The sustaining paradox is an affirmation of the gracious experience of God's presence and a holy fear of divine wrath toward sin and evil. We shall explore these themes in the exodus and in the figure of Moses; in the prophets and in the liturgical life in the Psalms; in sacrificial atonement; in the Day of Atonement. The themes of confession, repentance, forgiveness, and reconciliation in the New Testament are under headings of: righteous judgment, unbounded love, repentance, and forgiveness and community.

Chapter 4. A Brief History of Transgression and Reconciliation among Christians

In the first century Christians were already perplexed by questions about forgiveness, such as: Does baptism cancel all sin? If so, why do we still sin? What sins are serious, what trivial? What is unforgivable? How often can one be forgiven? Should sinners be banished or shunned? In what way and for how long does one need to repent? In the second century we find the gradual development of procedures for penance and the foundations of the penitential system. Fourteen centuries later we have the Reformation, based on Luther's attack on the foundation of the penitential system and his preaching of the universal priesthood of all reconcilers. Other Protestant reforms will be described and analyzed. The more recent Protestant stasis will be especially underscored: the stagnation and decline in ministries of confession, repentance, forgiveness, and reconciliation, and the amnesia regarding scriptural themes; the ignorance of tradition and the prejudice concerning it; the emergence of social sciences and the tendency to rely on them (especially through psychotherapy and counseling). Finally, we will discuss the most promising Catholic reforms coming out of Vatican II and the development of the Sacrament of Reconciliation rather than Penance, and the impact of this revolution in sacramental thinking and practice.

Chapter 5. Forgiveness and Reconciliation through Moral Development in Families, Churches, Schools, and Communities

The need for a cooperative approach to moral education came out of our study of the four congregations. In order to understand the current situation we present a brief history of the way moral development has been approached in the United States. We do this with reference to the Constitution, the Bill of Rights, and the various Supreme Court decisions, and how we have sought to define the respective roles of family, religious institutions, public schools, and community organizations. We then review central theories of moral development (moral education, values clarification, and character education with attention to optional theories found in Johannes A. van der Ven's views). We identify the various levels of character education extant today: international and interreligious, national and state, and grassroots. This is done with a view to helping local churches and communities find specific resources to assist them in designing their own local programs. Such resources are listed and analyzed.

Chapter 6. A Four-Pronged Approach to Increasing Forgiveness, Reconciliation, and Moral Courage

It is increasingly clear that the church's strategy should include both (1) moral development of children, youth, and adults, and (2) educational, liturgical, pastoral, and sacramental life oriented toward the healing of personal and social moral failure and spiritual separation from God, others, and the self. In order to take a holistic approach to these two dimensions we propose a four-pronged strategy: (1) A strong, focused moral and spiritual education and liturgical/sacramental life in our congregations, (2) the church's cooperative role in community-based moral or character education and service learning, (3) the church's advocacy of legal and necessary study *about* religion and ethics in our public schools, and (4) the development of public churches that will take the lead in addressing public issues that often divide us, causing the need for confession, contrition, forgiveness, and reconciliation.

The above strategy is unpacked in dialogue with our current understanding of the dynamics and stages of moral development (from Piaget to Kohlberg and beyond), emotional intelligence (Daniel Goleman), and faith development (James Fowler). There is an attempt to integrate these and other theories with special attention to the faith community (Craig Dykstra). The cooperative character-building strategy for the total community should have strong but balanced leadership from churches. The roles of family, schools, churches, and community groups (local government, businesses, media, etc.) are sorted out and interrelated. Illustrations are given, coming out of the character-education movement in the United States and from around the world. The matter of the legal study about religion in our public schools is discussed and the current national agreements outlined. The important matter of public churches is analyzed in conversation with Martin Marty's seminal work and in relation to a proposal for Christian education for the public church coming from Charles Foster, Robert O'Gorman, and Jack Seymour. They see the task of Christian education to be the shaping of public character, forming a consciousness of the necessity of reconciling the world to God, of healing divisions — ethnic, cultural, racial, sexual, the "haves and the have-nots," and the religious (often the biggest source of divisiveness, sometimes clouded by economic and political factors). The public church must recover a prophetic voice and at the same time bring healing, forgiveness, and reconciliation. Employing James Fowler's seminal work on the criteria for an effective public church, we present two illustrations of strong public church approaches: The Seekers Church in Washington, D.C., and the many churches in the Catholic diocese of Cleveland, Ohio.

The final two chapters of the book are designed to underscore the crucial nature of a refocusing of educational and liturgical life with a consideration of the potential of an ecumenical Sacrament of Reconciliation.

Chapter 7. Moral and Spiritual Education
Linked to Sacramental/Liturgical Life

This chapter celebrates the revolution in sacramental theology in general and within Roman Catholic theology in particular. We revisit the views expressed in our book, *The Sacraments in Religious Education and Liturgy* (1985), in which we saw more openness within Protestantism to find new meaning in individual confession, repentance, forgiveness, and reconciliation along with corporate forms already present. We propose that the educational resources and methodologies within Roman Catholic and Orthodox communities have been reformed to the point that they may have transfer potential for Protestant churches. We present an overview of Roman Catholic and Orthodox curricular resources, critiquing them especially for their transfer potential. We then do a case study of one especially creative Roman Catholic church's educational and sacramental life. The study includes work with parents on moral development of their children and the deeper relational meaning of the Sacrament of Reconciliation; workshops for parents and the whole family from the second grade through high school; youth retreats, total faith community celebrations, etc. Other educational designs are discussed in relation to the responses of the participants in the four-congregation study. These include education in nonviolence, forgiveness education, moral education throughout the life cycles, marriage, and family education, action-reflection-action teams, etc. There is recognition that religious education and liturgy are interrelated in a powerful way.

Chapter 8. Dealing with Moral Failure:
Forgiveness and Reconciliation in Christian Worship

Here we discuss the liturgical traditions of forgiveness and reconciliation. What elements are needed for a viable and enduring ministry of reconciliation?

Specific possibilities of this ministry are discussed: an acknowledgment of transgression (sin and how it is related to goodness); the living work of grace and God's forgiveness; contrition and confession and their relation to repentance; ways for Christ's body to speak the word of forgiveness; help for living and accepting forgiveness — a community responsibility, not the pastor's alone; help to walk in a new way and to repair past damages.

It is our hope that your internal or external dialogue with a reading partner or members of a study group will be fruitful enough that you will continue the quest for educational and liturgical renewal as well as for strengthened moral fiber in your congregation and the wider community. We believe there is great potential in an ecumenical approach to forgiveness and reconciliation as well as a cooperative, community approach to moral development of our children, youth, families, congregational members, and wider society. We pray that you will see the relevance of the ministries possible for a public church, committed to bringing the consciousness of the reign of a loving, just, and merciful God into reality at all levels of our society.

CHAPTER 1

What People Are Really Thinking:
A Survey of Four Churches

I n considering seriously our ministries of confession, forgiveness, reconciliation, and the development of moral courage it is necessary to come
down from the heights of theological inquiry and biblical investigation and
enter into conversation with people in the churches who hopefully both receive and share these ministries. Any consideration of how things ought to
be needs to take realistic stock of how things are. We naturally have some
judgments about this on the basis of our own experience, but we wanted to
sample opinions and experiences of laypeople. While we did not have the resources to conduct an exhaustive and scientific survey, we did prepare a survey of attitudes concerning confession, forgiveness, reconciliation, and
moral fidelity or failure, and we met with small groups of laypeople (15 to
25) who generously gave of their time to respond to the survey. The congregations were from Roman Catholic, United Methodist, Southern Baptist,
and Pentecostal denominations. After the survey, these groups of laity met
with us a second time to discuss the results and to explore their ideas and experiences further with us. We then met subsequently with pastors to garner
their responses. We are extremely guarded in drawing hard and fast conclusions from these encounters. They are certainly not descriptive of denominations, or even of local congregations, but they are genuine and lively meetings of minds and feelings with real people concerning our subject matter.
The surveys and discussions tell us some important things, if not everything.
They are openings to and indications of a wider discussion that needs to take
place in our churches.

In selecting particular congregations for our survey we were aware that
there was no way to find *the* typical representative of any Christian denomi-

nation. We selected churches in central Ohio where we knew that members represented various strata of our society and culture.

The Catholic Church

Church and Values

The Catholics who participated in our survey were communicants at a prestigious church at the heart of a large metropolitan city. The congregation assembles from all over the city and is generally a sophisticated group drawn together by the appeal of good liturgy, fine historic architecture, good preaching, great music well performed, and sensitive attention to human need.

The Catholic laypeople who participated in our survey were generally confident and well informed in their church's understandings of what constituted faithfulness and transgression. "Our core values come from the church." They were of different minds about some things, but they were basically loyal to church teachings. They were clear in their awareness that the Bible and church teaching need interpretation, but were suspicious of "too much interpretation" and rationalizing of behaviors. While they were critical of our culture, its confused and lax morality, and our failure to inculcate basic values in new generations, they were painfully aware of the complexity of our lives today and the impossible demands and pressures on families. They understood the radically plural character of our culture and while they stood for a core of values, most were reluctant to try to force values on people. They acknowledged that we are often too quick to judge and too late to forgive.

Affirming the truth and continuity of core values in the tradition of the church did not mean that they ignored changes in that tradition. As one person put it, "The church used to condemn and judge you a lot; today is different, there is more love in it."

Sin and Guilt

Questions involving guilt revealed much uncertainty among this group of Christians, as they did with every group. They were, for instance, strong in their belief in original sin (A2), but unsure about guilt being a "universal human condition" (B1). They were seriously conflicted about whether God always punishes the guilty (B5) or whether the righteous and faithful find eternal life while the sinful and unrepentant are condemned to hell (G5).

In discussion about sin and/or guilt being "original" the group concluded that what was really the rock of their certainty was "original grace, original goodness." About sin and guilt one member observed, "If you ain't got it when you get into this world, it ain't going to take you long to get it."

Most of these Catholics admitted that while they affirm and accept God's forgiveness, after absolution they still struggle with guilt. "Feeling guilt free can be hard, even when you believe you are forgiven." The pastor in a follow-up interview did not find this conclusion inconsistent with his experience as a priest hearing personal confession. "Many will say at the end of confession, 'and I want to remember the sins of my past life.' If I say, 'did you confess them,' the person might say, 'yes, but I still want to say I am sorry for them.' This is certainly expression of lingering sorrow, if not guilt." The priest acknowledged that "many come to the Sacrament of Reconciliation with a limited idea of repentance and forgiveness. They don't necessarily have the sense of joy that they might have over the notion of the angels in heaven rejoicing over one repentant sinner. They may get a sense of a slate wiped clean, but forgiveness for them may not be a light which shows new possibilities."

Sacrament of Love

While these members were predominantly convinced that "confession of sin is necessary for faithful Christian living" (C1), most denied that "personal confession to a priest" was "necessary to receive God's forgiveness." That conclusion was no barrier to their strong affirmation of the rite of confession and absolution. "I love it," one member acclaimed. "I need it; it helps me to feel good about myself." Others in the group were movingly supportive of the values of this sacrament in their lives. The Sacrament of Reconciliation and Forgiveness is something very precious in the minds of the persons in this sample group. It clearly reinforces and in some sense creates in them the strong affirmation of the love of God they have experienced. In their view, the God who is all-forgiving never gives up on us. "Even in that last breath there is a chance to find God's love. We cannot know the mind of God, and we find it hard to accept God's love, but God does love us and pursues us even after death."

Self and Community

The perception of the Sacrament of Forgiveness was very personal and individual. When asked to expand on the "reconciliation" dimension of the sacrament, people generally expressed their concern about "getting right with God personally." "That is what *Confession* is — something with the individual. Coming together as a unit strengthens faith, but I don't need to be with a group of people to experience God." Or, "God is divine, he forgives, not the community. Forgiveness is through the priest; he represents God and acts for God." There was little sense of a role for the community of faith in forgiveness, or that the priest was a representative of the congregation as well as of God. On the survey less than a third of the respondents considered "reconciliation with the faith community an essential part of divine forgiveness" (E5). One of the questions on the survey concerned the importance of confession in public worship. Not much more than half considered it helpful, and in the subsequent discussion some were unaware that it was a part of regular worship. Reference by other members to its recurring role in the Mass and the place of the Lord's Prayer in worship brought recognition. The important distinction for these Christians is the sacramental one. The communal service of reconciliation and the confessional elements in worship may be helpful, but they are not sacramental. "The power of reconciliation was passed down from Peter to the priest, and when he is sitting in the confessional, he is Jesus."

There was, however, some clear articulation of a communal dimension on the part of some participants. "In the Mass, when we say the confession, I sense a solidarity. We are all alive together. In the past, growing up I didn't feel that way. It was all personal guilt. I was less aware of the fellowship." And it should be pointed out that in the survey all of the respondents agreed that "it is the role of every Christian to be a forgiver" (E4).

The pastor noted that in his experience as a confessor, adolescents have a greater sensitivity to the social aspect of sin, while for older Catholic adults sin is "something between me, my body, and God." He was encouraged that in the section of the survey evaluating parts of the liturgy helpful in a person's need for forgiveness the Sacrament of the Eucharist rated very high. He judged that prior to Vatican II this would not have been the case. He was disappointed that the passing of the peace rated as low as it did. In the group discussion one participant avowed that the forgiveness of the community might not be essential to the reconciling sacrament but that there is now a more significant role for the community. "It's a little more of the community than it is just God. What happens in the Mass, even the passing of the peace, is extremely important."

The priest of this parish expects that in the future there will be more of a corporate sense of reconciliation in the church because of the way that children are now introduced into the sacrament. It is a communal event. Children come with their classmates and families, and families are encouraged to enter into the sacrament. After the liturgy there is a celebration, with food and fellowship. The priest believes that this experience of children can create a new sensibility and understanding of reconciliation as something that happens among the body of Christians as well as within individuals.

Education

This group was especially affirmative of parent education concerning moral and spiritual development and of Bible study highlighting reconciliation. They were relatively supportive of the study of social problems that require forgiveness and of small groups where reconciliation can be experienced in communal support.

Society and Culture

Many in our group were aware and astute about the ways in which the subject we had gathered to discuss was manifested in society and culture. They identified problems relating to our consumer fixations, especially as this related to the effects of the media. They were insightful about the dynamics of contemporary family life. They saw societal manifestations of some of the ecclesial issues we were discussing, such as the obsession of our culture with confession and its exploitation on TV. They were very reluctant, though, to share any guilt for matters other than those for which they were personally responsible. Fewer than half expressed any feelings of guilt for evils in society, such as poverty, war, injustice, etc. (B6). "Why should I feel guilty for something I didn't do?" No sense of guilt was felt for societal evils in which we may be caught, whether we will or not, just because we are part of the societal structures. "I feel something, but not guilty. I feel anger about it, but if I didn't do it, I don't feel guilty." Some expressed feeling guilty for not doing something about various problems, but not guilty about causing them. "I need to be more proactive." In general the attitude was, "How can you be guilty for something you had no control over?"

Responses were mixed concerning the questions about social/political issues. Most were in agreement that nations should perform acts of restitution and reconciliation when appropriate, and that it was a good thing for the French Catholic Church to confess their collaboration with Nazis and ask Jews for forgiveness. Most disagreed with South Africa's amnesty policy. They thought that contrition was necessary. And many did not approve of or were unsure about President Clinton's apology for the syphilis experiment on black men.

The idea of a shared collective guilt in which we are caught because, willy-nilly, we are enmeshed in webs of wickedness for which we cannot extract ourselves, was not a shared sensibility among this group.

The United Methodist Church

The United Methodist congregation in our study has a membership of about five hundred and is located in a small town in a rural context experiencing the suburban expansion of a major city. There is a great deal of diversity in the church: all generations, many lines of work, but with little or no ethnic diversity. They see themselves as a family church, and a church "that has something for everyone." The congregation has seen marked growth in recent years due to urban sprawl in its direction. There is every indication that this growth will continue. They believe that they have also grown a great deal spiritually. The church has strong programs in the Emmaus movement (a United Methodist equivalent of the Roman Catholic Cursillo movement) and a United Methodist program called the *Discipleship Bible Study.* The building is used a lot by church and community. They have a very full schedule and are cramped for space. During the week there is a large day care program.

A Shared Life

This United Methodist congregation shares a rich fellowship. Many in the congregation have participated in small groups aimed at deepening spirituality, sacramental life, personal accountability, and responsibility to others. This has built among other things their sense of church as family. Their pastor believes that the church has benefited from these programs and developed a strong identity as a believing, caring community. He wishes that these enrichment programs had stronger "justice-making dimensions" to them and works to find ways to fill this lacuna. He sees himself and the other pastor of the church as fortunate receivers of the congregation's spiritual enrichment.

Original Potential

The people in our survey were pretty united in their ideas about what sin is, except for the sin that is original. Half of them believed in it. A third of them did not believe in it, and a few ducked the issue (A2). They were, appropriately and consistently, just as conflicted about whether guilt is a universal human condition (B1). One-third said "yes," one-third "no," and one-third "not sure." Discussion began with much questioning about "What is it?" They seemed generally to agree on a meaning of "inherently born bad." Most had trouble believing this, balking at accepting that "a baby was born bad." One brother concluded, "I believe in original sin, but I also believe in accountability. If a baby dies before he is accountable, he goes straight to heaven." Some surmised that maybe sin was original with teenagers, something that descended upon you at about age 15. The group coalesced generally around the idea that original sin was not being born bad exactly, but was a "condition" we are born with, a "potential." "Something not taught, but already in there." They pictured original sin as a universal and innate potential.

Guilt and the Moral Conscience

Discussion about guilt began with the lament about the many who have none, who just don't care. One person worked in a youth offender program and was appalled at the total lack of any sense of guilt on the part of many youth with whom she deals. "I feel guilty when I know I have done something wrong; it takes a sense of moral values." It was not a great deal of help to her to realize that some of the youth she sees have personality disorders or dysfunctional families; most didn't. One person in the group pointed out that guilt does not always express itself in us in the form of remorse. Sometimes, for instance, it can come out in the form of a medical problem.

In some ways these United Methodists see the church itself as responsible for some persons' deep sense of guilt. Some believed that the church in the past overemphasized sin and guilt as a way to convert people. "When I was young the church had a lot of guilt to pass around. Now things have seemed to swing the other way." Some believed that the church has gone from overdamning to oversoothing, so that personal and social sins are not named, repented of, or forgiven.

Guilt, Forgiveness, and Community

While most of the persons in this sample participated in spiritual enrichment groups in the church, their sense of sin and guilt is primarily individualistic. A third of the group either denied or were not sure whether the ministries of the church served to "relieve guilt and reorient life" (B2). For some, the church doesn't have a lot to do with it. One "doesn't need others. You can confess to God alone. God is the only person that matters; the group is not necessary." In actual fact, in groups, the people do hear confession and surround one another with forgiveness, but they do not really connect the forgiveness given in community and God's forgiveness, which is seen as something between God and an individual.

While there was solid agreement that every Christian should be a forgiver (E4), there was considerable puzzlement over the notion that reconciliation within the faith community might be an essential part of divine forgiveness (E5). Two-thirds of the group either denied or were unsure about a connection between reconciliation and forgiveness. What they were sure about was that "God teaches us to love one another," and that it is possible to be forgiven by God but not have the forgiveness of the faith community. "People who sin are the people who need us the most." There was even assent to the conclusion that "we aren't better because they sinned and we didn't." They believe that is a commonality, and that shunning the sinner is itself a sin. Where their church is in all of this is another matter. They see themselves as willing, but far short of the ideal. "We don't bridge the gap too well." On the other hand they were agreed that "if you don't forgive it hurts you a lot more than it does them."

A substantial majority of these United Methodists affirm that "personal repentance is necessary to be forgiven by God and others" (D1). When they were asked to identify helpful forms of repentance, that same majority named "going directly to the person you have offended and repenting honestly, seeking forgiveness and understanding" (D2). In discussion most admitted that this doesn't happen too often. "I think we should do this, but personally I am more apt to repent to God and not do something else about it." Another added, "It is easier to repent to God." And another, "If we would go to the offended we would get rid of a lot more guilt." Some felt that the important thing was "to make yourself better and not to sin again."

Repentance in public worship has not been much practiced in this community; they prefer private means, although many named the Lord's Supper as a helpful time of repentance and renewal.

Guilt, Forgiveness, and Society

One-third of the United Methodist participants confessed to feeling guilt "because of evils in society" (B6). Most experienced guilt "only about those things where we have some control." If social evils have not really touched us, we "should not feel guilty, but be thankful." There was some demur from this general conclusion. One person in the group recalled a difficult situation in a classroom where one first grader ethnically different from others was subjected to indignities. This affected her deeply and she identified her attitude as shame, if not real guilt. She knew she had not personally caused the hurt, but nevertheless could not but feel part of it.

In general there was no strong sense in the group of social evil and sinning as a web of interconnectedness in which as a society we are all caught.

Judgment

This United Methodist group was agreed that "God's love for us is unconditional" (G2), but unsure 50/50 about whether "God's righteousness and love make judgment inevitable" (G2). In discussion they were more agreed that God's righteousness implies judgment, but what judgment? A final judgment at the last, or is judgment and forgiveness a more continuing relationship with God in Christ? There was some sentiment for the idea that the real judgment was "made long ago when Adam fell." Jesus paid the "price" for this and all human sin, and in faith we can know that we are forgiven and saved. At the last judgment "the good news is that you will have Jesus there as your 'mouthpiece.'" If God is going to judge us someday, why worry about forgiveness now? Others believed that whatever is at the "last," judgment is taking place in life now, that we are judged "along the way, day by day." The role of the church in this process remained unclear.

Liturgy and Religious Education

Opinions about the parts of worship these United Methodists found helpful in discovering forgiveness (H) were all over the chart. As we have seen, they did not view public worship as primarily important in repentance/forgiveness, but on the survey and in discussion as we have seen they did consider the Eucharist as a time of special meaning. They also rated "times of silence for reflection" as very helpful.

Opinions also varied concerning preferred mode of education. Not surprisingly, what rated highest with these United Methodists was "small support groups where forgiveness or reconciliation can be experienced" (I). Bible study also rated very high.

Social/Political Issues

Only the first of the scenarios on the survey under this heading found this group generally united in opinion. President Clinton was right to ask forgiveness on behalf of the United States government for experiments relating to syphilis in black men. Other "pictures" of social and political "sin-repentance-forgiveness" elicited much variety in response. This is obviously not an area that most Christians have heard much about or thought much about in the context of Christian faith. Most awareness of sin, as the pastor pointed out, "doesn't get beyond personal sin."

The Southern Baptist Church

Our Southern Baptist sample is situated in a suburb of a capital city. The congregation is small but dedicated, only 150 members. The pastor has nurtured the congregation, founded in 1972, for six years. He is well educated with a doctor of theology degree.

When asked to describe the nature of the congregation the participants said the community was accepting, open, and caring, like a second family. One person said, "People like the smallness — its warmth as a community." The three young people in the group appeared to mirror these feelings as they participated freely in the discussions. One young person stated that he was even able to say in a talk that he didn't as yet believe in Christ as his savior but was still accepted as a part of the community.

It became evident that group members saw their congregation as a part of the moderate Southern Baptists nationally and in the state convention. One woman asserted, "Some conference people say that we are different, even weird!" When asked what popped out of a review of the survey findings there seemed to be more agreement on the nature of sin but more division over whether sin should cause guilt. (Laughter) The dialogue with the group brought forth the following discoveries:

The Nature of Sin

There was agreement that sin is doing things against God's will, living in a self-centered way, failing to love God and neighbor, and giving money and power too much value. The discussion ranged from sin as alienation from God to disobedience of God's will to both breaking a relationship of love and trust with God and being estranged from others. Some saw sin as interior — "I can be related closely to God and still sin." Others believed sin to be inherited. "We are born with it."

There was much wrestling with the concept of original sin. Several interpretations emerged. One was based on the disobedience of Adam and Eve. Another quoted Romans to the effect that all are born in sin but through Christ sin was overcome. A school counselor shared: "I grew up thinking I was born in original sin. Then I went to college and decided that we are all born with a clean slate. But, as a school counselor one of the things that just could not be overlooked was that all children are born with the capacity to hurt others, sometimes in a very destructive way. So, I no longer believe that children are born with a clean slate. . . . Children are necessarily self-centered, but I mean beyond that, they are sinful. To reach out and hurt another child, and to do it again and again says to me that there is more there than self-centeredness." A parent agreed, saying that she didn't have to teach her children how to lie. They already knew!

Not all agreed with original sin. Some saw the strong influences from society on children, resulting in the unbelievable acts of violence from children in the public schools. Some called for the teaching of the Christian faith in schools. Others flagged the problem of the separation of church and state as an important principle historically for Baptists. There was a general decrying of the lack of moral standards in society and a concern that there was not an awareness of sin on the part of many.

The Nature and Resolution of Guilt

The group probed the issue of guilt deeply but with humor. In respect to whether guilt is a universal condition, several views were shared. Some said that guilt is a personal matter. With regard to any given act, some feel guilty and others do not. We can justify anything. One said, "I think we all experience guilt. What we do about it is another matter." A woman built on this idea, saying, "From a Christian perspective, guilt is a universal condition. However, for others who have never heard or accepted the Word, someone who is making a million dollars a day and walking all over others, no."

There was a general agreement that guilt is related to the standards we are raised to accept. Evidence was cited concerning youth who express no guilt about drive-by killings in a drug war. After much discussion it was finally decided that guilt is not a universal condition but is related to the standards of behavior we have been taught.

The Importance of Free Will and Choice

The discussion about sin and guilt became conflicted when the concept of the Imago Dei was introduced. How can we be created good, in God's image, and still inherit original sin? The answer was free will and choice: "We are born good, in God's image, with free will, and it is our wrong choices that get us into sin. Isn't that why God put Jesus Christ in this world — to live as an example for us? He was tempted as we are and still chose the right." St. Paul was cited as an example when he said, ". . . the good that I would do, I do not, and the evil I would not do, I do. Who will save me from this body of death?" Some thought that Satan was the source of temptation. Others believed ". . . the great gift of freedom is the seedbed for a lot of our decisions that lead us into sinful choices; and yet, it is the same quality that leads to our creativity."

It was agreed that the church can produce guilt, and that it is the mission of the church to help us recognize our sin and release us from guilt so that the energy wasted on guilt can be used for creative ends.

Confession and Repentance Are Avenues to Forgiveness and Reconciliation

There was strong agreement that confession of sin is necessary for faithful Christian living (C-1). A similar response was recorded for repentance as necessary for forgiveness (D-1). As expected, there was 100 percent agreement that personal confession to a priest or minister was not necessary to receive God's forgiveness. Most thought confession to God was first; and then, confession to the person offended should follow in order for forgiveness and reconciliation to be authentic (C-4). There was negative reaction to the idea of public confession in corporate worship. While prayers of confession for the entire congregation are acceptable, personal confession in public was seen as hurtful often. Again, repentance should be directly to God through Christ, to be followed by ". . . going directly to the person you have offended and repenting honestly, seeking forgiveness and understanding." Other forms of repentance (going to the pastor, performing penitential prayers or deeds, participating in the sacraments, etc.) all had from 0 to 7 responses. The group believed that God is forgiving by nature and that it is the role of every Christian to be a forgiving person. The issue of God's willingness to forgive any and all sins evoked considerable discussion. The sin against the Holy Spirit was raised. One man said, "We all sin, but God cannot forgive if we deny

Christ before others." Another added, "God is forgiving by nature, but not if we do not accept Christ." There was a split between those who see forgiveness as an event or a process. Many pointed to Christ's death on the cross for the forgiveness of sins as the central event. Others saw forgiveness as an ongoing process because ". . . we continue to sin and need forgiveness throughout life."

Openness to Wider Knowledge While Still Believing That Salvation Is Only through Christ

Group members admitted that they had broken many of the Ten Commandments for which they and others were continually in need of forgiveness and reconciliation. There was an open stance taken about working with non-Christians to strengthen the moral fiber of society (F-2). This openness was seen, also, in the agreement that "God's love for us is unconditional" (G-1), and that "God forgives us when we honestly repent and are willing to change" (G-6). One mother stated, "Our grace lies in Jesus Christ. The Bible says that if you do not accept Jesus Christ you will not be saved. But, my son says, 'But Mom, they are good people.'" There was real struggle over the loving, forgiving nature of God and the judgment of God. One person summarized with these words: "God doesn't condemn us to hell. We do it. He is just following through like a good parent. If I choose to be disobedient and not accept Christ as my savior, I have to accept my fate. . . . That is what the Bible says."

The Tension between the Authority of the Bible and the Use of Reason, Experience, and Tradition in Discerning God's Will

Many in the group recognized the importance of insights from reason, common human experience, and from the great themes coming out of the influences of past decisions and leaders. This was especially true in the discussion about original sin and about people outside the church being moral. While there was some concern about always relying on what the Bible says, the issues discussed were mostly resolved by quoting from the Scripture as the final authority. Mostly, Scripture was quoted without the recognition that faithful Christians interpret Scripture in several different ways. Even though this community of Southern Baptists identifies itself as more moderate than the national church with its more fundamentalistic stance, there seems to be a tendency to interpret the Bible in a somewhat similar way.

The Tendency to See Forgiveness and Reconciliation as Individual and Pietistic Rather Than Social and Political

Such a tendency was seen in the resistance to the need for confession, forgiveness, and reconciliation within the body of Christ as well as, on a personal basis, with God through Christ. It was also evident in the section on social and political matters. In the latter there was uncertainty about President Clinton's confession and request for forgiveness concerning the government's experiment with African American men who had syphilis, rather than treating them (J-A). The same was true about Christians affirming the South African Truth Commission's offer of amnesty to persons who confess their crimes without necessarily expressing contrition or making amends (J-B). There is higher affirmation but still uncertainty about the Roman Catholic Church's confession of collaboration with the Nazis in the persecution of the Jews and the request for forgiveness (J-C). There was more agreement that nations have a moral obligation to redress wrong with acts of restitution and reconciliation (J-D). There was a tendency to recognize the importance of societal influences on human behavior, to approve moral education and development (high voting for moral and spiritual development programs for parents), and awareness that there are good, moral persons who are not Christians. Such an awareness may be in tension with the tendency to make individual commitment to Christ the keystone for the moral life.

Unique Views concerning Liturgical and Educational Life

The group's views concerning liturgical and educational life in the church were as follows. There was strong support for the sermon, Scripture, the prayer of confession in helping meet personal needs for forgiveness and reconciliation. There was much less support for elements such as Communion, the liturgy of forgiveness, and passing the peace. The element most affirmed was *silence* — a possible clue for the future. Music (hymns, anthems, etc.) was added, as was the value of books.

Religious education experiences that help the most were parent education, resources (books, tapes, videos), Bible study, small support groups, church school classes, and direct training in methods of forgiveness and reconciliation. It is interesting to note that parent education and direct training in methods of forgiveness and reconciliation have not been high on the list of approaches used or contemplated.

Storytelling, study of social problems where forgiveness and reconciliation are needed, training in nonviolence, preparation sessions for children and youth concerning sacramental life, marriage and family life groups, work teams, and youth groups all had some support but not very high. Some of these options may indicate lack of experience with the approach rather than lack of support if it were to be inaugurated in the future. One person added wisely, "Teaching others about forgiveness so that I understand it myself."

The Pentecostal Church

The focus group seemed to have a clear identity as a charismatic, Pentecostal church. Group members saw the church as spirit-filled, anointed with the unction of God to perform the tasks of ministry. The evidence of the presence of the Holy Spirit is ". . . in the walk, not just in the talk," not in speaking in tongues, which does take place. The church is a fellowship of over a thousand persons where ". . . the truth of God's Word is preached with integrity." The participants saw the church as Bible believing, informal, multiracial, multiethnic, and growing. They insisted that they do not label people. "We are co-laborers who are accountable, friendly, evangelical, seeking to reach out to the community." The group felt the church to be warm, loving, accepting. The pastoral leadership was seen as responsible, accessible, and focused. All are asked to participate in the healing and prophetic ministries of the church. The concept of a Spirit-filled community that "walks the walk" meant the following: "Your behavior is changed. You know right from wrong. Your prayer life is deepened. The Spirit teaches you, comforts you. The Spirit is an actual person, the third person of God." The group was animated in discussing the following beliefs.

The Nature of Sin and Salvation

The group rather quickly agreed that the major problem with reconciliation is whether or not persons have accepted Christ who reconciles us to God and others. The members present believed in original sin as a reality inherited by each person. While they agreed that we are born in the image of God, we cannot escape sin because ". . . we separate ourselves from God because of Adam and Eve's disobedience." There was much discussion about seeking reconciliation with non-Christians who are "not saved."

One woman said, "I see a compromise here. It is possible for a person to be moral without being Christian. The life we are taught to live is a lot different than for those who do not know Christ. There are some things you cannot be reconciled on if you hold Christian principles. The question is: What do you think of Jesus?" Another asserted, "Different denominations can come to the table; but the bottom line is: What does the Word say? We may agree on Jesus but not on the Word and how to interpret it." The group was asked about working with non-Christians in order to bring racial reconciliation or to bring peace in the Middle East between Jews and Arabs. Again, it was thought that some helpful steps can be taken, but no long-lasting reconciliation can take place unless each person finds Christ. One woman thought such an open approach is the social gospel. She said, "The question of working with non-Christians to improve the moral quality of life is the wrong place to start. We have to start by getting others to believe in Christ. Then, they will branch out and strengthen society. Me trying to get you to be good isn't going to cure you. What you need is a transformation — to accept Christ."

The survey results on the question of working with non-Christians to improve the moral quality of life indicated strong willingness to join non-Christians in such endeavors. What does this response mean in the light of the above views? The group agreed that a cooperative attitude is important and that a contribution can be made via modeling prior to anyone receiving Christ. We can be a "light in the world," but all of these efforts must end in the conversion of the non-Christian for true reconciliation to take place.

The Nature and Resolution of Guilt

The issue of guilt brought forth a lively discussion. There was agreement that guilt is a universal condition and that the church can hurt people by creating in them too much of a sense of guilt. One young man used the analogy that guilt is the smoke that lingers after a damaging fire. He said, "The fire has been put out (by Christ) but the smoke is still in the room and will be there until it goes out a window or door that has been opened." He concluded, "Guilt is not a healthy thing. To get past guilt allows us to use the energy for creative things."

The question concerning whether or not God always punishes the guilty (B-5) evoked: "He punishes the guilty but not always immediately. We can be forgiven, but we will be punished by not having peace of mind. That is the purpose of forgiveness. What comes to mind is, 'While we were yet sinners Christ died for us.' We deserve death but he brings life." Others suggested that without Christ we may not even be aware of sin, and not feel guilty. Without Christ the conscience is not sensitive. It was agreed that it is the mission of the church not to make us aware of our guilt but of our sin. That is the job of the preacher every Sunday.

The Relation of Confession and Repentance to Forgiveness and Reconciliation

There was total affirmation that confession is necessary for faithful Christian living. Also, there was agreement that confession to a priest or minister is not necessary in order to receive God's forgiveness. There was approval of private confession to God and a fear of public confession. Confession in corporate worship was not seen as important as confession in a small group where confidences can be kept and personal ministries can follow confession. The School of Inner Healing offered by the church was cited. The group also found support groups to be helpful (I-9).

The most meaningful form of repentance is going directly to the person offended and repenting. This approach was seen as positive because of what it does for the person who has confessed and repented. There were fewer people who found meaning in doing compensatory acts or deeds, performing penitential prayers, participating in the sacraments, denying yourself certain pleasures or privileges. Four persons felt that psychological or pastoral counseling can be positive.

The experience of forgiveness brought consistently high levels of relief from anxiety, feelings of being guilt free, of joy, wholeness, inner calm, peace, being grounded in God's love, and a desire to share God's love with others. The reason for this uniformly high level of agreement turned out to be the assumption that the above feelings were the result of having been forgiven by God through faith in Christ. The group felt that God is forgiving by nature, and that it is the role of every Christian to be a forgiver. There was a split concerning the question, "Will God forgive any and all sin?" (E-3). As expected, the major issue was the sin of blaspheming the Holy Spirit — with varying views concerning what this means. The issue of whether being reconciled with the body of Christ was as important as reconciliation on a private basis with God evoked the response that corporate reconciliation is secondary to reconciliation with God through Christ.

There was strong agreement that God's love is unconditional, that judgment is inevitable, and that God forgives when we honestly repent and are willing to change. In respect to God's judging us more by what we do than by what we think there was a firm belief that what is in the heart is the most important. The matter of reward or punishment in terms of heaven or hell was resolved in this way: "God is a loving God. He is not going to send anyone to hell. This is your choice. We send ourselves to hell by our choices. The consequence is hell. It is not God's action."

Unique Views of Liturgical and Educational Life

The most helpful liturgical elements in respect to forgiveness and reconciliation were the prayer of confession, the sermon, Scripture, and silence. In addition, there was private confession and prayer, going to the altar at specific times or freely at any time at the services — before communion, even during the preaching. Silence is highly valued at any time, not just during corporate worship.

In regard to religious education, members of the group valued Bible study, resource use, work teams (serving where conflict exists and healing is needed), small support groups, church school classes, and storytelling, plus direct training in methods of forgiveness and parent education concerning moral and spiritual development — in that order. In the discussion, parent education was identified as a higher need than originally thought. There is much teenage pregnancy ("They can be saved but still get into trouble"). It was thought that many youth still do not know how to be parents or how to handle their sexuality. This may be a big clue for future religious education for the church. There was strong support for programs already in operation: a women's study effort, a prison ministry, the pastor's Wednesday-evening Bible study and preaching, and the church's radio and television ministry. One additional idea was "reliance on the teaching of the Holy Spirit to convince my heart of the sin of unforgiveness."

Confusion about Social and Political Reconciliation

There was significant confusion about social and political reconciliation. The major agreement was about President Clinton's confession and request for forgiveness for the government's experimentation with African American men with syphilis rather than treating them (J-A). The Christian response to issues such as the South African Truth Commission's offer of amnesty, the confession and request for forgiveness of the Roman Catholic Church concerning its collaboration with the Nazis, and affirmative action was much more conflicted. The discussion ended with a call for people to move to a deeper level of forgiveness and reconciliation — from God through Christ.

"Most people are not saved," said one person. "So, they will not move to a deeper level." Another said, "I don't know if you can ever undo the damage done to blacks in this country. The only real answer is forgiveness from Christ. The enslavement and bondage of the mind will never be dealt with without Jesus Christ." Group members seemed to believe that effort to deal creatively and collegially with complex social and political issues has to take a secondary position to the effort to convert individuals to Christ in such social and political contexts. All effort to bring wider reconciliation in society is effort spent at a superficial level — not at the deepest and only really effective level.

Learning from Listening to What People Think

The Nature of God as Forgiving

Members of all four groups strongly affirmed that God's love is unconditional; but then some people put conditions on it (G1). These conditions were largely related to the necessity of persons confessing their sins either to God directly or through a priest (with some recognition of pastoral counseling as important). Other conditions had to do with seeking forgiveness from "a God who is forgiving by nature" except if someone commits a sin against the Holy Spirit (E3). In the case of sin against the Holy Spirit the Pentecostals saw no forgiveness as possible, and the Southern Baptists saw this sin as grave, possibly to be forgiven only by Christ's sacrifice for the forgiveness of the sin of Adam that we have inherited.

Southern Baptists believed that we are created good by a good God and that we are endowed with free will. It is the free will that is the source both of our creativity and our sin. Some thought Satan was the source of evil and temptation, but others saw "the great gift of freedom" as the seedbed of our sinful choices. The Pentecostals agreed by saying, "God is a loving God. He is not going to send anyone to hell. This is your choice. We send ourselves to hell by our choices." Roman Catholics emphasized God's unconditional love, but were more open about God's essential nature, saying, "We cannot know the mind of God, and we find it difficult to accept God's love; but, God does love us and pursues us even after death."

Most of the participants in all four groups saw God as central in forgiveness and reconciliation. The Catholics, revealing the importance of sharing within the body of Christ, still put confession and repentance before God via the priest in the Sacrament of Reconciliation first and repentance within the faith community second. Southern Baptists, United Methodists, and Pentecostals agreed on the order but emphasized direct confession to God and forgiveness from God, with the role of the community second (C2, D2).

Most agreed that God's judgment is inevitable but disagreed concerning whether or not judgment was daily along life's way or a final judgment (G2). According to the United Methodists, it is the righteousness in God's nature, along with love, that makes judgment inevitable. One said, "The good news is that you will have Jesus there as your 'mouthpiece' in the final judgment." Others in all four groups felt that judgment, forgiveness, and reconciliation are and should be taking place in life now.

Several important questions flow out of our study: How can the nature of God as good be integrated with the view of human nature as essentially good but inevitably sinful? What is the relation between God's unconditional love and forgiveness and God's righteousness and judgment? How can we integrate the experience of God's Holy Spirit with God's revelation through Scripture, reason, and tradition?

Confession and Repentance

The necessity of confession of sin got high marks among this sample of believers (C1). Strangely, by percent, more Protestants thought confession was imperative than did Catholics. United Methodists all thought confession was necessary for faithful Christian living, and they, arguably, are afforded less opportunity to confess sin than Christians in the other denominations. That may be why they were universally in favor. Not surprisingly, only one Protestant among all respondents thought confession to a priest or minister was a necessary step in finding God's forgiveness (C2). But then, fewer than one-third of our Catholic sample thought so. In discussion it was clear that these Catholics rated their own experience of personal confession to the priest as very positive; they still did not understand it as a necessity.

By large majorities Protestants did not find the confession of sin in public worship important or helpful (C3). This might be an alarming finding, but it is no surprise. Many Protestant churches have dropped the liturgy of confession and forgiveness from ordinary worship. Not a few will have an occasional public prayer of confession or prayer for pardon but sometimes followed by no corresponding word of forgiveness or reconciliation at all. The response confirms one's expectation. Catholics, on the other hand, had a higher estimation of the importance of their ordinary public worship for their expression of confession of sin and the hearing of forgiveness. As one parishioner put it, "The Mass helps with guilt." The sample of Catholic opinion was not, however, unanimous about this, and some expressed the opinion that in the Eucharist and other public reconciliation liturgies the *real* grace of forgiveness is not conveyed; this is reserved for private confession with the priest.

There was majority agreement that confession to an offended individual is important for confession and reconciliation (C4). United Methodists were the least affirmative with 9 negative or conceding "sometimes." Pentecostals and Southern Baptists were the most affirmative of this sort of person-to-person confession. Discussion of this issue elicited "confession" that the ideal is more honored than exercised. "It is easier to confess to God."

Response to the question about the advisability of support groups in the church where confession and forgiveness could be shared (C5) was a mixed bag. Only the Pentecostals were strongly positive. Discussion of this question revealed that the reality tended to be somewhat different than opinion expressed in the survey. There are many different sorts of groups in the churches and some of these offer important support to the members. A lot of what one person called "dumping" goes on, and there is correspondingly much forgiveness, acceptance, and reconciliation. It may be that among Christians, especially but not exclusively among Protestants, confession and absolution operate most effectively in the small group and in personal relationship experiences. Most Protestants are obviously not doing well with their traditional public confession and reconciliation in the liturgy. Maybe they never did. As an alternative to private confession and absolution it has not proved very effective. In the private confessional where sins are spoken, at least someone says to another someone, "Absolvo te." Protestants probably only think that they have dropped this model. It goes on sub rosa. Protestants have just never found a way to regularize Martin Luther's "priesthood of all believers" in church life. It happens even so, sort of. Some laypeople in our groups clearly saw the necessity of our church life to have a time and place for "garbage disposal" and recognized that there is a real burden of unresolved guilt, with no effective way to deal with it.

It did not escape these Christians that Americans, judging from what they see on TV, love to confess. They also recognized the distinction between confession and exhibitionism and deplored the daily assault of confessional entertainment.

Surely part of the negative or ambiguous response to the questions that relate issues of confession in the liturgy or church groups is the general penchant of these Christians, as different as they are, to see issues of guilt, confession, and reconciliation in personal and individual perspectives.

Probably the most hopeful revelation in this section of our survey is the strong positive response to the question (C1) that asks if confession of sin is necessary for Christian life. Were confession to be seriously implemented in our churches it would in most places require significant change. People seldom welcome change. If, however, they are asked about what is real and unreal, needed or unneeded, helpful or unhelpful, their answers often signal the desire for change.

If confession is necessary, is repentance (D) also necessary? Everybody thought so, with 3 exceptions and 3 on the fence (D1). This is a mirror image of response to the first question about confession (C1). Real admission of wrong requires a real effect in life. "God forgives, but if you don't repent, God holds you accountable because you didn't feel sorry and change your ways." This response in discussion is a good summary of the general consensus that repentance is critical to the goal of forgiveness and reconciliation.

As for the most helpful form of repentance (D2), the most popular among the options presented was overwhelmingly going directly to the person you have offended and repenting honestly, seeking forgiveness and understanding (D2b). There obviously is an important clue here — as in the similar attitude toward confession (C4) — about strategies in ministry and congregational life. The only response getting genuinely high marks was this one (D2b). Responses to other options were scattered. Catholics showed the highest approval of repentance to a minister or priest, but only slightly more than half. United Methodists and Catholics rated participating in sacraments (D2e) higher than others, but again only about half of the respondents. One write-in response, "going to God in prayer," is probably an option that should have been offered in the survey. Our equivalent, "performing penitential prayers or deeds" (D2e), got a positive response from about half of the respondents, except for Southern Baptists, where only 2 rated this a helpful option. Neither doing compensatory good deeds nor seeking counseling got strong support, and denying the self certain pleasures and privileges was a sorry loser, garnering the support of one lone respondent. And to think, time was when this was the preferred path of repentance: *sic transit dolor mundi.*

Sin and Guilt

It was to be expected that we would find much variety in understandings of sin and guilt. There was considerable demur, for instance, concerning belief in original sin (A2), with Catholics the most affirming and United Methodists the least (barely half). Group discussion yielded solid opinion among all groups that sin was universal if not original. Interestingly, among UMs and Catholics more people believed in original sin than believed that guilt is a universal human condition (B1). The unspoken assumption in this conclusion, apparently, is that we may all be sinners, but not necessarily guilty. Of all the categories of our survey, guilt — along with social/political issues — finds this sample of Christians most conflicted. Considering ourselves guilty is doubtless more threatening and less acceptable than the more abstract conclusion that all sin. In discussion of sin, human guilt, and their supposed inevitability, all groups wanted to place corresponding emphasis on original grace, and the subsequent conclusion that our God is loving, accepting, and forgiving. Adam and Eve came in for blame, as did Satan, but less than one might expect. The notion of a sinful newborn — "I cannot believe a baby is born bad" — was an often heard refrain. If sin is not an original fact, all seemed to agree that it was an "original potential."

One of the really noteworthy and stark findings in our survey and in subsequent discussions is the *individualism* of people's understanding of sin and guilt. While we found general decrying of sin in decaying moral standards and breakdown of the social fabric, especially the terrible pressure on families, we found little sense of personal guilt for "evils in society" (B6). The various collective sins, e.g., racism, pollution, war, poverty, injustice, etc., do not devolve to us as guilt unless we have taken some clearly recognizable personal action to cause them. This conclusion stood just as well for the more "communal" Catholics as it did for the more "individualistic" Protestants. Just walking around, participating in the culture, consuming, paying taxes, etc., do not give us a share in the guilt that ought to be assessed for the sins of society. No finding in the study is more disturbing than this one.

The majority of respondents to our survey conclude that the divine reality is pretty slipshod in the punishment of the guilty (B5). What seems to be their awareness of the moral ambiguity observable in earthly rewards and punishments puts one in mind of laments in the Psalms about the prosperity of the unrighteous (Ps. 73, etc.). One could expect that popular belief in punishment "on the other side" would produce a more equitable picture of a just God. It didn't. Either confidence in God's loving forgiveness or simple observance of the realities in an unjust world, or a combination of both drove the opinion of a large majority.

The largest number of respondents chose to define sin as a failure of love — specifically, the failure to love God and the neighbor (A4). They strongly condemned, but were more ambiguous about, sin as self-centeredness (A3) and overvaluing money and power (A5).

As for society being in deep trouble because of neglect of the laws of

God (A6), only the Pentecostals agreed with this judgment 100 percent. One surmises that the category *law* raises flags of caution and doubt in the minds of many Christians. UMs and Catholics agreed at roughly 3 to 1, while more than half of Southern Baptists disagreed, believing that our society was in serious trouble because we have neglected the laws of God.

One of the more shocking findings in our survey is the extent to which many Christians doubt that the ministries of the church serve to relieve guilt and reorient life (B3). At least a third of Catholics and UMs thought not or were unsure. More than half of Southern Baptists and Pentecostals marked "no" or "unsure." Something is seriously amiss here. What is revealed in the responses of these laypeople is a main reason we find ourselves engaged in this project, namely, the general neglect in our churches of ministries of repentance, confession, forgiveness, and reconciliation. This is a neglect apparently so severe that many Christians do not connect guilt and its relief with ministries of the church.

While our ecclesial ministries may not set us free from guilt, a substantial majority of respondents to our survey believed that these ministries can create a harmful guilt in us (B3). By a tally of 6 to 1 they recognize the danger that the church can infect us with too much of a sense of guilt. Correspondingly and interestingly, fewer respondents were sure that people could have guilty feelings that were unrelated to actual guilt (B8). Fifty-three were sure, 2 thought not, and 19 recognized that this could sometimes be the case. One of the important discoveries in group discussions of these issues was the extent to which some people were unable to distinguish guilt from guilt feelings. In some cases this was a matter of concluding that one wouldn't have guilt feelings if one were not guilty. In more cases this was simply the identification of feelings and facts.

Forgiveness is clearly something hard to hear. Almost half of respondents still struggle with guilt after believing that they have been forgiven (B4). Neither the typical Protestant general declaration of forgiveness, nor the Catholic confessional, nor the witness of the Spirit seems entirely convincing. As one Catholic said of confession, "Sometimes we feel we didn't get it all in. Inside we may not be sure." One person acknowledged in discussion that "It is difficult to accept that God loves me." Back in the early 1950s Paul Tillich wrote movingly about our difficulty finding the "courage to accept acceptance." It remains a serious difficulty.

Is it part of the mission of the church to make us aware of our guilt (B7)? Of participants who responded to this question, 40 said yes, 21 said no, and 11 were unsure. Significantly, more than half of our sample deny or doubt that the message of God's plumb line and our transgression is a legitimate part of Christian ministry. The theological, homiletical, and pastoral category of *judgment* is fading from our screen. The breakdown of responses among denominational groups was intriguing. UMs were negative or unsure on this question 14 to 4, while Catholics were affirmative on the question 10 to 3, and Baptists and Pentecostals responded 3 to 1 in the affirmative. While not unexpected, this set of answers is further evidence that in our "I'm OK, you're OK" society, judgment — even the judgment of God — is unrecognized by not a few as a legitimate part of the mission of the church. It would appear that this is especially so among Protestants.

Social and Political Issues

Our survey and the dialogue sessions repeatedly touched on various aspects of social and political forgiveness and reconciliation. One of the questions that pointed to a basic attitude of openness or closedness was the willingness to work with non-Christians in strengthening the fabric of society. All four groups indicated a strong willingness to do so, almost 100 percent in each church (F2). Yet there was a great resistance on the part of all four groups to identify with the evils in society on the level of any personal guilt (B6). The matter of feeling a sense of sin for breaking the ethical laws of society had more recognition of responsibility but with several unsure (A7). There are clues concerning genuine interest in social and political issues in the survey on the religious education needed. See the discussion below in Chapter 7 concerning the desire for study about social problems where forgiveness and reconciliation are needed, the interest in serving on work teams to change social conditions, or to learn how to solve problems nonviolently.

On the specific issues of public apology, confession, repentance, and the request for forgiveness, considerable lack of clarity and affirmation emerged. The Catholics did not approve of President Clinton's apology to the families of the black men who died as a result of participation in an ill-planned and ill-conducted syphilis study. The other three groups were largely affirmative (JA). Many were negative about the efforts of the South African Truth and Reconciliation Commission and its approach to forgiveness and reconciliation through the quest for truth and confession within the context of a policy of amnesty. Catholics were more affirmative but wanted persons to be contrite before receiving forgiveness (JB). The discussions concerning the South African approach were agonizing in tone and revealed the depths of many issues included in our study. Most were quick to see the importance of personal confession, repentance, and forgiveness but were much less secure about approaches to social violence and the way to heal divisions and deep hurts that come from armed struggles, murder, torture, and the destruction of property. The South African situation brought all such ambiguity to the surface.

While there were several "not sure" responses, most in all the groups supported the French Roman Catholics in their confession to the Jews regarding their collaboration with the Nazis during World War II. The Catholics generally affirmed the action (JC). Again, while there were several "not sure" responses, most agreed that nations should make a public apology and perform acts of restitution and reconciliation when they commit acts that profoundly injure innocent people (JD).

All in all, it appears that much more attention is needed in educational, liturgical, and service life of the church concerning the specific dynamics of social and political forgiveness and reconciliation. There is real resistance to the church getting involved. This is seen in the response to the question having to do with the church's involvement and responsibility for the social problems associated with crime, drugs, sexual abuse, homelessness, ethnic cleansing, etc. These trends clearly point to the need for refocused educational and liturgical life in the future.

Religious Education

While religious education must be seen in a wider way than can be captured in the questions we raised (i.e., as the changes that take place as a result of participation in the total life of the congregation), it is possible to see characteristic perceptions via the responses on the survey and the dialogues that followed.

One of the most significant findings has to do with the strong affirmation of parent education concerning moral and spiritual development. All four church groups gave from over 50 to 90 percent approval (Ia). Even the Pentecostals with their firm emphasis on conversion and life in the Holy Spirit recognized that many teenage girls who had "been saved" had not been given sound moral education and had become pregnant and eventually mothers without clear guidance and direction. Another universally supported aspect of religious education was Bible study concerning reconciliation (Ig). Bible study has made a significant recovery within most congregations recently, including the Catholics who traditionally left interpretation to the priests and nuns. While Protestants have always lifted up Scripture study, there has been a renewed emphasis with the introduction of more intensive programs such as the Disciple Bible study program of the United Methodists and many others. These new studies call for covenantal commitment of time and preparation. The Pentecostal church has Bible study every Wednesday night, led by the pastor and televised to the wider community. Southern Baptists have a long history of Christian education centered in the Bible.

All the focus groups affirmed the importance of small support groups in dealing with forgiveness and reconciliation, with Catholics the lowest. The Pentecostals preferred confessing to God first and receiving forgiveness directly from God through Christ but recognized the importance of support from others (Ij). They have supportive group life in a women's study group and a prison ministry group.

The United Methodists have a strong emphasis on small groups that deepen personal spirituality, accountability, and responsibility to others. Such groups create a sense of the church as family. (Nationally, United Methodists have developed Emmaus groups for adults and Chrysalis groups for youth.) The same is true of the smaller Southern Baptist church in which members think of themselves as a family where everyone is important and gives and receives acceptance, forgiveness, and renewal. Catholics, too, have created the Cursillo movement with its sense of Christian community and much interpersonal support. The same pattern can be found in marriage preparation programs such as the Catholic Cana program and the marriage enrichment programs of Protestant churches.

The creative use of resources (curricula, books, tapes, videos, CDs, etc.) was selected as next in importance by Pentecostals, United Methodists, and Southern Baptists. The Catholics gave it less support. Storytelling was low for Catholics (2 out of 13) and more important for Pentecostals and Southern Baptists, with United Methodists in between. The study of social problems was not very high for most of the groups, except for the Southern Baptists, who placed it higher (Id). This is interesting because United Methodists have a history of more attention to social concerns and the Southern Baptists have a history of more attention to personal faith. Another unexpected finding: training in nonviolent methods was quite low for Catholics and United Methodists and somewhat more affirmed by Pentecostals and Southern Baptists (Je).

It was quite interesting that preparation of children and youth for sacramental life was quite modestly supported by all four groups. Given the more recent emphasis within the Roman Catholic Church on catechesis regarding the Eucharist and the Sacrament of Reconciliation, one might expect more support from Catholics. However, the priest where the study was made sees such support coming in the future. He believes there will be more of a corporate sense of reconciliation in the congregations of tomorrow because of the way children and youth are now introduced to sacramental life. This fresh approach is discussed in considerable detail in Chapter 7.

Marriage and family life education was somewhat supported by Pentecostals and United Methodists, more strongly supported by Southern Baptists, and less so by Catholics (1 out of 13). Church school classes were not important to Catholics, probably because of their parochial school pattern. Such classes were important for the other groups, especially the Southern Baptists, with their long history of training coming from the National Sunday School Board. Again, youth groups had zero importance for Catholics, probably because of their different patterns, while they were modestly supported by Pentecostals and United Methodists. The Southern Baptists had more youth in their focus group and their support was higher.

We decided to add two categories that are somewhat new (work teams dealing with reconciliation and direct training in forgiveness) in order to see if participants already had some experience with them or had positive responses to the ideas. Work teams (to study and serve where conflicts exist and healing is needed) received stronger support from Southern Baptists and United Methodists and very little support from Pentecostals and Catholics (Il). Direct training in methods of forgiveness and reconciliation (a process being researched and developed by Dr. Robert Enright of the University of Wisconsin and described in Chapter 7) received significant affirmation from Pentecostals and Southern Baptists, with modest support from Catholics and United Methodists (Im).

The survey information was used not as a definitive finding but as the basis for dialogue concerning the local educational efforts. There was either rejoicing about their selections or an awareness of omissions as "wake-up calls" for possible future improvement.

Liturgy

Our position is that religious education and liturgy are interrelated and reinforcing but with unique identities and functions. While for the most part they function powerfully when they are cooperative they can and should be at times in creative tension. In this study we separated the roles in order to discern how they are perceived to be helpful in bringing persons to forgiveness and reconciliation. The survey and the dialogues assessed the power of varying aspects of the congregation's worship life.

As was expected, Catholics valued highly the Sacrament of Reconciliation (Hf). The same rating was given to the Sacrament of the Eucharist. Since the other three churches do not participate in the Sacrament of Reconciliation per se, it makes sense that they would rate it much lower. All did, with the exception of the United Methodists who affirmed it. Again, it was expected that the Southern Baptists and the Pentecostals would be less sacramental and they were. The United Methodists joined the Catholics in valuing the Eucharist quite highly (He).

One of the most striking findings was the universal value placed on silence in dealing with issues of forgiveness and reconciliation (Hi). Southern Baptists were the highest with 22 out of 25 favoring it. Such a finding should not be overlooked. Much more attention should be paid to training in the practice of meditation and the use of silence in the spiritual life. Another unexpected finding was the low value placed on the relational ritual of passing the peace by all four groups. This may be because there was less direct connection in their minds with forgiveness and reconciliation or with the irregular use of the ritual. The sermon and Scripture were valued by all. The Pentecostals had a Bible study and sermon on forgiveness and reconciliation on Wednesday evening during our time with them. This was by chance — but it was quite a powerful, non-legalistic, relational approach to the issues of sin, guilt, confession, repentance, forgiveness, and reconciliation. It culminated with opportunity for persons to come forward to share their burdens and to receive God's forgiveness and renewal. All was done privately with the pastor in a confidential meeting of souls.

The liturgy of forgiveness was strongly rated by Catholics (12/13) and to some degree by United Methodists, but was quite low for Southern Baptists and Pentecostals (Hb). Also, the Lord's Prayer was high for Catholics and United Methodists but low for Southern Baptists and Pentecostals. The prayer of confession was affirmed by all four groups (Hc). This is significant because of the finding that so many congregations are omitting prayers of confession in corporate worship.

All four groups made additional suggestions that were quite helpful. The Southern Baptists listed the importance of music, especially hymns, as did the Catholics and the United Methodists. Catholics mentioned architecture and "being a liturgical minister." The Pentecostals highlighted an important drama ministry in which several were involved. They also added the importance of praise and prayer services along with individual, personal prayer.

One person added, "remembering what I have done wrong and working to stay in fellowship with the Lord." Books such as Max Lucado's *In the Grip of Grace* were mentioned.

Are Forgiveness, Reconciliation, and Moral Courage Really Possible? (The Nature of Human Nature)

W hen the nature of human nature is explored it is tempting to be either too optimistic or too pessimistic. If it can correctly be said that human beings are created in the image of God, Imago Dei, a cataloging of all of our positive human qualities of creativity, love, trust, and capacity for righteousness, forgiveness, and reconciliation can follow. If it can be said that it is our human nature to be centered in ourselves and to fall into patterns of anxiety and self-protection, a cataloging of the seven deadly sins can follow. Some of our thinkers have avoided these two conflicting assumptions and have said that human nature is neither positive nor negative but rather is neutral (tabula rasa). Whether a person becomes positive or negative depends on the quality of the environment in which he or she grows and matures. The problem is, of course, that there is some truth in each of the above assumptions. Our study of the four churches found much struggle about whether human nature is basically good or caught in original sin.

It is our position that *all of life is sacred.* This assumption flows out of our belief that the whole universe "belongs to God and is the gift of God to us, uniting us to creation and all people in celebration of the sacredness of all life and a belonging to one another in the Spirit."[1] We shall unpack the meaning of this basic assumption as we discuss the following issues.

First, we will attempt to identify some of the positive moral qualities that are clearly at the heart of the human condition. If we assume that we are created in the image of God, as sacred beings, what do we bring with us into

1. Robert L. Browning and Roy A. Reed, *The Sacraments in Religious Education Liturgy: An Ecumenical Model* (Birmingham, Ala.: Religious Education Press, 1985), p. 120.

life? This will be done as we probe biblical and theological assumptions as well as the creative thought of social scientist James A. Wilson. Second, we will seek to face the reasons why we as human beings repeatedly fail to treat one another as sacred and instead tend to use one another in order to deal with our anxieties and to find security and meaning (our sin). Our discussion of the nature of sin and anxiety will draw on various insights of Søren Kierkegaard, Reinhold Niebuhr, and Gregory Jones. Third, we will explore the relation of human nature to our quest for moral courage and universal justice. In doing so, we shall examine the assumptions about human nature in various approaches to moral education, especially that of Lawrence Kohlberg and his supporters and critics. Finally, we shall discuss whether or not we as human beings have the capacity for and necessity of giving and receiving forgiveness and being reconciled with those who have offended or hurt us or whom we have offended or hurt deeply. The creative research of Robert Enright and Everett Worthington and their associates will be of signal importance in our conversation.

Imago Dei: If Each of Us Is Sacred, What Are the Qualities in Human Nature on Which We May Build?

First of all, why can it be said that each person (and all of creation) is sacred and worthy of our love, nurture, care, and forgiveness? It is, of course, impossible to prove that all of life is sacred and that each one of us is to be treated as holy. It *is* possible to discover the truth of such an assumption by living it, by risking, by putting our faith into action in our attitudes and decisions. It *is* possible to allow ourselves to be inspired to make such discovery through the scriptures and the guidance of present-day spiritual leaders. We can agree with the psalmist about God's presence in each of our lives. "For it was you who formed my inward parts; You knit me together in my mother's womb. I praise you, for I am fearfully and wonderfully made. Wonderful are your works; that I know very well" (Ps. 139:13-14). We can emphasize the gifts God has given each of us for service to others in his name. We can say yes to Jesus' high view of human potential. "You are the light of the world. A city built on a hill cannot be hid. No one after lighting a lamp puts it under a bushel basket, but on the lampstand, and it gives light to all in the house. In the same way, let your light shine before others, so that they may see your good works and give glory to your Father in heaven" (Matt. 5:14-16).

If we assume that all in God's human family are sacred, we will find it to be the norm not the exception to follow Jesus' teaching, which is deceptively simple but has been identified in moral development theory as the highest form of moral behavior: namely the Golden Rule. "In everything do to others as you would have them do to you; so this is the law and the prophets" (Matt. 17:12). And why would each of us so treat others? Because the other is of infinite value as such; because the other has been created by God, "fearfully and wonderfully made" in God's image, and therefore sacred. Morever, if all of life is sacramental, each of us can allow Christ, the primordial sacrament, to shine though us. We, then, can become a living sacrament to others.

Such a perspective on faith can have a profound effect on our relations with human beings of all races and creeds and also with nature. Albert Schweitzer took such a position with his "reverence for life" philosophy and with his sacrificial ministry in Africa. The Jewish scholar Martin Buber has inspired people of many faiths to see the holy in our everyday relationships. Buber maintained that each person is really an I-thou or an I-it, not just an I. He saw deeply that as human beings we *are* the way we relate to others. We can see others as sacred, precious Thous through which the Eternal Thou moves or as *things,* as *its* that we use for our purposes rather than for their own ends.

In his classic book *I and Thou,* Buber said that the mysterious truth in all human relations is that when we treat others as Thous, as sacred beings of unique and infinite value, we become Thous ourselves. Also, when we treat other persons as things, or its, we become it-like ourselves, wooden and unspontaneous. Buber also called for us to treat the world of things, the world of nature with respect, as a world given to us by God. He was realistic, however. He knew how easy it is for us to treat others as things to be moved around to meet our needs, to provide security for our insecure and fragile lives. Therefore, we as human beings are always in the situation of having to admit that we have treated other persons, Thous, as its, and therefore we must ask for forgiveness and re-enact the relationship of I-thou-ness. When we treat others as sacred, as valuable in and of themselves, we will meet the eternal Thou and be lifted up for living another day. Such a perspective is put in challenging terms by Jesus in the Sermon on the Mount. "You have heard that it was said, 'You shall love your neighbor and hate your enemy.' But I say to you, Love your enemies and pray for those who persecute you, so that you may be children of your Father in heaven; for he makes the sun rise on the evil and the good, and sends rain on the righteous and the unrighteous. For if you love those who love you, what reward do you have. . . . Be perfect, therefore, as your heavenly Father is perfect" (Matt. 6:43-46a, 48). The admonition to be perfect gives most of us pause. Yet, Jesus' challenge does help us to look more deeply at our own lives, to evaluate whether or not we, in our inner selves, want to love others, even our enemies, as sacred Thous, worthy of our forgiveness, understanding, and love. Such is especially true today with major divisions between people who see themselves as enemies in Afghanistan, Bosnia, Kosovo, Ireland, South Africa, India/Pakistan, Burma, and yes, in the United States with our racial and ethnic struggles.

If we agree that human beings are sacred, having been "wonderfully formed" by God in God's image, what evidence do we have of positive quali-ties within human nature that can be nurtured and on which we can build a responsible, caring, and reconciling society? Great philosophers from Plato and Aristotle on to Aquinas and contemporary thinkers have sought to distill the evidence. One of the most helpful studies of human nature, in respect to identifying positive moral qualities present in human nature per se, is James A. Wilson's *The Moral Sense.* Wilson argues convincingly that ". . . peo-ple have a natural moral sense, a sense that is formed out of the interaction of their innate disposition with their earliest familial experience. To different degrees among different people, but to some important degree in just about all people, that moral sense shapes human behavior and judgments people make of the behavior of others."[2] Wilson disagrees with cultural anthropolo-gists who believe that universal moral values do not exist but are the result of diverse mores found in various cultures. Such a stance implies that "culture is everything and nature nothing; and secondly, no universal moral rules exist in all cultures."[3] Wilson maintains that such a position is wrong. He finds murder and incest to be wrong in all cultures, for instance. Wilson's study sought to discover in human nature certain revealing uniformities, which can be seen as "general, non-arbitrary and emotionally compelling about human nature."[4] Wilson recognized several possible moral sensibilities such as mod-esty, integrity, and courage, but came down on the following four examples of a moral sense in human nature in all cultures: *sympathy, fairness, self-control,* and *duty.* Let us look more closely at each of these.

Sympathy

Wilson found sympathy to be a universal human capacity to be affected by the feelings and experiences of others. This elemental sense of sympathy can be seen, of course, in simple relations between parents and children in all cul-

---

2. James A. Wilson, *The Moral Sense* (New York: Free Press, 1993), p. 2.
3. Wilson, *The Moral Sense,* p. 17.
4. Wilson, *The Moral Sense,* p. 16.

tures and between those who are present in emergencies and respond at the risk of their own safety or their very lives. It was evident during the Holocaust when non-Jews in Europe helped Jews avoid the Nazi death camps. In the latter case, in a study of four hundred people who helped Jews escape, the vast majority helped out of a selfless sense of ethics. "They felt a keen sense of sympathy for the victims . . . or they believed in some principle (justice, fair play) that made it wrong for anyone to be treated in this way."[5] The researchers, Samuel and Pearl Oliver, stated that the most amazing thing about those who helped was that they were ordinary people with an extraordinary willingness to alleviate suffering when they found it. Moreover, the rescuers had been very close to their parents, both mothers and fathers, and had learned from them the importance of "dependability, self-reliance and caring for others. These warm familial feelings extended to others: sympathetic rescuers saw people as basically good and had many close friends."[6] A smaller group of Christians who were rescuers came to the same conclusions. Wilson cites the self-sacrifice of ants for the survival of the colony. There is a genre of literature about the sensitivity of animals and their willingness to care selflessly. For example, Susan McElroy has collected many true stories in her book, *Animals as Teachers and Healers.*

> One of the most memorable stories was of a German shepherd covering a toddler with its body during a house fire. When the firefighters removed the dog's body, they were surprised to find the toddler still alive and suffering from only minor burns and smoke inhalation. The dog had been purchased to protect the family — it gave its life to do so.[7]

Wilson concludes that sympathy for persons who are not offspring and creatures that are not human is characteristic of humans in all cultures. In fact, we often think people are inhuman who act as if they have no sympathy for others in deep need. Such feelings of sympathy are the ground of the development of conscience and the interior judgments we make about the right or wrong behavior of others and of ourselves.

5. Wilson, *The Moral Sense,* p. 38.
6. Wilson, *The Moral Sense,* pp. 38-39.
7. Susan Chernak McElroy, *Animals as Teachers and Healers* (New York: Ballantine, 1996, 1997), p. 54.

Fairness

Wilson found that one of the very first moral judgments of children is, "That's not fair." Such an expression comes because of concern for property and is self-interested in orientation. However, by four years of age children will share even when it is not in their interest to do so and even where parents are not present. Several experiments have found four- and five-year-old children who, when given things they could share, go ahead and share with others without any specific direction and without any claims by other children.[8]

Why do children do this? Is it because they are taught by parents and others to be fair or is there something in their nature that is behind this behavior? Wilson cites Piaget who says that the answer is to be found in the "natural sociability of the child." Piaget found that children playing marbles expressed a sense of justice. "The sense of justice," he wrote, "though naturally capable of being reinforced by precepts and practical examples of the adult, is largely independent of those influences, and requires nothing more of the development than the mutual respect and solidarity which holds among children themselves. Children learn marbles from each other not from adults. The younger children were taught by the older ones; the former respected the rules because they had traditional authority, the latter because they were useful in facilitating social relations!"[9]

The issue of fairness changes as persons develop. It is especially evident in middle childhood. However, it is always present, especially in relation to the ownership of property. Wilson agrees with Aristotle that fairness is best dealt with when persons have private property rather than property in common. The latter makes for arguments over fair distribution. Also, people will work harder to improve something they own and will be indifferent about property that is everyone's. Finally, Aristotle believed that people get pleasure out of sharing something they own with others. Aristotle concludes in *Politics* that having and sharing are "innate human sentiments."[10]

Wilson agrees with philosopher John Rawls that ". . . moral feelings are a normal feature of human life, and indeed a precondition of people deciding on the rules by which to live. Rawls asks us to imagine a person who lacks any sense of fairness, who never acts justly except as self-interest and expediency require. . . . Such a person would be less than human."[11]

8. Wilson, *The Moral Sense*, p. 57.
9. Wilson, *The Moral Sense*, p. 58.
10. Wilson, *The Moral Sense*, p. 77.
11. Wilson, *The Moral Sense*, p. 78.

Self-Control

Wilson ties self-control to the historic emphasis on temperance, indicating that Aristotle placed temperance beside justice and courage as qualities of character that anyone should possess if evaluated as good. "Self-control acquires moral standing in the same way that sympathy and fairness do," says Wilson. "Just as most people cannot imagine living in a society in which self-indulgence, self-centeredness, and self-dealing are accepted standards of right conduct, so they cannot imagine living a life devoted to such principles and still calling it human."[12]

Self-control has to do with the firmness of the person's self-understanding and sense of direction in life. If the individual has long-term goals and purposes, the ability to control the self in relation to deserved but conflicting short-term goals increases greatly. This struggle of the self is related to the quality of self-transcendence, which makes it possible for the self always to be thinking ahead — to the state of interior life that will be evident in the future. For instance, desiring a reputation for honesty and integrity in the future can motivate a person to resist temptation now.

It is clear that the ability of the person to control the self rather than to give in to impulses regarding consequences is exceedingly important. It is strange that self-control is not more emphasized and affirmed in a society in which there is so much individual and social cost to impulsivity seen in smoking, drug addiction, predatory sexuality, and crime.

Such an emphasis on self-control has been affirmed in several character education programs recently. One of the important national efforts is the Communitarian Network and its affirmation of two qualities of character necessary for self-integration and societal responsibility: the qualities of *self-discipline* and *empathy*. Amitai Etzioni, University Professor at George Washington University and founder of the Network, urges schools to employ these two character traits as ways not only to build character but also to evaluate the total educational program of the school. Etzioni also emphasizes the importance of recognizing the tendencies to be found in human nature and to use those to engage students, teachers, parents, and community leaders in the moral development of all participants.[13] It is not difficult to relate these two aspects of human capacity, self-discipline and empathy, to the qualities of sympathy and fairness that Wilson sees as universal.

12. Wilson, *The Moral Sense*, p. 82.
13. Amitai Etzioni, *The New Golden Rule: Community and Morality in a Democratic Society* (New York: Basic Books, 1996), p. 185.

Duty

When we are quick to respond to human need and do our duty in society, we are living out a basic human desire for attachment to others, says Wilson. It is this basic fact about human nature that is behind our development of a conscience. Recent research has altered the Freudian view that conscience comes from repression of the id and internalization of societal norms via the superego. It has been discovered that "people with the strongest conscience will not be those with the most powerful repressed aggressiveness but those with the most powerfully developed affiliation. . . . Attachment, not fear, is associated with late moral development. . . . Conscience is not simply imposed on us, it is in part something we impose on ourselves as we think through what it means to be human and on what terms we can live with ourselves."[14]

Duty is the disposition to honor our obligations without any hope of reward or any fear of punishment. Wilson believes that persons reveal themselves to be moral not merely by being true to their commitments but by honoring them even when it is not in their interest to do so. In studies of Good Samaritan behavior, of people who went forward to help crime victims, it was found that conscience was a central factor. Some acted quickly out of anger. Others acted out of principle. What they saw was wrong and they were selfless in responding.

Such reactions relate clearly to an implied view of justice or the lack of it. We shall return to this observation later in our discussion of moral development within and beyond the faith community.

Why and How We Fall into the Sin of Separation from Self, Others, and God — through Pride or Self-Abnegation — and Are Repeatedly in Need of Confession, Forgiveness, and Reconciliation

The greatest of all gifts from God is the gift of Spirit. This gift, however, bringing with it the power of self-transcendence, is the precondition that produces anxiety. The gift of Spirit also brings a marvelous reality of human freedom. In the light of the fact that as human beings we have been created in God's image, we can see in ourselves the natural qualities of sympathy, fairness, self-control, duty, and other indications of a moral sense. Because of God's gift of Spirit we are aware of ourselves and our freedom to respond to life as we wish. This awareness makes us know that we are both finite (we know we will die) and in-

14. Wilson, *The Moral Sense*, pp. 107-15.

finite (our gift of Spirit makes us long for eternal meaning and destiny during this life and beyond). Each person then is a synthesis of the natural, the finite, and the spiritual, the infinite. The result of this ability to transcend the self is the cause of our creativity and our anxiety, which can lead to despair. This inner condition calls for a centering in the love of God in faith in order for the self to be unified and given a sense of direction, purpose, and empowerment to love self, others, and God.[15] Kierkegaard, a man who was himself often plagued with a deep despair, saw despair itself as a gift from God. It is a gift because it is the result of our spiritual nature, the result of our ability to transcend ourselves to deal with our human freedom, to make decisions in order to handle our anxiety over our past, present, and future. Human nature is such that we are always in need of relating ourselves to ourselves by finding the true center of our being either in our Creator or in some other center of power and meaning which unifies the self and gives our spiritual nature grounding and unity. We discover finally that the only center with eternal meaning is the true God of love who created us and sustains us from day to day. Kierkegaard, according to many, profoundly understood the psychological dynamics of human life and faith when he concluded, "By relating itself to its own self and by willing to be itself, the self is grounded transparently in the Power which constituted it! And this formula . . . is the definition of faith."[16]

Building on Kierkegaard's views, the theologian Reinhold Niebuhr says that anxiety is the "inevitable concomitant of the paradox of freedom and finiteness . . . it is the internal precondition of sin."[17] Anxiety is not sin, but it is the result of not being loved perfectly by parents and peers, and of not being able to love others selflessly and spontaneously. When we realize we are not fully loved, treated as sacred, we attempt to protect ourselves, to build some castle of human security, often at the expense of our relationships with others. Instead of loving and trusting others as sacred Thous we tend to mask our insecurities by appearing to love selflessly but actually using others to build up our egos, our realm of influence and power. We do not do this because we are caught in the context of original sin into which we are born, a punishment, which is the result of the primordial willful acts of Adam and Eve. No. We as free agents existentially "fall" into the sin of inordinate and unhealthy self-love and self-protection. This "fall" is not unlike the original fall symbol-

15. Søren Kierkegaard, *The Sickness unto Death* (Princeton: Princeton University Press, 1944), p. 21.

16. Kierkegaard, *The Sickness unto Death*, p. 216.

17. Reinhold Niebuhr, *The Nature and Destiny of Man*, vol. 1 (New York: Scribner's, 1941), p. 182. See also Don S. Browning, *Religious Thought and the Modern Psychologies* (Philadelphia: Fortress, 1987), pp. 20-29 for a penetrating analysis of Niebuhr's significance.

ized by the temptation of Adam and Eve in the classic biblical story. It is not a punishment from God. Rather, it is the result of the gift from God of freedom and the natural gift of knowledge and the potential of human love.

Niebuhr wisely recognized that anxiety is the ". . . internal description of the state of temptation. It must not be identified with sin because there is always the ideal possibility that faith would purge anxiety of the tendency toward sinful self-assertion. The ideal possibility is that faith in the ultimate security of God's love would overcome all immediate insecurities of nature and history. That is why Christian orthodoxy has consistently defined unbelief as the root of sin which precedes pride."[18] Niebuhr's view was often called neo-orthodox. Such was the case because he did not take the scriptures literally. Rather, he saw the biblical stories as profound symbols of much deeper existential truth about the nature of human nature and the nature of God's forgiveness and reconciliation that are inevitably needed by every human being. The inevitability of sin is because of the way all of us finally deal with the gift of being born in God's image with wonderful creative potential and born free with endless decisions before us about how we will use our creative potential and our freedom, especially in light of our power of self-transcendence.

Kierkegaard recognized within his own life that he was in angst because he found himself willing to be himself but was unable to become the self that God had made possible. Also, he was in despair because he was unable *not* to be himself, to escape from the self that God had given him in all of its uniqueness and potential. Such an internal struggle helped Kierkegaard discover more deeply the relational nature of the self as well as the transcendent nature of the self. This sense of transcendence makes it possible for human beings to be able to stand above themselves and to discover their great potential as well as their limitations, their tendency to use others, to make sacred persons into "its" or things. Of course, because of this same gift of Spirit and the concomitant gift of self-transcendence, the self feels guilt and shame. Niebuhr saw clearly that the inevitability of the misuse of the gift of human freedom does not release us from responsibility for our "fall" into the sin of pride which separates us from God, from others, and from ourselves. We have two directions to go: either into remorse or repentance. Niebuhr asserts, "The remorse and repentance which are consequent upon such contemplation are similar in their acknowledgement of freedom and responsibility and their implied assertion of it. They differ in the fact that repentance is the expression of freedom and faith while remorse is the expression of freedom without faith."[19]

18. Niebuhr, *The Nature and Destiny of Man,* pp. 182-83.
19. Niebuhr, *The Nature and Destiny of Man,* p. 255.

When we fall into remorse we can find ourselves in patterns of unhealthy guilt or unhealthy shame. Unhealthy guilt is when we are feeling guilty for having the sexual feelings that accompany our normal male and female sexual development. Healthy guilt takes place when we act on such feelings irresponsibly, hurting another and ourself. Unhealthy shame is when we feel embarrassed and inferior because of an incident related to losing a job or having a failure known by others. Healthy shame is a shame that we recognize because we have not lived up to our own standards. Healthy shame is rooted in our convictions. As James and Evelyn Whitehead assert, "With proper care, a positive sense of shame matures into a resident strength in us — a virtue. . . . A positive sense of shame flowers in a multitude of virtues, with humility the most basic. By alerting us to the limits of our strength and gifts, shame keeps us humble. Humility is a realistic and flexible sense of self, which bends before adversity and even failure, but does not shatter. A healthy sense of shame allows us to be humbled without being humiliated."[20]

Healthy guilt and shame can bring us to the place where we can repent of our self-serving actions and attitudes that caused the hurt in the first place, can open the door to our willingness to ask for forgiveness from God and from those hurt, and finally to forgive ourselves and to act out our renewed relationship of trust, justice, and care.

As Kierkegaard and Niebuhr both recognize, remorse and despair are gifts that accompany our spiritual nature and are the result of our search for ultimate meaning, the result of our standing before God in freedom and finitude. Niebuhr sums it up for us when he states that "all experiences of an uneasy conscience, of remorse and of repentance are therefore religious experiences, though they are not always explicitly or consciously religious. Experiences of repentance, in distinction to remorse, presuppose some knowledge of God. . . . For without the knowledge of divine love remorse cannot be transmuted into repentance."[21]

L. Gregory Jones clarifies the nature of sin when he says that sin is not only our pride, resulting in our anxiety. It is also the opposite: self-abnegation or "hiding" from God and others. God loves all that God has created, human beings and all of nature. God created all human beings and nature for loving communion with God and one another. We become our most fulfilled selves when we are in loving communion with God and one another. Yet, because of our quest to protect ourselves we fall into patterns of rejecting the reality of

20. James D. Whitehead and Evelyn Eaton Whitehead, *Shadows of the Heart: A Spirituality of Our Painful Emotions* (New York: Crossroad/Herder, 1996), pp. 111-12.
21. Niebuhr, *The Nature and Destiny of Man,* p. 257.

communion. We become ". . . isolated and divided individuals obsessively concerned with preserving or sustaining a sense of 'self.' As a result, the musical harmony of God's self-giving communion is transmitted into the cacophony of self-asserting or self-abnegating selves unable to hear one another."[22]

Jones reminds us, also, that we are born into a world where the sin of separation is very much in evidence. We are born not into original sin and punishment from God for disobedience. However, because of the past sins of separation from God, others, and self, we "inherit" a brokenness and fragmentation that are present because of what we have done to one another (such as violence, adultery, lying, racism) or what we have failed to do for one another (such as abandoning those who suffer, neglecting the physical and emotional needs of others, or not being just or honest in our relationships). Therefore, there is much need of forgiveness very early in life. In order to move forward in freedom we need finally to forgive those who have hurt us without even knowing us. Forgiveness, then, not only frees us from self-doubt and inner pain, it opens the door to communion with God and others.[23] Of course, young children have to mature as selves, with the power of self-transcendence becoming more and more operational, before they have the capacity to forgive the sins of those who have gone before them (e.g., being born into a family/community suffering from racial or ethnic discrimination), or forgiving those who have used us for their own ends (e.g., living in a family with parents who have physically or sexually abused us).

It can be said, then, that human beings are born in the image of God, with gifts of creativity and a capacity to love and trust. They are also born with a moral sense that imbues them with a need to develop a loving and kind community, and with the gifts of freedom and spirit that make self-transcendence possible. But these gifts create the possibility of anxiety about how to handle our freedom, how to meet our deep need to be loved and to love. It is in this state of anxiety that we tend to seek securities that are self-centered or self-abnegating. We thus fall into the sin of separation from our Creator, from others whom we begin to use instead of affirm as infinitely valuable in themselves, and we separate ourselves from ourselves in inner turmoil and doubt. It is this dynamic interaction that brings about the need for education and nurture to affirm our great natural, human, God-given potential — a general education and a religious education that are positive and affirming of the uniqueness of each person, building on the gifts God has given

22. L. Gregory Jones, *Embodying Forgiveness: A Theological Analysis* (Grand Rapids: Eerdmans, 1995), p. 61.

23. Jones, *Embodying Forgiveness*, p. 63.

to each. Beyond this, each person experiences a psychological struggle and "fall" that lead to varying degrees of self-striving and self-hiding — conditions that can only be repaired by finding a true center of power, a center of love and trust that will always be adequate and genuine, a faithful orientation to the Creator God whose love created us and whose love and righteousness have been revealed to us in Christ, and whose ongoing love, forgiveness, and richness are promised through the Holy Spirit in touch with our spiritual nature. This final dynamic calls for a Christian religious education and for participation in the loving, serving, forgiving, reconciling corporate body of Christ in worship. It is within this community of faith that we can be inspired to discern the sacredness of all of life, the sacredness of each person and of the whole natural order. It is within this community of faith that we can be honest with ourselves and with one another concerning our repeated temptations to lose sight of God's will and way for our lives and to confess openly and honestly our tendency to fall into the sin of separation of ourselves from others. Also we need to confess: our tendency to forget the sacredness of our children, our spouses, our work associates, those who are competing for the resources of the earth; our tendency to separate ourselves from trusting and loving communion with God; and our tendency to separate ourselves from ourselves (being unable to will to be the self we know we can become or being unable to *not* be the self we have been born to be). These dynamics are the preconditions that lead us to explore our need for confession, for forgiveness from God, others, and ourselves.

The Relation of Human Nature to the Quest for Universal Justice

That human nature is basically good, the Imago Dei, is a presupposition of much moral education today. This is true, especially of moral education grounded in Socrates' belief that knowledge of the good is always within and has to be drawn out through dialogue. The Socratic method assumes an open and honest questioning, an exchange of ideas, a testing of the adequacy of ideas, and a relating of them to everyday life. Such a dialogical process will evoke more and more understanding of the good that is intuitively already known.

Lawrence Kohlberg's research on the purpose of moral education (universal justice) and the stages of moral development is anchored in the belief that human nature is essentially good. Kohlberg believed that the transmission of cultural values through the family, the schools, community norms, and laws was not only inevitable but mostly positive. However, the "bag of virtues" approach has to be judged by the only genuinely normative value: universal justice for all people in all situations. Kohlberg questioned efforts to find consensus on the values to be taught (such as respect, responsibility, honesty, integrity, trustworthiness, courage, etc.). When these values are taught directly, the learner is passive. The best way for the moral fiber of the child or youth to be developed is through dialogue, or what Kohlberg called progressive interactions. Dialogue brings out the goodness already intuitively known; the dialogue must be progressive because the child goes through various stages of mental development that call for ever more rigorous and persistent reasoning about moral and ethical dilemmas. The most powerful way to bring out the good is to present moral dilemmas that are better solved by thinking that is one stage above where the person is. The moral dilemma creates a disequilibrium that opens the person to a higher form of justice, bringing back a sense of equilibrium. Each successive stage grows in the direction of universal justice and universal civil rights.

Kohlberg recognized that the schools cannot be neutral in values. The schools must be absolutely clear that they not only teach the values of democracy — of the rule of law, of the consensual values of honesty, integrity, respect and responsibility — but all of these virtues must be focused on and tested by universal justice: the Golden Rule projected to all individuals, all nations, all institutions. Kohlberg's research of the stages of moral development discovered that the concept of justice was present in some form in the early stages ("pre-conventional" and "conventional" in his six-stage theory) but that decision-making guided by the principle of universal justice was only at the fifth and sixth stages ("post-conventional" thinking). Such a decision was not just an intellectual matter. It involved action. It is a matter of deep commitment that would call for personal risk-taking similar to a Martin Luther King or a Gandhi. The principle of universal justice often calls for the person involved to seek to change conventional laws that are unjust. Civil disobedience may be necessary if unjust laws and practices are to be changed over time.

Kohlberg maintains that justice is not a trait of character. "It is a moral principle," he writes. "By a moral principle I mean a mode of choosing that is universal, a rule of choosing that we want all people to adopt always in all situations. We know it is alright to be dishonest and steal to save a life because one person's right to life comes before another person's right to property. A moral principle is a principle for resolving conflicting claims. . . . There is only one principled basis for resolving claims: justice and equality. . . . A moral principle is not only a rule of action but a reason for action. As a reason for action, justice is called respect for people. . . . Because morally mature people are governed by the principle of justice rather than by a set of rules, there are not many moral virtues but *one*."[24]

Because universal justice and universal rights are the norms for evaluating all other virtues that are affirmed in society, the "bag of virtues" approach to teaching morals and ethics was criticized by Kohlberg and his followers. We shall return to this discussion in Chapter 5 when we assess the strengths and weaknesses of various theories of moral and character education.

Kohlberg was not naïve about human nature. He was appreciative but critical of romantic notions about education as a process of educing the good already present within the child in a way that frees the individual for inner-directioned growth. Dialogue is needed, but also philosophical wrestling with what the ends of education should be. The use of reason is essential to test and refine the ends of education so that learners will be growing in a direction that will not only be personally fulfilling but fulfilling and positive for all other persons. This unifying purpose is the achieving of universal justice and the rights and responsibilities that go with it.

Kohlberg's work has been critiqued by many. One of the most significant critiques comes from Carol Gilligan. She found that Kohlberg's research was too male oriented and that the end product of justice was important but also more male oriented. Her research with women found that women are more oriented toward an ethic of care and a higher concern for relationships and nonviolence. She calls for a recognition of the importance in education of both justice and caring. She concludes, "While an ethic of justice proceeds from the premise of equality — that everyone should be treated the same — an ethic of care rests on the premise of non-violence — that no one should be hurt. In the representation of maturity, both perspectives converge in the realization that just as inequality adversely affects both parties in an unequal relationship, so too violence is destructive for everyone involved. This dialogue between fairness and care not only provides a better understanding of relations between the sexes but also gives rise to a more comprehensive portrayal of adult work and family relationships."[25]

Let us now face the fact that the Imago Dei, the goodness inherent in the human soul, becomes distorted because of the gift of human freedom and the inherent quest to be loved and to love. Keeping in mind Reinhold Niebuhr's perceptive discussion of how this process works, we will explore

---

24. Lawrence Kohlberg, *The Philosophy of Moral Development*, vol. 1 (San Francisco: Harper & Row, 1981), pp. 39-40.

25. Carol Gilligan, *In a Different Voice: Psychological Theory and Women's Development* (Cambridge, Mass.: Harvard University Press, 1982), p. 174.

the human capacity for forgiveness and reconciliation on individual and societal levels.

The Human Capacity for and Necessity of Forgiveness and Reconciliation

One of the most encouraging recent developments in the discussion of human nature is the research on the human capacity to forgive. The research has been undertaken by Robert Enright and the Human Development Study Group at the University of Wisconsin–Madison and was started after Enright realized that the dominant Kohlbergian model of moral development was focused primarily on the issue of justice and ignored the whole matter of mercy. Enright found that a focus on mercy, benevolence, forgiveness and reconciliation evoked a whole new set of questions about human nature and development as well as a much deeper picture of human potential. His research has produced a rich dialogue with philosophers, psychotherapists, theologians, moral development theorists, educators, and other helping professionals.

Enright has sought to define forgiveness (distinguishing it from condoning, legal pardoning, excusing, personal weakness, a perpetuation of injustice, seeking moral superiority over the offenders, inducing inferiority in the offenders, etc.) and to identify a process model of the actual steps to healthy forgiveness. His model not only releases the offended person from internal negative feelings and wasted energy but establishes the preconditions for reconciliation if the offender responds to the forgiveness in a positive way. Enright has centered his research on the dynamics of forgiveness and not on reconciliation. He sees reconciliation as an important and hoped-for outcome of forgiveness, but as a process he has not included it per se in his research. He is moving very close to the study of reconciliation in his recent attempt to work with leaders in the former Yugoslavia in regard to the deep hurts that have taken place between Orthodox Serbians, Muslim Bosnians, Catholic Croatians, etc.[26]

Enright defines forgiveness, following the work of philosopher J. North (1987), in this way: "Forgiveness is the overcoming of negative affect and judgment toward the offenders, not by denying ourselves the right to such affect and judgment, but by endeavoring to view the offender with compassion,

---

26. Robert D. Enright, Elizabeth A. Gassin, Tomislau Longinorie, and David Loudon, "Forgiveness as a Solution to Social Crisis" (paper presented at the Conference on Morality and Social Crisis, Belgrade, Serbia, December 1994).

benevolence, and love while recognizing that he or she has abandoned the right to them."[27] Enright refines North's work by adding affective, cognitive, and behavioral elements. When a person forgives another who has hurt him or her deeply, certain negative emotions are drained away — such as anger, hatred, resentment, sadness, and contempt — however slowly this is accomplished. In terms of the thinking process, the person ceases to plan revenge or to rehearse over and over patterns of attack. In terms of behavior, the person ceases to act out the negative feelings and mental strategies. The negative emotions are replaced by more neutral and eventually by more positive feelings, including willingness to help the other. At the cognitive level the offended realizes he or she has the right to negative feelings and thoughts, but *decides* to forgo them. At the behavioral level the person is willing to take steps toward reconciliation, perhaps making overtures in that direction if the offender responds in a positive way.[28]

Enright defines forgiveness as an interpersonal matter. Forgiveness follows a "deep, long-lasting injury or hurt from the other person. The injury might be psychological, emotional, physical or moral" — and could involve all of these at once. The injury is objective — not merely a perception by the one offended. Forgiveness research moves toward the human potential for mercy and love but it also sees itself as an extension of the moral-development focus on justice. The offended cannot feel hurt without a sense of justice, without feeling the offender has been unfair. The offender does not have to apologize for the offended to forgive. The act of forgiveness is an interior act, made because the offender is a human being deserving forgiveness and another chance. Forgiveness and reconciliation are different realities. Forgiveness involves one person. Reconciliation involves two or more persons. To forgive another does not mean that the other is ready for reconciliation and wants it. Forgiveness does remove the interior barriers in the offended one, making possible reconciliation.[29]

In relation to the nature of human nature the capacity to forgive is a reflection of a loving God whose very nature is one of both justice and mercy, one of righteousness and forgiveness. The Imago Dei concept says that we as human beings were created in the image of a loving and just God and that we have been given those same qualities as a gift to be used in our relationships

27. Robert D. Enright and the Human Development Group, "Moral Development of Forgiveness," in W. Kurtines, *Handbook of Moral Behavior and Development*, vol. 1, ed. J. Gewirtz (Hillsdale, N.J.: Erlbaum, 1991), p. 126.

28. Enright et al., "Moral Development of Forgiveness," p. 127.

29. Enright et al., "Moral Development of Forgiveness," p. 129.

with others. The doctrine of Imago Dei says that humans have the capacity to imitate God as a forgiver.[30]

The strength of Enright's research on forgiveness can be seen in his *process model of forgiveness*, which can be very helpful in providing concrete steps for education, counseling, psychiatry, and other helping professions. The process model has been employed, evaluated, and refined in interactions with high school and college students, with friendship conflicts in Korea, with parentally love-deprived adolescents, with female incest survivors, with elderly females, and with same-gender parents.

Enright's process model is sensitive to developmental stages of moral thinking and to developmental styles or soft stages of forgiveness. The table on page 66 illustrates how the Kohlbergian stages of moral thinking (Justice) correlate with the soft stages of forgiveness (Mercy).

Enright's studies reveal that there are significant differences in reasoning about forgiveness between children, adolescents, and adults, as might be assumed. Adolescents are moving into Stage 3 (7th graders) and consolidating into Stage 3 (10th graders). Children are in Stage 2 and adults are primarily in Stage 4. The only instances of Stage 6 reasoning were in adult samples.[31]

The actual process of forgiveness can be followed all the way through to an internal change of heart, decision to forgive, and release, and it is best done by late adolescents and adults. Religious education of children and youth can greatly assist them in taking as many steps as possible in their thinking, feeling, and actions at an intuitive level and as a support for the validity of Stage 6 thinking and feeling — namely that every person, including the person who offended, is a sacred human being of equal worth and deserving of the free gift of forgiveness. The process of forgiveness comprises several elements, indicated in the illustration on page 67.

In the educational or therapeutic interventions with persons seeking to deal with the pain and hurt calling for forgiveness, there are several steps to take to make the above process genuinely helpful. The offended person needs to be enabled to look deeply at the nature of the hurt, the interior psychological reactions that have emerged, the defense mechanisms that are present to keep the hurt alive and unrelieved. It is very important to invite open expressions of feelings, including anger and resentment, the admission of shame or regret if present. The sharing of intense feelings of hurt and blame (cathexis) is very important in order to unblock feelings that may be inhibiting the abil-

---

30. Enright et al., "Moral Development of Forgiveness," p. 129.

31. Robert D. Enright, Maria J. D. Santos, Radhi H. Al-Mabuk, "The Adolescent as Forgiver," *Journal of Adolescence* 12 (1989): 106.

Stages of Justice

1 Heteronomous Morality. I believe that justice should be decided by the authority, by the one who can punish.

2 Individualism. I have a sense of reciprocity that defines justice for me. If you help me, I must help you.

3 Mutual Interpersonal Expectations. Here, I reason that the group consensus should decide what is right and wrong. I go along so that others close to me will like me.

4 Social System and Conscience. Societal laws are my guides to justice. I uphold laws, except in extreme cases, to have an orderly society.

5 Social Contract. I am aware that people hold a variety of opinions. One usually should uphold the values and rules of one's group. Some nonrelative values (life, liberty) must be upheld regardless of majority opinion.

6 Universal Ethical Principles. My sense of justice is based on maintaining the individual rights of all persons. People are ends in themselves and should be treated as such.

Styles of Forgiveness

1 Revengeful Forgiveness. I can forgive someone who wrongs me only if I can punish him to a similar degree to my own pain.

2 Conditional or Restitutional Forgiveness. If I get back what was taken away from me, then I can forgive. Or, if I feel guilty about withholding forgiveness, then I can forgive to relieve my guilt.

3 Expectational Forgiveness. I can forgive if others put pressure on me to forgive. I forgive because other people expect it.

4 Lawful Expectational Forgiveness. I forgive because my religion demands it. Notice that this is not Stage 2 in which I forgive to relieve my own guilt about withholding forgiveness.

5 Forgiveness as Social Harmony. I forgive because it restores harmony or good relations in society. Forgiveness decreases friction and outright conflict in society. Note that forgiveness is a way to control society; it is a way of maintaining peaceful relations.

6 Forgiveness as Love. I forgive because it promotes a true sense of love. Because I must truly care for each person, a hurtful act on her part does not alter that sense of love. This kind of relationship keeps open the possibility of reconciliation and closes the door on revenge. Note that forgiveness is no longer dependent on a social context, as in Stage 5. The forgiver does not control the other by forgiving, he releases her.

Note: This table is an extrapolation from Enright et al. (1989). Reprinted with permission.

	1		2		3	
Injury →	Experiencing of negative psychological consequences	→	Need for resolution	→	Deciding among strategies: will it be a justice or mercy strategy	→

	4		5		6	
→	Forgiveness motive	→	Decision to forgive	→	Execution of internal forgiveness strategies	→

	7			
→	Need for action ↓ ↓ ↘	Execution of behavioral reconciliation strategies →	Release ↑ ↑ ↑ →	↗

ity of the person to consider forgiveness. The awareness and sharing of the many rehearsals of ways to resolve the conflict are also crucial in order for the offended to be able to admit that other strategies of revenge or demand for justice have failed. These sharings may bring awareness that the injured party may be comparing self to the person who caused the injury with the views that the injured is often better off. Discussion of the possibly altered "just world" view can open the deeper understanding the person has about life itself and its purpose and destiny. These deeper probings may then lead to "a change of heart," a conversion, or new insights that the old strategies are not working. A cognitive decision may then be made to forgive the offender. This is not an easy step, but it was made by many people in the experimental groups studied. The results of this decision to forgive unfolded in the following way.

The person begins to *reframe* this situation by viewing the wrongdoer in context, "getting inside the other's shoes." Empathy and compassion begin to grow. Then comes a genuine acceptance of the pain that has been inflicted, along with a realization that the offended person has also needed forgiveness in the past — or maybe in the situation at hand in terms of hurtful things said or done. Often there is a realization that the injured has been permanently changed in certain ways. Even though the hurt and internal change are real, there is a clear decrease in negative feelings and thoughts and an increase in positive feelings and thoughts toward the offender and maybe toward self and/or (in the case of a "religious" person) toward God.

Finally, the last step is an awareness of an internal, emotional release from the negative feelings of the guilt and anxiety, from the accumulated weight of self-doubt or low self-esteem that may have been present.[32]

Whether or not the persons going through these steps identify themselves as religious (actively involved in worship, Bible study, service, etc.) is important. This is especially true at this point of deciding to embrace forgiveness as a strategy. *Support* for such a decision as well as *inspiration* to see all persons as children of God, worthy of forgiveness and renewal, are significant positive factors in such persons. There was little mention of what the specific theological views of God, sin, confession, and forgiveness were in the various descriptions of the importance of religion. Since this earlier research, Enright and colleagues have studied differing world religions in respect to forgiveness. Joseph Elder's research has found that forgiveness is a central concept in Judeo-Christian-Muslim cosmology but not in Buddhist-Hindu. In the latter the loss of Karma is central. Karma says that every virtuous act is rewarded and every sinful act is punished in an inexorable manner — in this life or later. No process of repentance or forgiveness can affect the outcome. Justice will be done. Buddhism identifies three poisons in life: ignorance, attachment, and hatred. These poisons are the causes of suffering. There is no place for revenge because the law of Karma will bring justice. Therefore there is no place for forgiveness. There is a big place for wisdom and compassion for all sentient beings. The Dalai Lama, perhaps the Buddhist most involved in trying to heal the world's hurts, is a supporter of the emphasis on forgiveness, largely because he recognizes that there are many parallels between forgiveness and "the dynamics of acquiring wisdom and overcoming ignorance, attachment and hatred endorsed by Buddhism."[33] Much more study of the place of basic belief in world religions and philosophies needs to be done and will be continued by new organizations such as the International Forgiveness Institute, which provides grants to graduate students and professors who wish to study the wide range of forgiveness issues emerging as a result of the work of Enright et al.[34]

32. Robert D. Enright, Elizabeth A Gassin, and Ching-Ru Wu, "Forgiveness: A Development View," *Journal of Moral Education* 2 (1992): 107-9.

33. Joseph W. Elder, "Expanding Options: The Challenge of Forgiveness," in Robert D. Enright and Joanna North, eds., *Exploring Forgiveness* (Madison: University of Wisconsin Press, 1998), pp. 158-59.

34. Elder, "Expanding Options," p. 60.

One additional insight from Enright's work is worthy of attention here. Enright tries to integrate Kohlberg's structural approach to the development of justice in all human relationships with his forgiveness model with its emphases on mercy or love in all relationships. One difference he highlights is Kohlberg's emphasis on *reciprocity* in human relationships (with the Golden Rule as the culmination of growth in Stage 6) and his own emphasis on *identity* as the central element in human relationships (forgiveness not because of equality of actions but because each person is essentially sacred). The latter reality makes it possible to love unconditionally and to forgive even when the other person doesn't deserve it.[35] Enright traces these differences in thought from Piaget on to Kohlberg and other thinkers such as Carol Gilligan (in her focus on caring relationships in moral development), Turiel, Eisenberg and Brabeck, etc.[36]

Enright and his study group members have identified twenty steps in the forgiveness process in dialogue with the research of others from many fields of inquiry. We shall return to these steps when we discuss specific educational and liturgical designs for enhancing the possibility of forgiveness and reconciliation within and beyond the church.[37]

Reconciliation

The process of reconciliation has been more difficult than that of forgiveness. Two or more people are always involved with their own unique perceptions of the past, their specific feelings of hurt, anger, guilt, fear, shame, and lack of trust. On an interpersonal level, if one person has forgiven the one perceived to be the primary offender (infidelity, for instance), a giant step has been taken, making reconciliation more possible. However, as experience and research have indicated, the one who has been deeply hurt but has genuinely forgiven may elect not to try to reconcile. Such a stance may be taken by someone who, for instance, has been sexually abused by a fam-

35. Robert D. Enright and the Human Development Study Group, "Piaget on Moral Development of Forgiveness: Identity or Reciprocity?" *Journal of Human Development* 37 (1994): 63-80.

36. Robert D. Enright and Joanna North, eds., *Exploring Forgiveness* (Madison: University of Wisconsin Press, 1998), p. 59.

37. Enright and North, *Exploring Forgiveness*, p. 59. See also *Campaign for Forgiveness Research*, with Jimmy Carter, Desmond Tutu, Robert Coles, Ruby Bridges, and Elizabeth Elliot as co-chairs: Goal to raise $10 million. Find online at http://www.Templeton.org/forgiveness/forgivenessresearch.asp.

ily member or who has witnessed the murder of a mother or sibling by a father. Still, there are countless stories about deeply hurt people whose faith has motivated them to take the first steps toward reconciliation with the offender.

On the social, political, and religious levels, great numbers of individuals are involved with their varying perceptions of hurt, anger, fear, and lack of trust. The process of reconciliation becomes very complicated indeed. There are many stories in the media about the difficulty of reconciliation at these levels, but also a few concerning successful efforts. In the Introduction, we flagged meaningful and significant patterns of forgiveness and reconciliation, the South African Truth and Reconciliation Commission being a primary example.

We are emotionally fatigued by the constant reports concerning the failures in negotiation between Israel and the Palestinian Authority, between Pakistan and India, and with the complicated violence between Indian Muslims, Hindus, and Christians, and on and on around the world. We are in need of hopeful signs of the effectiveness of known approaches to conflict resolution, mediation, and third-party negotiations that lead to stability, reconciliation, and peace.

One such illustration is the story of the Irish Peacemakers, recently selected as winners of the Profiles in Courage Award. Michael Daly writes a detailed description of the many leaders who took the incredible number of twists and turns to reach the 1998 Good Friday Peace Agreement that was later confirmed by the people of Northern Ireland and Ireland. The story told in *Profiles in Courage for Our Time* (2002) makes it clear that the role of former Senator George Mitchell was crucial. He was willing to take repeated rejection, continuing episodes of violence (3,574 men, women, and children were killed during what was known as the Troubles), and long periods of waiting for confirmation of agreements from many different parties in the conflict. Many leaders who sought a way toward peace were killed. Leaders who stayed in dialogue with Mitchell literally risked their lives. One of these leaders was Monica McWilliams. She is the founder of a political party, the Northern Ireland Women's Coalition, which inspired many to break through the divisions between Catholics and Protestants. She was able to bring Catholic and Protestant women together to work for an era of trust, justice, and peace for their families and for the nation. Through the grassroots organization of Women in Northern Ireland the party won a seat at the negotiation table.

George Mitchell praised all at the table for their true valor. He said, "It doesn't take courage to shoot a policeman in the back of the head, or to murder an unarmed taxi driver. . . . What takes courage is to compete in the arena of democracy, where the tools are persuasion, fairness, and common decency." British Prime Minister Tony Blair exulted, "Courage has triumphed!"[38]

George Mitchell knew the importance of making a set of ground rules about how to proceed: how to deal with diversity of experience and opinion, how to make agreements and change them in the light of new realities. These ground rules were called the Mitchell Principles. Participants who stayed in the process had to agree to honor those principles. Mitchell, of course, took a similar process to the Middle East struggle between Israel and the Palestinians. The difficulty in both settings was the continuation of violence during the process. Suicide bombings from Palestinians and military responses or initiatives from the Israelis have kept the process confused or put on hold. Other third-party efforts from the United States and Saudi Arabia have sought to keep the peace process alive.

Everett Worthington has found similar elements in the process toward reconciliation at the interpersonal, social, political, and religious levels. He studied such fields as primatology (how nonhuman primates repair conflict), child-child conflict, restorative justice, international conflict negotiations, political reconciliation, and religious dialogues. He found four planks that make up the bridge to reconciliation.

The four planks are: (1) We *decide* whether, how, and when to reconcile. (2) We *discuss* past and present transgressions with a "soft attitude." (3) We *detoxify* our poisonous past relationship. (4) We *devote* ourselves to building up a relationship of mutual valuing. These four planks sound deceptively simple, but they involve many steps. Worthington identifies barriers that emerge in the process of communication. At the interpersonal level some of the barriers are internal ("I don't want to give up my right to see him or her suffer"; "I feel vulnerable to being hurt or rejected again," etc.).[39] In each case, Worthington's research points to a way to climb over the barriers. Worthington presents tested strategies for each of the four planks along with charts that detail typical problems. His steps are especially helpful when related to an interpersonal reconciliation but can also be effective at social, political, and religious levels.

Worthington is a Christian and interrelates his scientifically refined suggestions with religious motivations. For instance, he agrees that confes-

---

38. Caroline Kennedy, ed., *Profiles in Courage for Our Time* (New York: Hyperion, 2002), p. 245.

39. Everett Worthington, Jr., *Five Steps to Forgiveness: The Art and Science of Forgiving* (New York: Crown, 2001), pp. 161-68.

sion of transgressions (without excuses) is essential. Also, expressions of re-pentance and contrition are central. He has discovered that offers of apology for specific hurts can open the door to offers of forgiveness and the accep-tance of forgiveness.

A soft, more descriptive, rather than a harsh, blaming style of speaking should be one of the ground rules. Each party should focus on ways to change his or her own attitudes and behaviors rather than focus only on changes the other party should make.

Detoxification is usually needed in order to move on. It may be neces-sary for those involved to go back through their previous pattern of behavior — stonewalling (the silence treatment), defensiveness, or extreme criticism — to some past normalcy or toward some ideal state of future reconcilia-tion. Such a process can help the parties decode and better understand why past ways of communicating and solving problems have failed. New agree-ments concerning better ways to communicate can become more possible. Those involved need to detoxify negative expectations and move on to risk more positive, hopeful expectations. The more positive expectation should be real, however. It is realistic to expect some failures in trustworthiness along the way. "The process of reconciliation is one step backward and two steps forward."[40]

Worthington's final plank is devotion. It takes commitment and devo-tion to stay on the bridge to reconciliation. Often religious faith empowers our devotion to the tasks required for reconciliation to be achieved. Worthington's research has discovered that it is possible, during the process, to develop a forgiving and reconciling character and basic attitude. Parties studied have been able to express their grief about past failures and also de-velop new agreements to deal creatively with the root causes of those failures. Devotion involves developing empathy for the other(s), understanding why conflicts emerged, building trusting, loving new relationships honestly, and facing new issues as they emerge.

Such a process calls for open communication, a win-win rather than a lose-win approach. It is often very helpful to look carefully at the unwritten contract of the past and assess the elements needed in a written contract to guide the future. Such a step has been shown to help couples seeking reconcil-iation. Writing or rewriting contracts is especially needed at the social, politi-cal, and religious levels.[41]

40. Worthington, *Five Steps to Forgiveness*, p. 243.
41. Robert D. Enright, *Forgiveness Is a Choice: A Step-by-Step Process for Resolving Anger and Restoring Hope* (Washington, D.C.: American Psychological Association, 2001), p. 270.

Another element in reconciliation is the concrete attempt to make amends for past hurts. Seeking to repair past damage gives evidence of sincerity and good faith. Such is true in interpersonal reconciliation, but it is even more essential in sound political and religious reconciliation — a discovery made by the South African Truth and Reconciliation Commission even though amnesty was granted.[42]

In conclusion, we can say with confidence that forgiveness, reconciliation, and moral courage are possible for human beings. They are qualities of life that are by-products of our creation in God's image. They are possible because we have the gift of free will, the gift of choice. We can choose to forgive and be reconciled with those we have offended or hurt or who have offended and hurt us. We can forgive and be reconciled because we have been forgiven by God through Christ.

There are different levels of need for forgiveness and reconciliation. We can learn as children in our families to forgive and be reconciled because we have been forgiven and enfolded in the loving arms of our parents. We can experience the depth of God's love for us through the depth of love received and shared in the body of Christ, the church. We can recognize what it means to be in ministry to one another — in a loving and honest climate in the actual family or a surrogate family where love, and honesty about our striving for self-protection, contrition, forgiveness, and reconciliation, become "habits of the heart." As we grow in faith from stage to stage we can be strengthened to deal openly with the moral and ethical issues that emerge and increasingly accept responsibility for our own decisions. In these gifted communities of faith, we can be honest about our failings, accept God's grace, and be guided by God's truth. We can forgive and accept forgiveness so that the life of love and justice for all can be experienced.

However, we know how easy it is to get absorbed in our own patterns of pride or self-abnegation. This is especially true when we have experienced a deep hurt or offense that engenders anger, bitterness, and the desire for revenge. The studies of forgiveness and reconciliation cited here all indicate that we can learn how to go through the process of forgiveness and that we can be prepared to be reconciled with those who have hurt us. In the process our faith in God's love and forgiveness can greatly strengthen us to take the difficult steps needed to move on to full forgiveness and genuine desire for reconciliation. The supportive Christian community, the inspiration from the stories of others who have been freed by their acts of forgiveness and reconciliation, the sacramental and liturgical occasions for confession, repen-

---

42. Desmond Tutu, *No Future without Forgiveness* (New York: Doubleday, 1999), p. 165.

tance, contrition, the acceptance of forgiveness and reconciliation from God and one another — all are central realities for the Christian journey.

While research studies can help us know the pathways, guidance from Christian sources of inspiration is essential to our pilgrimage.[43]

43. See Lewis Smedes, *The Art of Forgiving* (Nashville: Moorings, a division of Random House, 1966); Johann Christoph Arnold, *Seventy-Times Seven: The Power of Forgiveness* (Farmington, Pa.: Plough, 1997); Johann Christoph Arnold, *Why Forgive?* (Farmington, Pa.: Plough, 2000); L. William Countryman, *Forgiven and Forgiving* (Harrisburg, Pa.: Morehouse, 1998); Joan Mueller, *Is Forgiveness Possible?* (Collegeville, Minn.: Liturgical Press, 1998); Dennis Linn, *Don't Forgive Too Soon* (New York: Paulist, 1997); *Forgiveness Forum,* the website of Dr. Douglas K. Showalter, where you can share your story of forgiveness, reconciliation, and quest for moral grounding and be inspired by others' stories (www.vsg.cape.com/~dougshow/index.htm/).

CHAPTER 3

Forgiveness and Reconciliation in the Bible: The Relation of Justice and Mercy

The Hebrew Bible

An Ancient Memory

Forgiving is more than action among the people of the Word; it is an identity. And as such it is an inheritance and an ancient memory. We hear its most distant echoes in the pentateuchal prayer of Moses:

> O Lord, I pray, let the Lord go with us. Although this is a stiff-necked people pardon our iniquity and our sins, and take us for your inheritance. (Ex. 34:9)

In this tradition there is no quality that is more decisive in the image of the Holy One than this image of mercy at the heart of creation. It is, of course, not self-evident that mercy is a dominant quality of what we know as nature, personality, or reality itself. It is rather a remembered grace among believers and a continuing experience. The people of the Word call it revelation, and it turns out that because it is revelation about God, it is also revelation about what kind of people the believers are called to be. This understanding is declared succinctly in Leviticus 11:45: "You shall be holy, for I am holy." This analogy of human nature with divine nature is inevitable for a people who understand their created nature as in the image of God (Gen. 1:26).

Not a few observers have claimed the opposite: humanity created God in its own image. This, of course, is true since we have only human minds to reason with and our worldly experience to bring to bear on any question. The believer's image of God is constructed out of what we see as the better parts of nature and of our human natures. God is beautiful, God is good, God is just, God is merciful, and so on. Our human ideas about God are naturally projections of our human experiences, longings, etc. The wonder that still compels these thoughts and affections is our irrepressible fascination with the relation between our projections about God and the "screen" upon which these projections are made, the divine reality itself.

Credo: In Paradox

Searching the Holy Book for a complete and coherent understanding of our topic or any topic, one runs inevitably into contradictions, paradoxes, and confusions. These cannot be eliminated. What can be established, however, are main lines of understanding, of ideals and of practice. We will attempt to find these.

Moses could pray for his people in the words of Exodus 34:9 quoted above, because he believed in the "creed" articulated as the Word of the Lord a few verses earlier:

> The Lord, the Lord is a God merciful and gracious, slow to anger
> and abounding in steadfast love and faithfulness,
> keeping steadfast love for the thousandth generation,
> forgiving iniquity and transgression and sin,
> yet by no means clearing the guilty,
> but visiting the iniquity of parents upon the children,
> and the children's children,
> to the third and the fourth generation. (Ex. 34:6-7)

This is the Word of the Lord, spoken out of the cloud to Moses on Mt. Sinai. Moses' immediate response is the prayer for mercy for his people (Ex. 34:9). Small wonder! The Word out of the cloud on Sinai was a seriously mixed message. To paraphrase: "I am a God of infinite mercy; I am a God of absolute justice." This fundamental paradox remains unresolved in the whole story of God's revelation to the people of the Word. It stands at the beginning starkly expressed in the Word to Moses out of the cloud, and it is spoken at the end of the Christian scriptures in the *Book of the Apocalypse* (Rev. 20–21) and everywhere in between. We think that this unresolved paradox becomes unbalanced as the story evolves, and that while the absolutes of justice and mercy remain, the witness of the faithful and of the Word itself is that the Almighty "fudges" in the direction of mercy, and wills that we should do the same.

Intercession and Atonement

One of the continuing tableaus in the Hebrew Bible is the picture of the leaders of the people and prophets among them exhorting the people to righteousness and interceding for them at the throne of the Almighty. Surely the most eloquent and moving of these scenes is the beautiful prayer of Solomon at the dedication of the temple in Jerusalem in the tenth century:

> But will God indeed dwell on the earth? Even heaven and the highest heaven cannot contain you, much less this house that I have built! Regard your servant's prayer and his plea, O Lord my God, heeding the cry and the prayer that your servant prays to you today; that your eyes may be open night and day toward this house, the place of which you said, "My name shall be there," that you may heed the prayer that your servant makes toward this place. Hear the plea of your servant and of your people Israel when they pray toward this place; O hear in heaven your dwelling place; heed and forgive. (1 Kings 8:27-30; cf. 2 Chr. 6)

Solomon underlines repeatedly his plea for the people's forgiveness: "If they sin against you . . . and you are angry with them . . . yet if they come to their senses and repent, and plead with you . . . then hear in heaven your dwelling place and forgive your people" (1 Kings 8:46-50).

So, more than a thousand years before the Christian era, theology and liturgy were in place for repentance, confession, forgiveness, and reconciliation.

Sacrifice

These themes were, of course, part of the liturgy of sacrifice in the temple. Temple sacrifice and its liturgy functioned to assuage guilt and rebuild peace with both God and neighbors. Atonement offerings of "clean" animals and sometimes offerings of cereals and wines connected individuals and sometimes a whole people with guilts and special needs before the throne of the Almighty. "You shall lay your hand on the head of the burnt offering, and it shall be acceptable in your behalf as atonement for you" (Lev. 1:4. See Lev. 1–7 for a description of the cultus of sacrifice). To approach the altar was to acknowledge need and guilt and unworthiness. There were caveats to allay the fears that this system was automatically efficacious. (See Num. 15:30-31.) Even so, there were misgivings and critics.

Specified ritual procedures of a religious establishment for relief of offenses against God and neighbor can have serious shortcomings, particularly since the religious institution usually has a vested financial interest in rites of atonement. They are open to criticisms of insincerity and corruption. And there is no shortage of such criticism about the sacrificial "system" in Israel, the words of God echoed by the eighth-century prophet Amos being the most eloquent.

> I hate, I despise your festivals and take no delight in your
> > solemn assemblies. Even though you offer me your
> > burnt offerings and grain offerings,
> > I will not accept them;
> and the offerings of well-being of your fatted animals
> > I will not look upon.
> Take away from me the noise of your songs;
> I will not listen to the melody of your harps.
> > But let justice roll down like waters,
> > and righteousness like an ever-flowing stream.
> > > > (Amos 5:21-24; cf. Isa. 1:10-20; Hos. 6:6)

What has been called propitiation, that is, doing something "toward God," an act of prayer, of penitence, of service, can be a legitimate and important part of reconciliation with God and neighbor, although an activity subject to abuse. Indeed, while the sensibilities of our twenty-first century are far removed from the idea and practice of animal sacrifice as a means of atonement before God, we should realize that the concept and language of sacrifice are by no means merely antique expression. They are found through the whole Bible and are an essential language of understanding for contemporary people of the Word. Part of the prophetic reaction to sacrifice included an enlargement of the meaning of the language, for instance, the designation of prayer as incense and the lifting up of hands as an evening sacrifice (Ps. 141:2). Rejection of ideas of God's need for food or its aroma, or appeasement of anger, or other primitive concepts, still leaves the themes of *gift* and *communion* as relevant inheritances from the cult of temple sacrifice. What does one do to atone for the moral failure to which we are prone? Two sides of contrition and rehabilitation in the tradition of the Bible have been and continue to be gifts:

benefits and deeds that intend recompense and renewed communion — prayerful return to God and to the fellowship of the covenant. These themes of temple sacrifice remain relevant.

As we shall see, for Christians the image of sacrifice inevitably became part of the understanding of the meaning of Jesus. It is a basic motif of New Testament writers and will always be at the heart of the Christian understanding of God's purposes in Jesus of Nazareth. St. Paul frames sacrifice as the essence of worship, praying that believers will present themselves "as a living sacrifice, holy and acceptable to God, which is your spiritual worship" (Rom. 12:1).

Psalmody

We can begin to understand a larger meaning of sacrifice if we attend to some of the songs of Hebrew worship. The Psalms of the Hebrew Bible are a window into the theology of sacrifice. They are apparently mostly post-exilic creations that were compiled and edited over six centuries, and ideals of sacrifice in these hymns are greatly influenced by the witness of the prophets. Even so, they have roots in more ancient language, and surely in the language of sacrificial worship. The penitential psalms, such as Psalms 51 and 130, are especially revealing pictures of the character and spiritual milieu of confession and forgiveness in Israel. They reveal something much deeper than a barren pacifying bribe in the slaughter of animals.

> Have mercy on me, O God according to your steadfast love;
>> according to your abundant mercy
>> blot out my transgressions.
> Wash me thoroughly from my iniquity and cleanse me from my sin.
>> > (Ps. 51:1-2)

> You desire truth in the inward being;
>> therefore teach me wisdom in my secret heart. (v. 6)

> Do not cast me away from your presence,
>> and do not take your holy spirit from me.
> Restore to me the joy of your salvation,
>> and sustain in me a willing spirit. (vv. 11-12)

Psalm 130, the *de profundis,* is the appointed Psalm among Christians for Ash Wednesday.

> Out of the depths I cry to you, O Lord.
>> Lord, hear my voice.
> Let your ears be attentive
>> to the voice of my supplications. (vv. 1-2)

> O Israel, hope in the Lord!
>> For with the Lord there is steadfast love,
>> and with him is great power to redeem.
> It is he who will redeem Israel
>> from all its iniquities. (vv. 7-8)

The songs of worship remain the most reliable entree into the theology and spirituality of a worshiping people.

The Covenant

The God who condemns in judgment and the God who redeems in love are one being, and these polarities of character are joined together and joined to humanity by what in scriptural language is called the covenant. The covenant is about relationship, and about promises and responsibilities within relationship. The earliest expressions of the idea of covenant, such as those involving Noah (Gen. 8), Abraham (Gen. 17), and Joseph (Gen. 48), are revealing promises of God: to sustain the earth, to create a people, to give them a fruitful land. The Mosaic covenant, on the other hand, is about both the promises of God and also about human relationship to God and human responsibilities before God (Ex. 19–20). The covenant binds the people of God to moral laws. But it is more than a catalogue of laws and rules. It is also the framework that mediates the mercy of God, for the covenant is finally not based on human righteousness, but on the righteousness of God and God's mercy.

> Many times he delivered them, but they were rebellious in their purposes and were brought low through their iniquity.
> Nevertheless he regarded their distress when he heard their cry.
> For their sake he remembered his covenant and showed compassion according to the abundance of his steadfast love. (Ps. 106:43-45)

When Jeremiah envisions a new covenant it is the grace of a divine gift to the human heart.

> The days are surely coming, says the Lord, when I will make a new cove-
> nant with the house of Israel and the house of Judah. . . . I will put my law
> within them, and I will write it upon their hearts. . . . I will forgive their
> iniquity and remember their sin no more. (Jer. 31:31, 33b, 34b)

This does not mean that we should forget that God is jealous for righteousness.

> I am the Lord your God; sanctify yourselves, therefore, and be holy, for I
> am holy. You shall not defile yourselves. . . . For I am the Lord who
> brought you up from the land of Egypt, to be your God: you shall be holy,
> for I am holy. (Lev. 11:44-45)

These commands and laws are absolute; breaking them incurs divine wrath
and punishment. Nevertheless, the forgiving compassion expressed above in
Psalm 106 and Jeremiah 31 persists in shining through the cloud of wrath.
One can conclude that mercy in God is a deeper reality than justice.

Sin, Forgiveness, and Holiness

Forgiveness and our universal need for it implies, of course, our universal
separation, faithlessness, and disobedience to the laws of God, i.e., the various
injustices that incur the wrath of God. Why it is that we are given to moral
failure and to breaking the faith of the covenant has been and remains a mystery. At the beginning of the creation story as the Bible tells it there is a response line in the litany of creation: "and God saw that it was good" (Gen. 1).
The creation myth contains also the sad story of the fall from grace of the first
created pair of humans. Disobeying God's command, Adam and Eve dared to
eat the fruit of the tree of the knowledge of good and evil, and they were punished by expulsion from the garden of paradise and were cursed (Gen. 3:14-
19). What the wily serpent tempted them with was the promise that "You will
not die; for God knows that when you eat of it your eyes will be opened, and
you will be like God, knowing good and evil" (Gen. 3:4-5). So here we are told,
of the creation itself, that while it is good, the humanity in it is seriously
flawed from the outset. And the psalmist can lament, "Indeed, I was born
guilty, a sinner when my mother conceived me" (Ps. 51:5). This question of
"original sin" and the relation of good and evil in our natures seems every bit
as intractable and beset with contradictions today as it was when the first
chapters of Genesis were written as an explanation. Someone has observed

that original sin is the most obvious conclusion ever reached in the whole history of human thought. That would appear to be so. What the Bible calls sin does indeed abound: wickedness, hardness of heart, depravity, immorality, selfishness, lawlessness, and so on, *ad infinitum*. And sin is deadly. The classic seven: pride, covetousness, lust, gluttony, anger, sloth, indifference, do overtake and destroy us.

What we are generally asked to believe about these flaws in human nature is that while they are universal, they are not somehow constitutive of our humanity. They are unfortunate manifestations of our interaction with the "fallen" and wicked world into which we are innocently born. We make these circumlocutions because to admit that sinning is something we are naturally prone to is to admit that we are created that way, and this conclusion blames God. A great deal of what we call theology consists of making excuses for God. We would do better to pay attention to our creation myth and to recognize that we are beyond our depth in these rationalizations. The fruit of the tree of the knowledge of good and evil belongs to God; it is not finally available to us. It remains a mystery. We have enough to do to acknowledge both "original blessing" and "original sin" and try to find a way to walk in this wonderful and wicked world. That is to say, we may not be able to solve the age-old "problem" of good and evil, but we can choose sides.

Most of us have been nurtured on faith in the goodness of a loving God. It would be well for us to ponder that the positive of goodness is never sufficient unless it is yoked to the negative of anger about badness. That is, it is not enough for us to love; it is also necessary for us to be against the unlove. In a different world, we might just claim the positive, the love, but in this world where evil and wickedness abound it is necessary to enlist ourselves in efforts and causes that seek actively to oppose the ungodly. So, if we affirm the God of the biblical story, we can understand how the sinfulness of this world hurts, offends, and angers God. If there is such a thing as justice then there must be judgment. If there are moral laws, then there is some sort of plumb line on the basis of which we make judgments, as difficult and questionable as some of these might be. Naturally there is no need for mercy except within some realistic understanding of rule, of law, and subsequently of transgression and wickedness. Embracing mercy apart from the exercise of judgment is an indulgence in sentimentality.

How do the people of the Word know that they sin? There are, of course, the rules: don't lie, don't steal, don't murder. . . . But the rupture of covenant between the soul and God and the people of covenant is something more personal and spiritual than breaking rules. It is the destruction of a quality of life we call holy. We know we sin primarily because we know a holy

God; "You shall be holy, for I am holy" is the underlying, abiding "command-ment." Sin is a disfigurement of the holy image in humanity. And the Hebrew Bible is the story of God's will and work to restore holiness to creation.

Truth

An essential factor in reconciliation is truth. The Bible has a passion for truth. For our purposes the relevance of this passion for truth is the need we have to find our own truth. Looking to our own truth is often the discovery of what we are reluctant to acknowledge, but out of personal honesty can come confession, contrition, and the quest for reconciliation. Jeremiah understands exactly this link between truth and repentance.

> Everyone deceives his neighbor
> > and no one speaks the truth;
> they have taught their tongues to speak lies;
> > they commit iniquity and are weary to repent. (Jer. 9:5)

The very definition of sanctity, of those who can abide in God's holiness, is of a person of truth.

> O Lord, who shall sojourn in thy tent?
> > Who shall dwell in thy holy hill?
> He who walks blamelessly, and does what is right
> > and speaks truth from his heart. (Ps. 15:1-2)

The psalmist can even write God into the depths of the soul where truth can be seen and known.

> Search me, O God, and know my heart!
> > Try me and know my thoughts!
> And see if there be any wicked way in me,
> > and lead me in the way everlasting. (Ps. 139:23-24)

Most of us are aware of the unprecedented procedures undertaken in South Africa to cultivate reconciliation. Not everyone would recall that the commission established to accomplish this was called the "Truth and Reconciliation Commission." Lies, evasions, excuses vex the spirit. Truth is the doorway to reconciliation.

> The Lord is near to all who call upon him,
>> to all who call upon him in truth. (Ps. 145:18)

Love

One of the eighth-century prophets, Hosea, uses the metaphor of human love to illustrate God's suffering quest to remove the barriers of separation in sin and guilt, and to heal and renew a people healthy, holy in the Lord. His indictment is severe:

> Hear the word of the Lord, O people of Israel,
>> for the Lord has an indictment against the inhabitants of the land.
> There is no faithfulness or loyalty,
>> and no knowledge of God in the land.
> Swearing, lying and murder, and stealing
>> and adultery break out: bloodshed follows bloodshed.
> Therefore the land mourns and all who live in it languish
>> together with the wild animals and the birds of the air,
>>> even the fish of the sea are perishing. (Hos. 4:1-3)

A distressing picture of human and environmental degradation. Hosea pulls no punches in accusation, but his conclusions for his land and his people reflect the allegory that he creates in the first three chapters of his book, which describe Hosea's love for his faithless wife Gomer. Israel is like Gomer, faithless, wicked, unrepentant. Like the figure of Hosea vis-à-vis his wife, the Lord does not leave the people in their degradation but goes out to them to forgive, to save and to heal.

> I will heal their disloyalty; I will love them freely,
>> for my anger has turned from them.
> I will be like dew to Israel;
>> he shall blossom like the lily,
>> he shall strike root like the forests of Lebanon.
> His shoots shall spread out;
>> his beauty shall be like the olive tree,
>> and his fragrance like that of Lebanon.
> They shall again live beneath my shadow,
>> they shall flourish as a garden,
>> they shall blossom like the vine,
>>> their fragrance shall be like the wine of Lebanon. (Hos. 14:4-7)

This is not the image of a wrathful God intent on destruction and vengeance. It is the picture of a God who is angry with evil, and who judges, but who loves and who is seeking the lost, reaching out to them to forgive and heal and to bring them to a new life, a holy life.

Judgment, repentance, and forgiveness are such powerful themes in the faith of the Hebrew people that they are given place in the sanctorial of time. *Yom Kippur,* the day of atonement described in Leviticus 16, is a day when the faithful are particularly confronted with divine judgment and called to purification. "For on this day atonement shall be made for you, to cleanse you from all your sins" (Lev. 16:30). It is a time to recognize failures and shortcomings and to express these in confessional prayers. It is also a time to give thanks for forgiveness and blessings and to atone in almsgiving and in penitence. Giving atonement a time and a place in the yearly ritual cycle can be a temptation to formalism and "every devotion except the heart," but the witness of Isaiah 58 is sufficient testimony to an understanding that the call to repentance and atonement cannot be reduced to a matter of proper ritual observance.

> Is not this the fast that I choose: to loose the bonds of injustice,
>> to undo the thongs of the yoke, to let the oppressed go free,
>>> and to break every yoke?
> Is it not to share your bread with the hungry,
>> and bring the homeless poor into your house;
>>> when you see the naked, to cover them,
>> and not to hide yourself from your own kin? (58:6-7)

Forgiveness and justice are more than polarities within a puzzle. They are partners in the strategy of God to create a new day.

A New Covenant

God's Righteous Judgment

It has become commonplace to contrast the wrathful God of the Old Testament with the loving God of the New Testament, but only the most selective reading of the Bible could reach this conclusion. The story of Jesus begins with a call to confess sin and discover forgiveness. This is the challenge of John the Baptist to which Jesus responds. Jesus accepts the message of John and makes it his own, and he even threatens his hearers with divine punishment: "Unless you repent, you will all perish" (Luke 13:5). The kingdom of God that John and Jesus perceived as "coming" would be the time of blessing, but also the time of judgment when God will smite evil in his wrath.

In his sermon on the day of Pentecost, Peter preaches the coming "time" of God as the promise of salvation, but he is not backward about also calling it a time of divine wrath. He quotes the prophet Joel (2:28-32) to underline this threat, and makes it clear that only those who repent and call upon the name of the Lord will be saved (Acts 2:14-39). What Peter holds out is a life-line: "Save yourselves from this corrupt generation" (Acts 2:40). The apostle Paul in his letter to the Romans argues powerfully for the logic of God's legitimate wrath. What it gets down to for Paul is that "all, both Jews and Greeks, are under the power of sin" (Rom. 3:9). He reasons that since we know the law we know what sin is, and how universal it is, and understand that "the whole world may be held accountable to God" (Rom. 3:19). Paul is bold enough to plunge into the really deep theological waters and conclude, "For God has imprisoned all in disobedience so that he may be merciful to all" (Rom. 11:32). This terrifying logic will be echoed and debated often in Christian theology. Paul is not led to an ontological dualism by this line of reasoning, but to a hymn of praise to the *mysterium tremendum* and to grace.

> O the depth of the riches and wisdom and knowledge of God! How unsearchable are his judgments and how inscrutable his ways!
>
> For who has known the mind of the Lord
>   Or who has been his counselor?
> Or who has given a gift to him,
>   To receive a gift in return?
>
> For from him and through him and to him are all things. To him be the glory forever. Amen. (Rom 11:33-36. Quote from Is. 40 and Job 35.)

This lyric at the end of Romans 11 is followed by perhaps Paul's most compelling call to commitment and to a life lived in the values of a *new* world governed by love. He concludes the chapter, "Do not be overcome by evil, but overcome evil with good" (Rom. 12:21).

If the New Testament is a book about the love of God and the redemption of the world, it is not because its authors are naïve about the evil of the world or reticent in declaring God's terrible judgment upon evil and evildoers. Certainly Jesus was no less reluctant than the Hebrew prophets to proclaim God's judgment on an evil and disobedient people, and in very harsh language: "You snakes, you brood of vipers" (Matt. 23:33). Matthew 23 is a litany of vituperation against the hypocrisy of the religious leaders. "Woe to you" is the litany line, which Jesus seven times throws at the scribes and Pharisees whose falseness in the name of piety has so offended him. This is nasty stuff. It is not Jesus "meek and mild"; it is Jesus angry, judgmental, calling down enmity and woe upon evil masquerading as pious good. This prophet is bold in calling down "woe," even as he laments over it.

> Jerusalem, Jerusalem, the city that kills the prophets and stones those who are sent to it: How often have I desired to gather your children together as a hen gathers her brood under her wings, and you were not willing! (Matt. 23:37)

Jesus' message and ministry has a continuity with John the Baptist's message of God's judgment.

> Truly I tell you, among those born of women no one has arisen greater than John the Baptist. . . . From the days of John the Baptist until now the kingdom of heaven has suffered violence, and the violent take it by force. . . . For John came neither eating nor drinking, and they say, he has a demon. (Matt. 11:11-12, 18)

And Jesus' pronouncing of woe is not limited to individuals like scribes and Pharisees, but to whole peoples:

> Then he began to reproach the cities in which most of his deeds of power had been done, because they did not repent. "Woe to you Chorazin! Woe to you, Bethsaida! For if the deeds of power done in you had been done in Tyre and Sidon, they would have repented long ago in sackcloth and ashes. But I tell you, on the day of judgment it will be more tolerant for Tyre and Sidon than for you. And for you Capernaum. . . ." (Matt. 11:20-23a)

The divine judgment in the message of Jesus is not only comprehensive, as in these passages, but also comes as a surprise, not only in the sense that no one knows the day or the hour (Mark 13 and parallels) but in the sense that many who expect salvation will instead find destruction.

> There will be weeping and gnashing of teeth when you see Abraham and Isaac and Jacob and all the prophets in the kingdom of God and yourselves thrown out. These people will come from east and west, from north

and south, and will eat in the kingdom of God. Indeed, some who are last will be first; and some who are first will be last. (Luke 13:28-30)

Many Christians indulge a highly selective reading of the New Testament that screens out these themes of divine wrath and judgment. There are understandable reasons for this: the former penchant for overemphasizing the judgment theme; evangelism as fright and false guilt that some lay upon themselves for no discernible reason. Ignoring or forgetting this theme, however, is to seriously distort our image and understanding of Jesus himself and his witness.

Jesus' call to repentance for forgiveness of sins is not solely a condemnation of the evils of the world and the corruptions to which humanity is prone. It is more importantly a prophetic proclamation of God's great, persistent love:

> So he told them this parable: "What man of you, having a hundred sheep, if he has lost one of them, does not leave the ninety-nine in the wilderness, and go after the one which is lost until he finds it? And when he has found it, he lays it on his shoulders, rejoicing. And when he comes home, he calls together his friends and his neighbors, saying to them, 'Rejoice with me, for I have found my sheep which was lost.' Just so, I tell you there will be more joy in heaven over one sinner who repents than over ninety-nine righteous persons who need no repentance." (Luke 15:3-7)

Grace: God's Unbounded Love

In the perspective of the Bible, forgiveness is what stands between us and God's wrath over injustice and evil. Punishment may be deserved, but the message of the New Testament is that God did not send the Son into the world to condemn the world, but that through him the world might be saved (John 3:17; cf. John 12:47b). A primary theme in the story of Jesus is this particular outgoing, persistent love toward the wayward and the unrighteous. God is pictured as the relentless pursuer of souls in Jesus' parables, such as the ones about the lost sheep and the lost coin (Luke 15). In the parable of the prodigal son Jesus acknowledges a resentment caused by the divine bias toward the sinner, but its telling underlines a message of God's unlimited forgiveness (Luke 15). To fall into God's grace is to travel from death into life. "This brother of yours was dead and has come to life" (Luke 15:32b).

The scope of God's redeeming grace is not narrowly envisioned as redemption for individuals but as creation itself set free from its bonds to decay (Rom. 8). As St. Paul puts it, "Creation has been groaning in labor pains" (Rom. 8:22) awaiting the "fullness of time to gather up all things in him, things in heaven and things on earth" (Eph. 1:10).

This theme of a "fullness of time" is recorded in Luke's Gospel in his description of the beginnings of Jesus' ministry in his hometown synagogue at Nazareth. Jesus reads a lesson out of the prophet Isaiah (61:1-2; 58:6), a lesson about God's Spirit being upon him, and about good news for the burdened and the bound. It is about good news for those in the promise of release, recovery, and freedom. And Jesus binds himself to this promise saying, "Today the scripture has been fulfilled in our hearing" (Luke 4:21; cf. Matt. 4:14-16).

The Gospel writers consistently describe Jesus in terms of this prophetic intent. The healing of the paralytic is a paradigm of Jesus, his message, and his blessing. "Son, your sins are forgiven" (Mark 2:5). Several things are clarified in this story. Jesus acknowledges a connection between healing and forgiving, and he credits the faith of those who brought the paralytic to Jesus as having a power in his healing. "When Jesus saw their faith, he said to the paralytic, 'Son, your sins are forgiven'" (Mark 2:5). Jesus' detractors are shocked that he claims authority to forgive. He claims the authority forthrightly: "The Son of Man has authority on earth to forgive sins" (Mark 2:10). And in crediting the faith of the paralytic's friends as a power in his forgiveness and healing, Jesus demonstrates that his authority is something shared. This is a crucial understanding in the developing story of Jesus and his disciples.

Sin and Sickness

The equation Jesus makes between forgiving and healing raises questionable assumptions about the relation between sin and sickness. Concluding that sin is a necessary causality of sickness is not the logical conclusion to jump to in understanding this story. It would seem better to understand that the healings of Jesus are all symbols of his authority to forgive sin and to reconcile and restore humanity to fellowship with God. It is a persistent theme in the Hebrew Bible that human suffering is rooted in separation from God. In other words, the basic human affliction is not paralysis but sin. If in some larger sense that is true, then forgiveness itself is indeed healing.

In this story of the forgiving and healing of the paralytic no prior repentance on his part is indicated. This is worth pondering. Jesus does indeed call to repentance, as did John the Baptist (Mark 1:15), but his blessing of forgiveness does not always follow a repentance. In Luke 7:36-50 we find the story of a woman, identified as a sinner, who anoints the feet of Jesus. He says to her at the end of the story, "Your sins are forgiven" (Luke 7:48), and in front of the startled houseguests adds, "Your faith has saved you; go in peace" (Luke 7:50). Faith had also entered into the story of the forgiveness of the paralytic, but there it was the faith of his friends. With Jesus the steps on the road to forgiveness or healing are not wrapped up in a neatly prescribed formula. To the woman caught in adultery and facing possible death by stoning, Jesus could intercede without calling for her repentance. "Neither do I condemn you," he declared. "Go your way, and from now on do not sin again" (John 8:3-11). Jesus does not specifically forgive her, but declares a kind of amnesty and sends her back into life with hope. This amounts to forgiveness. On the other hand, the persistent themes of repentance and faith indicate to us what is normative, namely, as Mark describes the work of the apostles, "they went out and preached that men should repent" (Mark 6:12).

Sorrow for sin is a natural human reaction and, as Paul reminds us, it is integral to the gospel message: "I testified to both Jews and Greeks about repentance toward God and faith toward our Lord Jesus" (Acts 20:21). The New Testament presents this encounter with Christ as a new way to view the world. Repentance, forgiveness, and conversion are means toward a new mind that perceives differently.[1] Grace creates forgiveness and a forgiver, one whose new mind is turned to "premeditated mercy," a mind recreated into reconciliation.[2] Such a person, in New Testament perspective, has put off an "old nature which belongs to your former manner of life," and is renewed and has been "created after the likeness of God in true righteousness and holiness" (Eph. 4:22, 24). St. Paul especially is at pains to describe in some detail the character of such a "new being" (cf. Rom. 12; 1 Cor. 12 and 13; Gal. 5; Eph. 5).

Startlingly, in the Jesus story, his will to forgiveness extends even into his agonies on the cross. Before his tormentors he prays, "Father, forgive them; for they know not what they do" (Luke 23:34). And to those crucified with him, hearing the confession of one — "we are receiving the just reward for our deeds" (Luke 23:41) — Jesus could speak the word of pardon: "Truly I say to you, today you shall be with me in paradise" (Luke 23:43). Jesus is not only a forgiver; he is the embodiment of forgiveness.

So it is that Jesus' followers could claim, as Paul did, that "through this man forgiveness of sin is proclaimed to you" (Acts 13:38). And as did Peter,

---

1. L. William Countryman, *Forgiver and Forgiving* (Harrisburg, Pa.: Morehouse, 1998), p. 2.

2. Joseph Nassal, *Premeditated Mercy* (Leavenworth, Kans.: Forest of Peace Publications, 2000).

"God exalted him at his right hand as leader and Savior that he might give repentance to Israel and forgiveness of sins" (Acts 5:31). In his account of the appearance of the resurrected Christ to Paul on the Damascus road, Luke records Jesus as declaring to Paul that he was appointing him to bear witness to the people and "to open their eyes so that they may turn from darkness to light and from the powers of Satan to God, so that they may receive forgiveness of sins and a place among those who are sanctified by faith in me" (Acts 26:18). St. Paul is faithful to the preaching of the message and presents it as the challenge of a transforming new age in which God's forgiveness, manifested through the anointed Jesus and through believers, resonates throughout the world.

> From now on, therefore, we regard no one from a human point of view; even though we once regarded Christ from a human point of view, we regard him thus no longer. Therefore, if anyone is in Christ Jesus, he is a new creation; the old has passed away, behold, the new has come. All this is from God, who through Christ reconciled us to himself and gave us the ministry of reconciliation, that is, in Christ, God was reconciling the world to himself, not counting their trespasses against them, and entrusting to us the message of reconciliation. So we are ambassadors for Christ, God making his appeal through us. (2 Cor. 5:16-20)

Repentance

Grace may abound, but sadly, so do evil and sin. Repentance is the twin of the powerful message of the forgiveness of sins (Luke 24:47). Indeed, the gospel story begins with the theme of repentance. Jesus is drawn to John the Baptist and his baptism of repentance for the forgiveness of sins (Mark 1:4), and after John's arrest he begins his own ministry, announcing, "The time is fulfilled, and the kingdom of God is at hand; repent and believe in the gospel" (Mark 1:15).

At Pentecost, when the apostles and other believers reassembled, Peter assumed leadership and preached a sermon challenging his hearers to:

> Repent and be baptized every one of you in the name of Jesus Christ for the forgiveness of your sins; and you shall receive the gift of the Holy Spirit. For the promise is to you and to your children and to all that are far off, every one whom the Lord our God calls to him. (Acts 2:38-39)

This is a call to enter into the baptism that Jesus accepted from John the Baptist, and to this are added two other essential meanings of baptism: the name of Jesus Christ, and the gift of the Holy Spirit. Baptism into the "name" is what creates a Christian community. (This liturgical formula evolves, probably already in the first century, to baptism into the Trinitarian name.)[3] The gift of the Holy Spirit, while not a part of John's baptism, is associated by Christians with the baptism of Jesus because of Jesus' experience of the blessing of the Holy Spirit at his baptism. We see, thus, the picture of Christian baptism in Peter's Pentecost sermon as a sort of recapitulation of the baptism of Jesus in the life of the believers. Put another way, it is an image of Christian baptism as into Christ's baptism. The words of Jesus, "Can you be baptized with the baptism with which I am baptized?" (Mark 10:38), are addressed to every believer in every baptism.

We can see the coalescence of these meanings, experiences, and potencies of baptism in the scene in Ephesus where Paul encounters persons who had only been baptized into the baptism of John. "And Paul said, 'John baptized with the baptism of repentance, telling the people to believe in the one who was to come after him, that is, Jesus.' On hearing this, they were baptized in the name of the Lord Jesus. And when Paul had laid his hands upon them the Holy Spirit came on them" (Acts 19:4-6a). It is important to realize that Christian baptism does not supplant John's baptism of repentance for the forgiveness of sins; it includes it. The New Testament authors are not unmindful of the pervasiveness of sin ("For God has imprisoned all in disobedience so that he may be merciful to all" [Rom. 11:32]), or of the necessity of repentance, confession, and renewal: "If we say we have no sin, we deceive ourselves, and the truth is not in us. If we confess our sins, he is faithful and just, and will forgive our sins and cleanse us from all unrighteousness" (1 John 1:8-9).

There is a caveat to the unbounded grace of God which Jesus declares in a confrontation with scribes: "Truly, I say to you, all sins will be forgiven the sons of men, and whatever blasphemies they utter; but whoever blasphemes against the Holy Spirit never has forgiveness, but is guilty of an eternal sin" (Mark 3:28-29; cf. Matt. 12:31-32; Luke 12:10). This passage has puzzled believers. What can it mean to say all sins are forgiven and then exclude one sin? The dispute with the scribes concerns the power by which Jesus casts out demons, and they have raised the question whether it is not by the power of Satan (Mark 3:20-22). Jesus sees this as "an obstinate rejection of the Spirit's work in

---

3. Didache, 7.

God's kingdom, and thus a rejection of God himself."[4] The unforgivable sin against the Holy Spirit is to call evil and unholy that which is truly holy.[5]

Forgiveness and Community

We sinners may need forgiveness one by one; but forgiveness, as Jesus sees it, is no private matter. Probably the clearest indication of just how social forgiveness is for Jesus is his response to the disciples' request that he teach them how to pray. He presents them an interactive image of forgiveness: "and forgive us our sins, as we forgive those who sin against us" (Matt. 6:12).[6] Forgiveness in the perspective of the Lord's Prayer is not a static event in which, by accepting Jesus Christ as Lord and Savior, one is automatically enlisted among the elect, or by signing one's name to the proper creed one is spared judgment and punishment. Forgiveness as it is expressed in Jesus' prayer is rather a rhythm of receiving and bestowing, of getting and giving. Forgiveness so seen is not a status one achieves; it is rather a life into which one enters. Jesus has what we might call a functional/interpersonal idea of forgiveness. It is something real as it happens, as we enter into its reality: "Whenever you stand praying, forgive, if you have anything against anyone; so that your Father also who is in heaven may forgive you your trespasses" (Mark 11:25; cf. Matt. 6:14-15; 18:35).

Forgiving as you have been forgiven is also the burden of Jesus' parable of the unmerciful servant (Matt. 18:23-35). The kingdom of heaven is like a king who forgave a large debt of a servant because of his pleas. That same servant forced one of his own servants into prison for a debt. The king then ordered the first servant into prison because he did not show mercy to a fellow servant. Jesus' story concludes: "So also my heavenly father will do to every one of you, if you do not forgive your brother from your heart" (Matt. 18:35).

Jesus tries to lay down some principles for his followers to guide them in the difficult interpersonal relationships that can arise relating to forgiveness:

> If your brother sins against you, go and tell him his fault, between you and him alone. If he listens to you, you have gained your brother. But if

---

4. Gary S. Shogren, *The Anchor Dictionary of the Bible,* vol. 2 (New York: Doubleday, 1992), p. 837.

5. Mary Ann Tolbert, *Sowing the Gospel* (Minneapolis: Fortress, 1989), p. 147.

6. Ecumenical text.

he does not listen, take one or two others along with you, that every word may be confirmed by the evidence of one or two witnesses. If he refuses to listen to them, tell it to the church, and if he refuses to listen even to the church, let him be to you as a Gentile and a tax collector. (Matt. 18:15-17)[7]

That is, let him be as an outcast. The specificity of this three-step procedure may be useful, but in the end, Jesus refuses to set a limit on forgiveness:

If your brother sins, rebuke him, and if he repents, forgive him; and if he sins against you seven times in the day, and turns to you seven times, and says "I repent," you must forgive him. (Luke 17:4)

As Matthew tells the story, Peter asks Jesus how many times he should forgive a brother who sins against him — seven times maybe (Matt. 18:21)? "Jesus said to him, 'I do not say to you seven times, but seventy times seven'" (Matt. 18:22). The magnitude of mercy is infinite. Maybe the simplest way in which Jesus put this entire matter is in the beatitudes: "Blessed are the merciful, for they shall obtain mercy" (Matt. 5:7).

One of the ways to extend mercy is to be wary about passing judgment. Jesus makes specific warnings about the dangers of our readiness to judge others:

Judge not, that you be not judged. For with the judgment you pronounce you will be judged, and the measure you give will be the measure you get. Why do you see the speck that is in your brother's eye, but do not notice the log that is in your own eye? Or how can you say to your brother, "Let me take the speck out of your eye," when there is the log in your own eye? You hypocrite, first take the log out of your own eye, and then you will see clearly to take the speck out of your brother's eye. (Matt. 7:1-5; cf. Luke 6:37-38, 41-42; Mark 4:24)

Some observers conclude that our forgiveness is in large measure based upon awareness of our own flaws and faults.[8] Jesus is one such insightful observer. Another commonplace of human psychological and scriptural wisdom Jesus

---

7. Such a procedure is based on Leviticus 19:17 and has parallels in the Qumran community. Daniel J. Harrington, *The Gospel of Matthew* (Collegeville, Minn.: Liturgical Press, 1991), p. 271.

8. Cf. John Patton, *Is Human Forgiveness Possible?* (Nashville: Abingdon, 1985).

underlined is what we call the Golden Rule: "Whatever you wish that men would do to you, do so to them, for this is the law and the prophets" (Matt. 22:39-40; Luke 6:31).

Jesus is baptized by John, responding to his call to repentance for forgiveness of sins. When John is arrested Jesus takes up his mantle and his message and inspired by the Holy Spirit preaches "good news," calling disciples into forgiven life in the new time of the kingdom of God. He teaches in synagogues, exorcizes evil spirits, heals, preaches to crowds, maintains a private life of prayer, and appoints twelve apostles who will be near him and commissioned by him. These are bold moves in which Jesus accepts an authority, attracts attention and followers, and stirs up controversy (Mark 1–3).

In the fourth chapter of Mark, Jesus, teaching a large crowd, tells them the parable of the sower (cf. Matt. 13; Luke 8). The story is a kind of allegory of his own life and ministry. The message of Jesus, as the seed of the sower, falls along the wayside — eaten by birds (false, misguided religious leaders); is sown in rocky ground — cannot root, withers and dies (disciples); is sown among thorns — choked out (Herod and his ilk); is sown on good earth — brings forth abundant grain (those who have faith and repent and are saved). To these later is revealed the secret of the kingdom of God, the gift of faith in the God who forgives and blesses abundantly (Mark 4:10-12).

> Though the Gospel uses the concrete metaphors of earth to represent the kingdom of God, the mystery of the kingdom is not agricultural but human. It is the human heart, not land that is the seat of God's domain. . . . Jesus is the messenger of God's good news that the kingdom of God has already come. Those who believe what he says reveal God's rule in their own hearts; that is, for those who have faith that the kingdom has come, it has come in them.[9]

Those who hear, and are faithful and fruitful enter into the new age of the kingdom of God — which is, however, no real novelty. It is rather faithfulness to God's covenant call into holiness:

> Think not that I have come to abolish the law and the prophets; I have come not to abolish them but to fulfill them. For truly, I say to you, till heaven and earth pass away, not an iota, not a dot will pass from the law until all is accomplished. Whoever then relaxes one of the least of these commandments and teaches men so, shall be called least in the kingdom

9. Tolbert, *Sowing the Gospel*, p. 173.

of heaven. For I tell you, unless your righteousness exceeds that of the scribes and Pharisees, you will never enter the kingdom of heaven. (Matt. 5:17-20)

Ministry of Forgiveness

Fulfilling the law means going beyond the requirements of the law and finding one's self in the righteousness of God. This is the bold disclosing of Jesus' Sermon on the Mount (Matt. 5–6). Obedience to rules is not living faith. Seeking first the kingdom of God and God's righteousness (Matt. 6:33) is to discover oneself reconciled within the forgiving and energizing embrace of God's love. Going beyond the rules — the law — into a new creation, St. Paul compares it to adoption:

But when the time had fully come, God sent forth his son . . . so we might receive adoption as sons. And because you are sons, God has sent the Spirit of his son into our hearts, crying, "Abba! Father!" So through God you are no longer a slave, but a son, and if a son then an heir. (Gal. 4:4-7)

And in this new creation there is a new freedom: "For all of you as were baptized into Christ have put on Christ. There is neither Jew nor Greek, there is neither slave nor free, there is neither male nor female, for you are all one in Christ Jesus" (Gal. 3:27-29). All of this is the gift of God who through Christ reconciles us to himself (2 Cor. 5:18) and commissions us as reconcilers: "So we are ambassadors for Christ, God making his appeal through us" (2 Cor. 5:20). The ministry of reconciliation is entrusted to us (2 Cor. 5:19). Another way to put this is to say that the ministry of forgiving and reconciling is a sharing in the mind of God. Participating in this way of life is to become, as St. Paul put it, "stewards of the mysteries of God" (1 Cor. 4:1).

This ministry is both personal and social in equal measure. When Jesus sent his apostles out in mission, he bestowed on them the authority to purge unclean spirits, to heal the sick (Mark 6; Matt. 10; Luke 9), and I think we can add, recalling the story of the forgiving and healing of the paralytic (Mark 2; Matt. 9; Luke 5), to forgive the repentant. Mark sums up their mission: "They went out and preached that men should repent. And they cast out many demons, and anointed with oil many that were sick and healed them." In these accounts Jesus does not specifically confer authority on his apostles to forgive sin, but elsewhere he does.

> Truly, I say to you, whatever you bind on earth shall be bound in heaven, and whatever you loose on earth shall be loosed in heaven. Again I say to you, if two of you agree on earth about anything they ask, it will be done for them by my Father in heaven. For where two or three are gathered in my name, there I am in the midst of them. (Matt. 16:18-20)

And in the Gospel of John:

> Jesus said to them again, "Peace be with you. As the Father has sent me, even so I send you." And when he had said this, he breathed on them, and said to them, "Receive the Holy Spirit. If you forgive the sins of any, they are forgiven; if you retain the sins of any they are retained." (John 20:21-23)

Christians have disagreed about just how wide this apostolic commission extends. Is it the task of an ordained clergy or is it part of the interpersonal dynamism of the larger Christian community? It would seem that Jesus' illustrative teachings, such as the parable of the sheep and the goats in the great judgment (Matt. 25:31-46), the Lord's Prayer (Matt. 6:12), and the role of the paralytic's friends in his forgiveness/healing, indicate the ministry of forgiveness is a shared gift in the whole body of Christ.

This matter of the authority to forgive becomes a critical issue in the Reformation. For Protestants, Luther's argument for a "priesthood of all believers" has been decisive, even if monumentally unsuccessful.

> A man's secret sins are forgiven him when he makes a voluntary confession before a brother in private, and, on reproof he asks for pardon and mends his ways. . . . One who has done wrong might lay bare his soul to whomsoever he chooses, and beg absolution, comfort, and Christ's very word from the mouth of his neighbor.[10]

There is evidence that the New Testament church practiced the manner of reconciliation Luther advocates, nowhere expressed more clearly than in the letter of James, which ironically Luther had little regard for: "Confess your sins to one another, and pray for one another that you may be healed" (James 5:16; cf. Matt. 18:17; 1 Cor. 5:10-13; 2 Cor. 2:5-11; 1 John 5:16). In the context of the mercy of God that Jesus proclaims, the acceptance of forgiveness involves

---

10. Martin Luther, "The Sacrament of Penance," in *Martin Luther, Selections from His Writings*, ed. Jn. Dillenberger (New York: Doubleday, 1961), p. 321.

a desire to share it. The call to repent and discover forgiveness in Christ is a call into a holy life, a life among the saints. It echoes the word of God to Israel: "Consecrate yourselves therefore and be holy. . . . For I am the Lord who brought you up out of the land of Egypt, to be your God; you shall therefore be holy, for I am holy" (Lev. 11:44, 45; cf. 1 Peter 1:16). Mercy is more than a blessing, it is a vocation.

> But you are a chosen race, a royal priesthood, a holy nation, God's own people, that you may declare the wonderful deeds of him who called you out of darkness into his marvelous light. Once you were no people but now you are God's people; once you had not received mercy but now you have received mercy. (1 Peter 2:8-12)

> Practice hospitality ungrudgingly to one another. As each has received a gift employ it for one another, as good stewards of God's varied grace. (1 Peter 4:9)

CHAPTER 4

A Brief History of Transgression
and Reconciliation among Christians

First Century

Reconciliation with God and neighbor was a primary concern in the nascent Christian community. It was also a problem. The problem had many sides to it, but essentially it comes down to this question: If baptism is for the forgiveness of sins (Acts 2:38), why do we continue to sin, and what do we do about it? Of course, no one knew why sinning persisted. Demonic powers and perversity in human nature were the most natural culprits at hand. What to do about it was a more difficult problem.

Re-baptism did not generally present itself as a solution. This was to doubt and profane divine forgiveness itself. Some new way needed to be found to repent of post-baptismal sin and find forgiveness. We can see the issue and some lines of possible solutions already in the work of New Testament authors. The author of Hebrews, the most rigorous moralist, strongly denies the possibility of repentance and reconciliation for anyone "enlightened," i.e., gifted with the Holy Spirit (baptism) and initiated into the new age, and yet sins deliberately, breaking the law of Moses. Such a one has fallen into apostasy, is condemned and unforgiven. No second chance (Heb. 6:4-8; 10:26-31; 12:16-17)! Paul admonishes the Corinthians to banish a certain man for a particular immorality, and characterizes this as "delivering him to Satan." What he means in seeing this as "the destruction of the flesh, that his spirit may be saved in the day of the Lord Jesus" (1 Cor. 5:1-5), is less than clear. In condemning the man, Paul at least holds out the hope of ultimate salvation. Clearly his main concern is that the church not be corrupted. We have seen in the Gospels that Jesus advises a particular procedure of fraternal correction for sins and misunderstandings (Matt. 18:15-17; Luke 17:3-4), and that disciples are urged to be generous in forgiveness (Matt. 18:22).

One might well conclude that any "way" that aimed for perfection ought to make room for generous forgiveness: "Be perfect, as your heavenly Father is perfect" (Matt. 5:48). So it stands to reason that sinners must pray for their own forgiveness (Matt. 6:12; Acts 8:22), and other believers need to join their prayers with them to intercede with God on their behalf (James 5:16; 1 John 5:16). And we find already in the New Testament communities some indications of the beginning of a penitential practice that included atoning good works of compensation. The clearest of these indications is Acts 26:20: "They should repent and turn to God and perform deeds worthy of their repentance" (cf. Matt. 3:8; Luke 7:47; James 21:25; Rev. 2:5).[1]

The problem that post-baptismal sin raised for these early Christians was not only the problem of *why* but also the problem of *what*. How was one to make judgments about what constituted serious transgression? One can see judgments emerging about qualities of sin — for instance, the ending of the first epistle of John (5:13-20), which concerns what is proper in prayer.

> And this is the confidence which we have in him, that if we ask anything according to his will he hears us. And if we know that he hears us in whatever we ask, we know that we have obtained the request made of him. If anyone sees his brother committing what is not a mortal sin, he will ask, and God will give him life. . . . There is sin which is mortal. I do not say that one is to pray for that. All wrongdoing is sin, but there is sin which is mortal.
>
> We know that anyone born of God does not sin, but He who was born of God keeps him, and the Evil one does not touch him. (1 John 5:14-18)

Two problems are posed in this passage: the issue of distinctions in the seriousness of sin, and the question that some sin may be unforgivable. While New Testament writers give repentance a prominent place, they do not specify structures of the church's life to support this or supervise it. In general the repentant sinner is welcomed, but there are reservations, and in the case of the author of Hebrews, denial of repentance.[2] These first Christians faced many perplexities about their common life, although most seemed to under-

---

1. Joseph Favazza, *The Order of Penitents* (Collegeville, Minn.: Liturgical Press, 1988), p. 71.

2. James Dallen, *The Reconciling Community* (Collegeville, Minn.: Liturgical Press, 1986), p. 2.

stand what principle to put first: "Above all hold unfailing your love for one another, since love covers a multitude of sins" (1 Peter 4:8).

Other Christians of the late New Testament era address themselves to these problems and recommended prayer, fasting, and charity as "remedies" for sin. These included the author of the Didache and Justin Martyr. The most interesting of them is probably St. Clement of Rome. In his first letter to the Corinthians (still a fractious community c. AD 96) he writes:

> Let us then also pray for those who have fallen into any sin, that meekness and humility may be given to them, so that they may submit, not unto us, but unto the will of God. For in this way they shall secure a fruitful and perfect remembrance from us, with sympathy for them, both in our prayers to God and our mention of them to the saints. Let us receive correction, beloved, on account of which no one should be displeased. These exhortations by which we admonish one another are both good [in themselves] and highly profitable for they tend to unite us to the will of God.[3]

Clement is here following patterns established by canonical authors (Matt. 18:15-20; Luke 17:3; 1 Cor. 6:1-6; Gal. 6:1; James 5:19-20), and he adds an administrative dimension that points toward disciplinary practice.

> Submit yourselves to the presbyters, and receive correction so as to repent, bending the knees of your hearts. Learn to be subject, laying aside the proud and arrogant self-confidence of your tongue. For it is better for you that you should occupy a humble but honorable place in the flock of Christ, than that, being highly exalted, you should be cast out from the hope of his people.[4]

Three important understandings are put forward here. First, penitents are to present themselves to the elders of the church. Second, if they are not repentant over misdeeds, they will be cast out of the church. Third, implicit in Clement's advice and prescription is the conclusion that repentance toward God and neighbor is accomplished in repentance and subsequent forgiveness within the fellowship of the church. Breaking God's law is no individual matter; it is a serious rupture of the Christian community, and God acts within the forgiving love of the Christian people. This latter point in the post-

---

3. *The Ante-Nicene Fathers*, vol. 1 (Grand Rapids: Eerdmans, 1956 [1885 edn.]), ch. 56, p. 20.

4. *The Ante-Nicene Fathers*, ch. 57.

apostolic witness established a connection between penitence and public worship, both in regard to confession and forgiveness and to possible banishment of the sinner.

Second Century

Evidences from the second century are very scarce and advance little our understanding of confession and forgiveness in the church. The most important witness is the document *Shepherd of Hermas* (c. 150). In Hermas's "revelation" capital sins are identified: apostasy, immorality, and murder, and arguments are put forward for repentance, forgiveness, and reconciliation even for such mortal sin, even after baptism. No rite or process is suggested for this, and Hermas wants unrepentant sinners banned and isolated. He also argues that reconciliation after baptism is possible only once. This turns out to be a provision adopted by most of the church for a long time.[5]

Irenaeus (d. c. 200) refers to penance in *Adversus Haeresus* often enough to indicate that confession was a common practice, but he gives no picture of a system for reconciliation or indicates specific actions of the repentant sinners.[6]

Third Century

By the third century evidences of structured forms of ecclesial penance, so-called public penance, are abundant. Also, it is observable that there are considerable differences in understanding and practice between the church of the west and of the east.

The clearest picture of penance in the west is found especially in the writings of African theologians Tertullian and Cyprian. Tertullian's contribution is mainly in two works, *De paenitentia* and *De pudicitia*.[7] The former he wrote while still a "Catholic," and the latter as a Montanist. In *De paenitentia* (c. 220) Tertullian excludes no sins from pardon. Believers are saved by baptism and second repentance, which can be offered once. The penitential process, referred to as exomologesis, is a rigorous discipline and indeed a special

---

5. Oscar D. Watkins, *A History of Penance* (New York: Burt Franklin, 1961 [originally published London, 1920]), pp. 47-72.

6. "Against Heresies," Chapter 3, number 3 and 4, *The Ante-Nicene Fathers*, pp. 414-17.

7. Watkins, *A History of Penance*, pp. 113-29; pp. 81-92.

"order" of penitential life. In the church penitents are segregated by location, by dress, and by particular penitential behaviors.

> Exomologesis, then, is a discipline which leads a man to prostrate and humble himself. It prescribes a way of life which, even in the matter of food and clothing, appeals to pity. It bids him to be in sackcloth and ashes, to cover his body with filthy rags, to plunge his soul into sorrow, to exchange sin for suffering. Moreover, it demands that you know only such food and drink as is plain; this means it is taken for the sake of your soul, not your belly. It requires that you sigh and weep and groan day and night to the Lord your God, that you prostrate yourself at the foot of the priests and kneel before the beloved God, making all the brethren commissioned ambassadors of your prayer for pardon.[8]

This is a process of "segregated penance within the life of the community"[9] that includes serious deprivations and humiliation intended not only to atone for wickedness, but to enlist the prayers of believers, lay and clergy, on the penitents' behalf. The separation includes denial of the Eucharist, and once reconciled and returned to communion, the forgiven sinner is not permitted to join the military or to marry, and indeed is ordered to lifelong continence. Note that Tertullian is not here making recommendations but describing what happens. Of course, when he converts to Montanism, Tertullian no longer supports these "liberal" procedures. Now, for mortal sin — apostasy, immorality, murder — one is cast out from the people of God, and kept out.[10]

Cyprian, bishop of Carthage, raises the other important voice out of Roman Africa. Cyprian was bishop during the period of the Decian persecution and in 249 he was forced to flee Carthage. On his return he faced the problem of "lapsed" Christians who now wanted to return to the fold. Indeed, prior to his arrival he was informed by letter by several *lapsi* in the latter half of 250 that they anxiously sought readmission to the church. Some had letters they had obtained from martyrs (those in prison who refused to sacrifice and were eventually martyred) granting their forgiveness and reconciliation. Martyrdom gave one a special status in the Christian community, and at least since mid-second century their intercession was commonly considered sufficient to reconcile an apostate to God. Cyprian denies these *lapsi* a return to

---

8. Favazza, *The Order of Penitents*, p. 194. *De Paen.* 9, 3-4.
9. Favazza, *The Order of Penitents*, p. 195.
10. Cf. *De Pudicitia* in Watkins, *A History of Penance*, pp. 114ff.

the *Pax ecclesiae* and informs all that they must wait on the decision of a council. Such a council did meet after Easter in 251 and decided that deathbed communion could be granted to the lapsed, made some allowance for individual circumstances, and shortened the period of penance, but in general held all to its disciplines. Renewal of persecution threatened in 252 and another council shortened the period of penance and decided to receive all the lapsed back into the church to unify the church and fortify it against the new threat.[11]

Cyprian's arguments against an easy reconciliation of the lapsed focus upon his concern for the unity of the church. Not surprisingly, considering his office, his concern for unity comes to center upon the role of the bishop. Obedience to the bishop is what guarantees the unity of the church. In fact the only sin that he identifies as beyond repentance is disobedience to the guidance of the bishop.[12] It is in Cyprian that we see for the first time a clear ecclesial/liturgical process for penance. It consists of three steps: penitential satisfactions, exomologesis, and the granting of the peace of the church. The first step consisted of personal works like fasting, prayer, and charity. Such acknowledgment of sin would exhibit intense sorrow, and include penitential dress and a segregated place in the church — all of this supervised by the clergy. The second phase, the exomologesis (confession), is apparently the actual confession of sin before the bishop. Some things about this are unclear, such as, was this done privately or before the congregation? Tertullian describes this action as taking place with the penitent on knees before the bishop and other clergy and the community.[13] The third step of penance was the granting of the *Pax ecclesiae*. This reconciliation had three moments: the laying on of hands by the bishop, the celebration of Eucharist on behalf of the reconciled, and admission to communion.

Both Tertullian and Cyprian recognize a distinction between mortal and venial sin, although not entirely clearly. For the latter they prescribe prayer, fasting, good works, and almsgiving as appropriate satisfactions.

A process of church penance develops in the eastern church along similar lines to that in the west but there are significant differences that become quite clear by the fourth century. The author of *Didascalia Apostolorum*, a church order in Syria in the early third century, describes a means of repentance and reconciliation that has much similarity with Cyprian. The role of

11. Cyprian, "Letter 33: The Problem of the Lapsed," in *Early Latin Theology*, ed. S. L. Greenslade (Philadelphia: Westminster, 1956), p. 143.

12. Favazza, *The Order of Penitents*, p. 208.

13. Karl Rahner, *Theological Investigations, Vol. XV: Penance in the Early Church* (New York: Crossroad, 1982), p. 154.

the bishop is critical; he dominates the process. The *Didascalia* calls for strict observance of Christian morality, but holds out the possibility of repentance even for grave sins. Such sinners are first isolated. If penitent, they are then examined by the bishop, who then assigns the period of time and the tasks (prayer, fasting, etc.) of penance. Penitents are barred from the Eucharist but they are allowed to participate in the ante-communion (Service of the Word). When the time and tasks of penance are completed the bishop receives the penitent back into the fellowship with the laying on of hands. One notes already in the *Didascalia* and other writings on penance from the eastern church an accent upon mercy different from that of Tertullian or Cyprian.

> You see, beloved and dear children, how abundant are the mercies of the Lord our God and his goodness and loving-kindness towards us, and how He exhorts them that have sinned to repent. And in many places He speaks of these things; and He gives no place to the thought of those who are hard of heart and wish to judge strictly and without mercy and to cast away altogether them that have sinned as though there were no repentance for them. But God is not so, but even sinners He calls to repentance and gives them hope; and those who have not sinned He teaches, and tells them that they should not suppose that we hear or partake in the sins of others. Simply, then, receive them that repent, rejoicing.[14]

There has been considerable discussion about the meaning of the laying on of hands in reconciliation in this period. Was this related to the laying on of hands in the baptismal ritual? The conclusion is generally in the negative. It does seem, however, that since so much is made of this rite as a second repentance there must have been some resonance between laying on of hands in the original ceremony of belonging and in this rite of return. One of the notable features of *Didascalia Apostolorum* is the lack of any mention of the unrepeatable nature of penance. It is possible that in the east in general, Alexandria excepted, penance was indeed repeatable.

In mid-third century, Origen describes an analogous system of reconciliation.[15] The role of the bishop is most important, but Origen insists on a bishop/confessor of holy character. He must be "someone of God."[16] In this regard we should note that here and commonly in the penitential instructions and understandings of the eastern church there is more the flavor of

---

14. *Didascalia Apostolorum*, ed. R. Hugh Connolly (Oxford: Clarendon, 1929), pp. 48-50.

15. Watkins, *A History of Penance*, pp. 132-42.

16. Rahner, *Theological Investigations*, pp. 283f.

spiritual counsel and direction than of juridical requirement. Which is not to say that the penitential discipline is relaxed or haphazard. The program Origen describes in essays, commentaries, and sermons is an unrepeatable forgiveness that begins with the isolation and exclusion of the petitioner.[17] Sin must then be revealed in confession to the bishop who will assign a regime of exomologesis and personal penitential acts. The penitent retains a limited status in the church. The bishop presides over the liturgy of reconciliation, laying hands upon the forgiven, and there is some indication with Origen that the whole church participates in this action.[18]

Development in a new direction in the east is first noticed in an anonymous letter to a fellow bishop by Gregory Thaumaturgus (the wonder worker), bishop of Neocaesarea (d. c. 270-275). Advising this colleague about procedures in penance, Gregory suggests some progressive steps in penance.[19] These are presented in a full statement in the last paragraph of his letter. Scholars are generally convinced that this ending of the letter is gloss, bringing Gregory's "stages" into conformity with what had become common fourth-century practice. The grades of penance recommended are in the first place, weeping and mourning, expressing sorrow for sin; second, listening, standing in the narthex hearing the service of the Word; third, falling down, prostrating oneself in the nave before all the congregation; fourth, standing with the faithful hearing the Word with the people in the nave; the last stage of "graded" penance is restoration to communion with the faithful. The concept recommended itself widely and the system spread rapidly throughout Cappadocia and Galatia and the churches of Syria. By the fourth century it was common procedure. The grades are referenced in the canons of the Council of Nicea (325).[20] In the east, the popularity of the system endured throughout the fourth century.

Summary

Several things impress one about these modes of penance in both east and west as the church comes to imperial legitimacy in the Edict of Milan (313). One is the strictness of its discipline and its unrepeatable and punishing char-

---

17. Ernest F. Latko, *Origen's Concept of Penance* (Quebec City: Faculty of Theology, 1949), pp. 100ff.

18. Rahner, *Theological Investigations*, pp. 291-304.

19. *St. Gregory Thaumaturgus*, ed. Michael Slussen, *The Fathers of the Church*, vol. 98 (Washington, D.C.: Catholic University of America Press, 1998), pp. 147-51.

20. Peter L'Huiller, *The Church of the Ancient Councils* (Crestwood, N.Y.: St. Vladimir's, 1956), pp. 17-100; cf. canon 11, p. 65 and canon 12, p. 67.

acter for most of the church. Two is the lack of an "absolution" in the liturgies. One does not find a proclamation of pardon issued by the bishop, no formula of "absolvo te." The act of reconciliation is the blessing gesture of the bishop in the laying on of hands, and reconciliation with the whole church in the readmission to communion. Liturgical gesture and action dominate, not declaration. Three is the different flavor of penance established between east and west by the fourth century.

Circumstances and the nature of penance itself eventually forced changes in the ways Christians sought and found forgiveness. One of the general provisions in the several schemes of penance was the right of every Christian to confess sin and find reconciliation at the time of death. This right and the stringency of the systems themselves led many, maybe most Christians, to postpone penance until the deathbed. Indeed, it convinced not a few "believers" to postpone baptism until before death, including the emperor Constantine, and far from thinking of himself as less than a real Christian, Constantine considered himself one of the apostles. Another factor leading finally to the breakdown of the penitential orders was the success of Christianity in the empire. Once the empire embraced the faith multitudes flocked into the church, in no small measure for the same political/cultural reasons they had embraced the cult of the emperors in the past.

The creation of Christendom changed the church radically. The system of ecclesial penance endured failingly into the early Middle Ages, greatly lamented in some quarters. Especially from mid-fifth century through the tenth century, there was much confusion about the considerable variety and competition of methods.

A New Model

Seeds of a quite different plan of penance sprouted in the far north, even beyond the reaches of the vanishing empire. Public church penance was unknown in the British Isles.[21] The organization of the church had taken on a unique character in Ireland owing particularly to the lack of urban centers and the class political system. Monasteries were the centers of church life and they functioned as a sort of county parish centers. Laypeople were part of monastic life as well as monks and clergy. In this climate penance evolved as a private matter and a personal encounter with a "soul friend." Penitence was seen in this Christian milieu in severe and rigorous terms; fasting and serious

---

21. Watkins, *A History of Penance*, p. 752.

self-denial were common in penance, but the manner was private and personal. This dimension of reconciliation was not totally absent from canonical penance, especially in the east, and there are indeed evidences that from the seventh century, in some places, persons could go to a priest and under supervision do assigned penance.[22] It is a practice that expands definitely under the influence of Celtic and Anglo-Saxon monastic practice.

The islands of the north had been isolated from the continent from the mid-fourth century. Institutions of learning flourished there however, largely because of the isolation from the chaos on the continent. They were privy to classical and early Christian texts, and they read Greek and Latin. One of the primal influences on the Celtic penitential method was eastern monasticism, especially the writings of Cassian.[23]

> Most of the penitentials were compiled by careful students of Cassian, and a number of these have been arranged on the plan of the eight vices first systematized in his writings.[24]

The Celtic penitentials were handbooks for the use of the ministers of penance. They listed transgressions and prescribed a balancing regime of penance. One of the earliest of the penitentials is that of the Irish monastic scholar Finnian, compiled mid-sixth century. An example of one of the 53 articles of his handbook:

> #5. If one of the clerics or ministers of God makes strife, he shall do penance for a week with bread and water and seek pardon from God and his neighbor, with full confession and humility; and thus can he be reconciled to God and his neighbor.[25]

Finnian's penitential is more thorough than the few that preceded it and is based on the identification of deadly sins in Jerome and Cassian.

In this way to forgiveness of the Celtic church there is no public dimension, no liturgical expression, and hence no involvement or participation of the community as such in reconciliation. There is also no recourse to the bishop. A priest is sufficient to hear confession and assign penance. There is

---

22. Hugh Connolly, *The Irish Penitentials* (Dublin: Four Courts Press, 1995), p. 15.

23. Dallen, *The Reconciling Community*, p. 7.

24. *John Cassian: The Conferences*, ed. Boniface Ramsey (New York: Paulist, 1997), pp. 177-209.

25. John T. McNeill and Helen Garner, *Medieval Handbooks of Penance* (New York: Columbia University Press, 1938), p. 19.

evidence that a monk could assume this role as well. Also, in contrast to church penance, this Celtic practice is repeatable. In the Irish monastery, confessions were made to a spiritual guide known as an *anamchara*, which means soul-friend. Every monk had a soul-friend to whom he could "manifest his conscience."[26] It was not in origin an official act of the church but a form of spiritual direction, a healing dialogue.[27] This personal dialogic relationship eventually evolves into a systematic method that exceeded the confines of a monastery, encompassing lesser clergy and laity.

This new penance was carried to the continent by Celtic and Anglo-Saxon missionaries. The most effective of these was the Irish monk Columbanus, whose penitential, much influenced by Finnian, begins with these words:

> True penance is not to commit things deserving of penance but to lament such things as have been committed. . . . Diversity of offences causes diversity of penances. Doctors of the body compound their medicines in diverse kinds. . . . So also should spiritual doctors treat with diverse kinds of cures the wounds of souls, their sicknesses, pains, ailments, and infirmities.[28]

Columbanus founded monasteries in France and Lombardy. He was a forceful and charismatic personality, and his message of repentance, confession, and salvation was welcomed by common people and by the aristocracy, if not much appreciated by local bishops.

> Penance healed guilt and drove out fear. Its discipline helped to make sense of misfortune and deflected divine anger provoked by human depravity. And if sin could be wiped out by the discipline of penance, could not the offering to God — in a society where every cog of social intercourse was oiled by the giving of gifts — of a monastery, richly endowed, splendidly furnished, peopled by the founders' own kin, turned monks expert in prayer, buy His favor?[29]

This new "tariff" penance solved some problems existing in church penance that were especially vexing for the upper classes. The old way was humiliating

---

26. McNeill and Garner, *Medieval Handbooks of Penance*, p. 88.

27. Connolly, *The Irish Penitentials*, p. 14.

28. Connolly, *The Irish Penitentials*, pp. 16f.

29. Richard Fletcher, *The Barbarian Conversion* (New York: Henry Holt, 1997), p. 140. Cf. Watkins, *A History of Penance*, pp. 615-22; *Medieval Handbooks of Penance*, pp. 249-65.

in its stringent mandates. Stern regulations concerning marriage, sex, vocation, and isolation were disruptive of family and civic life. Columbanus's foundations were rural on the Irish model, and this too appealed to the aristocrats, who were governors of the rural world. The new way of liberation from temporal and eternal damnation was popular, as reported by Jonas of Elmo, Columbanus's biographer: "From all sides the people flocked together to the medicaments of penance."[30]

It is not the case that the old model of penance disappeared quietly. There was conflict. Perhaps nowhere are the issues formed better than in the dissonance between Alcuin of York (c. 740-804) and Theodulf of Orléans (c. 750-821). Both were great scholars and major figures in the Carolingian Renaissance. Alcuin, the Englishman, knew and favored the new penance. Theodulf, bishop of Orléans, had reservations and worked to oppose, even outlaw the penitentials.

> For the confession which we make to the priests brings us this support, that we wash away the stains of our sins when we receive at their hands salutary council, the very wholesome observances of penance, or the exchange of prayers. But the confession which we make to God alone is helpful in this, that in so far as we are mindful of our sins, so far God is forgetful of them; and conversely, in so far as we forget them, so far God remembers them.[31]

Theodulf was concerned that the new methods would be too easy, even insincere — that real contrition could be subverted in the forms of a rush to forgiveness. This issue did, in fact, become a fundamental complaint in the revolt of the Reformation to come. Back at the time of the turn of the centuries, from eight to nine, Theodulf won some battles in council decisions, but lost the war. No small part of the credit for this victory must be given to the reign of Charles the Great between 768 and 814 and of his immediate successors. The ideals and reforms of the Carolingian era provided a basis of education and communication that could refine and promote the new penance. Interestingly, the leader who played almost no role at all in this reform of penance was the pope.

---

30. Watkins, *A History of Penance,* pp. 620, 758.
31. Capitulary I, canon 30. In Watkins, *A History of Penance,* p. 694.

Sacrament and Obligation

By the mid-twelfth century Peter Lombard in the *Sentences* — a text that educated centuries of churchmen — set forth a theology of penance that identifies it as one of seven sacraments and outlined its fourfold shape: contrition before God, confession to the priest, absolution pronounced by the priest, and satisfactions prescribed by the priest as appropriate atonement for the sin confessed. Lombard sets no precedents here; he rather systematizes what had been by his day established theory and practice. As the system evolved to this era, confession gradually overtook in importance the activity of satisfaction, and the "period of satisfaction had been so shortened that it had effectively been absorbed within the confession."[32] At the fourth Lateran Council (1215), understood by the Latin church as the twelfth ecumenical council, the Sacrament of Penance imposed upon all adult Christians the duty of confessing as well as receiving communion at least once yearly.

Not until the eleventh century is there evidence of general indulgences. In early centuries we have seen that unusual powers of forgiveness were allowed to martyrs and confessors. These later powers of indulgence "were acts of jurisdiction by ecclesiastical authority remitting ecclesiastical penances upon performance of acts of piety or charity, usually pilgrimages to certain churches or the giving of alms."[33] A pilgrimage, a crusade, an offering could be a suitable substitute for sacramental penance.

Revolt

Warnings of abuse in such substitutions were not rare in this period but they were not notably effective. One such protest led to open revolt. In 1517, on All Hallows' Eve, the Augustinian monk Martin Luther nailed 95 theses to the door of the castle church in Wittenberg. His preface to these debating points read:

> Out of love and concern for the truth, and with the object of eliciting it, the following heads will be the subject of a public discussion at Wittenberg under the presidency of the reverend father, Martin Luther, Augustinian, Master of Arts and Sacred Theology, and duly appointed Lecturer

32. Dallen, *The Reconciling Community*, p. 149.

33. Monika K. Hellwig, *Sign of Reconciliation and Conversion: The Sacrament of Penance for Our Time* (Collegeville, Minn.: Liturgical Press, 1982), p. 124.

on these subjects in that place. He requests that whoever cannot be present personally to debate the matter orally will do so in absence in writing.

1. When our Lord and Master, Jesus Christ said "Repent," He called for the entire life of believers to be one of penitence.[34]

And there are 94 more. In the theses and other writings[35] of the period, Luther is saying to holy mother church that she is using quantitative means to accomplish what is a qualitative matter. Essentially his whole point is subsumed in the first thesis.

We have seen the possibility of this corruption of the "new" penance forecast by Theodulf of Orléans eight centuries ago. Another way to put Luther's protest, in terms of the structure of the Sacrament of Penance — contrition, confession, absolution, satisfaction — is to say that he accused authorities in the church of twisting the sacrament so that a particular "satisfaction," in this case the giving of money, could accomplish the other parts of the sacrament, especially "contrition," without these actually happening. It is hard to imagine a monk out in a Germanic province going up against the great and powerful church in this way. He knew he had some basis of support. Even so, it was a brave, reckless, and dangerous action. The Reformation has many causes, but it was the corruption of the church's Sacrament of Forgiveness that sparked the conflagration.

Luther's discovery in St. Paul that the just shall live by grace through faith[36] transformed him personally and spiritually. It formed in him a way of thinking and living redemption and sanctification that was at odds with much of the theological/ecclesial/liturgical/spiritual tradition he inherited. Luther discovered in Paul that the opposite of sin is not righteousness but faith.

> Since all have sinned and fall short of the glory of God, they are justified by his grace as a gift, through the redemption which is in Christ Jesus. (Rom. 3:23-24)

On this understanding Luther did not want to abolish a sense of sin in human self-understanding. He rather "cut every traditional element of discipline out of the theory of justification and made it as purely a theory of consolation as he

---

34. John Dillenberger, ed., *Martin Luther, Selections from His Writings*, "The Ninety Five Theses" (New York: Anchor, 1961), pp. 490-500.

35. Luther, "Preface to Latin Writings," "Freedom of a Christian," in Dillenberger, pp. 5, 43-52.

36. Romans 3.

could."[37] Contrition is not superseded, but it is a lifelong task. Along with accepting the gift of grace every Christian must accept the reality of sin, even of his or her total depravity. Luther did not mean by "total depravity" that everything a person did was depraved. He meant that depravity, sin and wickedness, can invade any and every part of life. Put another way, he meant that there is no part of one's existence, not thinking, or feeling, or any part of identity and activity that was exempt from wickedness. What drove Luther to solace in St. Paul was his own quest for righteousness. He couldn't find a completely pure motive. There was always the possibility of some seedy prompting.[38] This means that for even the most pious Christian there is no pure life. Even at our best we exist before God as righteous and as a sinner: *simul justus et peccator*. This was Luther's anthropology. Penance in this understanding is surely sorrow over faults and failings and continued quest throughout life for a deeper trust in God's accepting mercy, and the commitment to live out the revealed qualities of that mercy.[39] What it definitely is not, is the penitential *modus vivendi* established in the western church between the seventh and twelfth centuries.

Make no mistake, Luther believed in grace, but he also believed in confession of sin.

> There are two sorts of confession. . . . One of them consists in confession to God alone; the other is confession to one's neighbor alone, and asking his forgiveness. Both are included in the Lord's Prayer, in which we say: "Forgive us our trespasses, as we forgive them that trespass against us." Indeed the whole prayer is really a confession. What, in fact, does our prayer mean, but that we confess that we do not do what we ought to do, and that we ask for God's grace and the joy of a good conscience? Such confession ought to be made constantly all our lives, for it pertains to the Christian to recognize himself to be a sinner and to ask for grace.[40]

Luther maintained that before coming to God in confession we ought first "to confess to each other and forgive each other."[41] And he understood that be-

---

37. Thomas N. Tentler, *Sin and Confession on the Eve of the Reformation* (Princeton: Princeton University Press, 1977), p. 355.

38. Paul Tillich, *A History of Christian Thought* (unpublished lecture stenographically recorded and transcribed during Spring semester, 1953, at Union Theological Seminary in New York by Peter H. John), pp. 201f.

39. Tillich, *A History of Christian Thought*, pp. 190-95.

40. Martin Luther, "A Short Exhortation to Confession," from Luther's Great Catechism (1529), in Max Thurian, *Confession* (London: SCM, 1958), pp. 142f.

41. Luther, "A Short Exhortation to Confession," p. 143.

yond general guilt — "the total depravity" — there is particular guilt that stains our lives and for which we need to "disburden ourselves to a brother, and seek from him, as often as we wish, counsel and consolation."[42] This ministry of forgiveness extends to all Christians.

> Because we have one baptism, one gospel, one faith, and are all equally Christians. . . . When a pope or bishop anoints, grants tonsures, consecrates, dresses differently from laymen, he may make a hypocrite of a man, or an anointed image, but never a Christian or a spiritually-minded man. The fact is that our baptism consecrates us all without exception, and makes us all priests. As St. Peter says, I Peter 2[:9], "You are a royal priesthood and a realm of priests."[43]

While absolution may be within the capacity of every Christian it turns out that in the "order" of the church it devolves basically upon the clergy. In the Small Catechism of 1529, Luther provides for confession and absolution.

> Confession comprises two things. Firstly, one must confess one's sins; secondly, one must receive absolution or pardon from the confessor as from God himself, and doubt not, but firmly believe, that by this means our sins are forgiven before God in heaven.[44]

He provides instruction about what sins are to be confessed and a brief format for doing this with a confessor. What does not get developed is a systematic or even unsystematic program for exercising this ministry as a lay priesthood. Of course such confession and absolution happened, but given the novelty of the idea, the state of the church, the chaos and confusion of the times, Luther's reform of penance pretty much kept this as a lay-clergy encounter. And, given Luther's theology of grace, sin, and salvation, it stands to reason that private confession/absolution was bound to wane. What Protestants put in its place was general confession, corporate confession within the liturgy.

The reformers and their successors in Protestantism all provide for confession of sin in the liturgies they appoint for public worship. A consideration of their services for the Lord's Supper is illustrative. Luther's reforms of the liturgy, the Latin *Formula Missae* of 1523 and the *Deutsche Messe* of 1526, are

42. Luther, "A Short Exhortation to Confession," p. 143.
43. Luther (Dillenberger, 1958), pp. 407f.
44. Luther, "A Short Exhortation to Confession," p. 147.

both more or less essays on the character of the liturgy and how to do it than they are liturgical texts. In 1523 he places a public absolution at the end of the eucharistic prayer, following the Lord's Prayer. It is introduced by the sharing of "the peace of the Lord." The absolution he sees as "the one and most worthy preparation for the Lord's Table if it be apprehended by faith and not otherwise than though it came from the mouth of Christ himself. On account of this I wish it to be announced with face turned to the people."[45] The Lord's Prayer in this case serves as the people's confession. Luther does not require private confession before communion, but sees it as "useful and not to be despised."[46] In any event his fencing of the table is so severe that the requirements for participation are a fitting substitute for private confession.[47] In the German liturgy of 1526 Luther stresses again serious preparation for communion.[48] In this prescription for the liturgy Luther follows the sermon with the Lord's Prayer and what he calls an "admonition." This is a sort of "bidding" prayer that includes an underlining of the forgiveness asked for in the Jesus Prayer, but the service contains no confession and no absolution as such. One must remember that Luther does advocate pre-communion penance and creates a small liturgy for this in 1529. Such private penance endured in Lutheranism for a time. Most contemporary Lutheran liturgical books, while not including confession specifically in the liturgy, do provide a separate order for confession and forgiveness and do allow its use within the liturgy, in a rubric prior to general prayers.[49]

Other Reformers

The *Action or Use of the Lord's Supper* by Ulrich Zwingli appeared in 1525. It contains no liturgy of confession and forgiveness, but Zwingli like Luther does fence the table, and he promises particulars on the manner of exclusion.

> We are also prepared, in keeping with divine ordinances to exclude from this Supper all those who defile the body of Christ with intolerable stains and blemishes, because a communion of Christians and a pure, devout life ought to follow this memorial of Christ's passion and thanksgiving

---

45. Bard Thompson, *Liturgies of the Western Church* (New York: World Publishing Company, 1961), pp. 112f.

46. Thompson, *Liturgies of the Western Church*, p. 117.

47. Thompson, *Liturgies of the Western Church*, pp. 115-19.

48. Thompson, *Liturgies of the Western Church*, pp. 123-29.

49. Cf. *Lutheran Book of Worship* (Minneapolis: Augsburg, 1978), pp. 56, 65.

for His death. In what manner this shall be done will be explained in a separate booklet, since time is not left to do it now.[50]

Martin Bucer begins his Strasbourg liturgy of 1539 with three optional corporate prayers of confession, the first prayer composed in the first person plural and the other two in the singular. The third is quite lengthy and in ten paragraphs confesses to violating all of the Ten Commandments. For the complete sinner, one supposes. Maybe the list could be contemplated in silence. The public confession is followed by the pastor reading 1 Timothy 1:15, and an absolution.

John Calvin considered confession the proper beginning of worship to be followed by absolution. "It is no mean or trivial consolation to have Christ's ambassador present, furnished with the mandate of reconciliation."[51] He follows this practice in Strasbourg, but in Geneva he found opposition to the absolution and was forced to abandon its use. He was similarly thwarted by the town council from having the Lord's Supper every Sunday. English and Scotch Puritans follow Calvin in placing confession of sin at the outset of liturgy.[52] The Westminster Directory of 1644 includes confession as part of the pastoral prayer before the sermon.[53] It is common that the descendants of Calvin and the Puritans in their worship books in our day include confession and "Declaration of Forgiveness," or "Assurance of Pardon," or a statement of similar designation at the beginning of the liturgy.[54]

Reform in the English church as on the continent reduced the number of sacraments from seven to the two judged to be dominical: baptism and the Lord's Supper, and no liturgical order of penance was created. The initial liturgical reform in English was a penitential order to be inserted in the Latin mass prior to the people's communion. It was printed for public use a year following the death of Henry VIII: *The Order of the Communion* (1548). It included elements that would appear, as is, in the first prayer book of 1549: an exhortation of self-examination, the invitation, a general confession, an absolution with "comfortable words" (appropriate Scripture sentences), and the "prayers of humble access." This public penance was then followed by the ad-

---

50. Thompson, *Liturgies of the Western Church*, p. 150.

51. Thompson, *Liturgies of the Western Church*, p. 191.

52. Thompson, *Liturgies of the Western Church*. Cf. John Knox, "The Forme of Prayers (1556)," pp. 287ff.; "The Middlebury Liturgy (1586)," pp. 311ff.; Richard Baxter, "The Savoy Liturgy (1661)," pp. 375ff.

53. Thompson, *Liturgies of the Western Church*, pp. 345ff.

54. *Book of Common Worship* (Louisville: Westminster/John Knox, 1993), pp. 52-57, 87-89; *The New Century Hymnal* (Cleveland: Pilgrim, 1995), pp. 2-3, 14-15, 21-22; *Rejoice in the Lord* (Grand Rapids: Eerdmans, 1985), pp. 560-61.

ministration of communion. This order endures to the present, minus the preliminary exhortation. By the 1552 revision of the liturgy, this penitential rite had moved from its position before the people's communion to just before the consecrating prayer. This penitential preparation to receive the communion was inspired probably by the Lutheran liturgy of Cologne created by Bucer and Melanchthon (1543).[55] Framed by Thomas Cranmer, this unit of prayer has endured in Anglican and Methodist liturgy to the present time, and has been very influential ecumenically.

The Priest.

Christ our Pascall lambe is offred up for us, once for al, when he bare our sinnes on hys body upon the crosse, for he is the very lambe of God, that taketh away the sinnes of the worlde: wherefore let us kepe a ioyfull and holy feast with the Lorde.

> *Here the priest shall turne hym toward those that come to the Holy Communion, and shall saye.*

You that do truly and earnestly repent you of your synnes to almightie God, and be in loue and charitie with your neighbors, and entende to lede a newe life, folowying the commaundements of God, and walkyng from hencefurth in his holy wayes: draw nere and take this holy Sacrament to your comforte, make your humble confession to almightie God, and to his holy church here gathered together in hys name, mekly knelying upon your knees.

> *Then shall thys generall Confession bee made, in the name of al those that are minded to receiue the holy Communion, eyther by one of them, or els by one of the ministers, or by the prieste hymselfe, all kneling humbly upon their knees.*

Almyghtie GOD father of oure Lord Jesus Christ, maker of all thynges, jidge of all men, we knowlege and bewaile our manyfold synnes and wyckednes, which we from tyme to tyme, most greuously haue committed, by thought, word and dede, against thy diuine maiestie, prouokyng most justly thy wrath and indignacion against us, we do earnestly repent & be hartely sory for these our misdoinges, the remembrance of them is greuous unto us, the burthen of them is intollerable: haue mercye upon us, haue mercie upon us, moste mercifull father, for thy sonne our Lorde

---

55. Thompson, *Liturgies of the Western Church*, pp. 229f.

Jesus Christes sake, forgeue us all that is past, and graunt that we may euer hereafter, serue and please thee in neunes of life, to the honor and glory of they name: Through Jesus Christe our Lorde.

Then shall the Prieste stande up, and turnyng himselfe to the people, say thus.

Almightie GOD our haeuenly father, who of his great mercie, hath promysed forgeuenesse of synnes to all them, whiche with hartye repentaunce and true fayth, turne unto him: haue mercy upon you, pardon and delyuer you from all youre sinnes, confirme and strengthen you in all goodnes, and bring you to euerlasting lyfe: through Jesus Christ our Lord. Amen.

Then shall the Priest also say.

Heare what coumfortable woordes our sauiour Christ sayeth, to all that truly turne to him.

Come unto me all that trauell and bee heauy laden, and I shall refreshe you. God so loued the worlde that he gaue his onely begotten sonne, to the ende that al that beleue in hym, shoulde not perishe, but haue lyfe euerlasting.

Heare also what saint Paul sayeth.

This is a true saying, and woorthie of all men, to bee receiued, that Jesus Christe came into thys worlde to saue sinners.

Heare also what saint John sayeth.

If any man sinne, we haue an aduocate with the father, Jesus Christ the righteous, and he is the propiciacion for our sinnes.

Then shall the Priest turnying him to gods boord knele down, and say in the name of all of them, that shall receyue the Communion, this prayer following.

We do not presume to come to this thy table (o mercifull lord) trusting in our owne righteousness, but in thy manifold & great mercies: we be not woorthie so much as to gather up the cromes under thy table, but thou art the same lorde whose propertie is always to haue mercie: Graunt us therefore (gracious lorde) so to eate the fleshe of thy dere sonne Jesus Christ, and to drynke his bloud in these holy Misteries, that we may conntinuallye dwell in hym, and he in us, that oure synfull bodyes may bee made cleane by his body, and our soules washed through hys most precious bloud. Amen.

> *Then shall the Prieste firste receiue the Communion in both kindes himselfe, and next deliuer it to other Ministers, if any be there presente (that they may bee ready to helpe the chiefe Minister) and after to the people.*[56]

Certainly in Protestantism, no liturgical text for reconciliation has had more resonance than this one.

In the rubrics of the Anglican Book of Common Prayer of 1559 as part of the liturgy for the visitation of the sick there is opportunity suggested for private confession and absolution, but no general provision is made for private penance. Even so, private penance has never died out in Anglicanism or in other churches of the Reformation.

A Continuing Ministry

It is by no means the case, even through monumental upheavals, that everybody immediately stopped all past practices and adopted new ones. Church penitence in Protestantism has endured, though mainly in public liturgies, in exhortations to prayer delivered by the clergy, and as one of the common themes in the pastoral prayer that usually preceded the sermon in the Puritan and free churches. Private penance has not died out in the churches of the Reformation. Segments of Lutheranism have always maintained a private penance, and so have the Anglicans, especially where the Oxford Movement in England in the nineteenth century brought some revival of the "sacrament." Other movements advancing spirituality, communality, or social reform, such as Taizé or Iona, have had a penitential aspect to them. One should also not forget that a great deal of what comes under the heading of "pastoral care" in our churches is hearing of confession, if not always joined to absolution.[57]

Orthodoxy has continued a ministry of repentance and forgiveness. There is considerable variety in method and frequency, and there have been

---

56. Thompson, "The Book of Common Prayer (1549)," *Liturgies of the Western Church*, pp. 259-61.

57. Cf. *The Theory and Practice of Penance*, ed. H. S. Box (London: SPCK, 1935); *Confession and Absolution*, ed. M. Dudley and G. Powell (London: SPCK, 1990); Hyde Clark, *To Declare God's Forgiveness* (Morehouse-Barlow, 1984); Georgia Harkness, *The Ministry of Reconciliation* (Nashville: Abingdon, 1971); G. W. Bowman, *The Dynamics of Confession* (Richmond, Va.: John Knox, 1969); Max Thurian, *Confession* (London: SCM, 1958); Ted Jennings, *The Liturgy of Liberation* (Nashville: Abingdon, 1988).

times such as during the Ottoman Empire in the Balkans when it was discontinued for a time. Individual priests generally have considerable discretion about methods and times. Confession is considered necessary before communion, especially if one has committed grave sin, or been absent from communion for a long time. There is no confessional booth, and penitent and confessor meet face to face. The sacrament is considered a form of spiritual healing. As a rite it consists of confession, dialogue, and the priest's prayers to God on behalf of the penitent.[58] Penances may be prescribed, such as "spiritual reading," fasting, increased prayer, prostrations, charitable works, and exclusion from Holy Communion for a specified time.[59] Liturgical prayer for general confession was introduced in Russia early in the twentieth century. Its use is not considered a substitute for private penance.

In the Roman Catholic Church sacramental private penance, as defined in 1215 at Lateran IV, underlined at the Council of Trent in 1563, and codified as ritual in the *Rituale Romanum* of 1614, has endured with few alterations until review and reform were mandated by Vatican Council II in the "Constitution on the Liturgy," in 1963. Liturgical reform in Catholicism begins really in the mid-nineteenth century in Benedictine communities in France, Belgium, and Germany.[60] It spread early in the twentieth century to Holland, Italy, and England, and to the United States. By the time of the Second World War the movement had begun to affect worship in some local parishes. Liturgical reformers made use of scholarship that by mid-twentieth century had opened up knowledge of texts and understandings of the early church that were previously unknown, or dimly known, or even misunderstood.[61] The first five centuries of Christian life have profoundly influenced liturgical reform. Increased scriptural scholarship has also played a role. Catholic reformers aimed also to make worship more relevant to modern Christian life. This has meant simplifying rites and reeducating laity and clergy about their roles in liturgy, especially the need for active lay participation. Owing primarily to theological and doctrinal issues, it would take ten years for the Catholic Church to get from the call to reform in Vatican II, to a revised penitential rit-

58. *A Manual of Eastern Orthodox Prayers* (London: SPCK, 1983), pp. 51-60.

59. Alciviadis C. Calivas, "The Sacramental Life of the Orthodox Church," in *Orthodox Ministry ACCESS*, http://www.goarch.org/access/Companion_to_Orthodox_Church/sacramental_life.html.

60. Herman Wegman, *Christian Worship in East and West* (New York: Pueblo, 1985), pp. 351ff.

61. Dom Gregory Dix, *The Shape of the Liturgy* (London: A. & C. Black, 1945); Louis Bouyer, *Eucharist* (Notre Dame: Notre Dame University Press, 1968 [published in France, 1966]).

ual.[62] A committee of scholars first met in Rome in February 1967. They established four criteria for revision of the rite:

1. The nature of sin as an offense against both God and the church.
2. Simultaneous reconciliation with God and the church.
3. The whole church collaborating with the sinner's effort at conversion through its charity, example, and prayers.
4. The value of the Sacrament of Penance in fostering Christian life.[63]

The committee finished its work by the end of 1969 and its report and a draft of liturgy was submitted to a special commission of the newly formed Congregation for Divine Worship. After lengthy processing through the bureaucracy, Paul VI approved the final text and it was promulgated late in 1973.[64] The contents of the new ritual include:

1. Explanation of the new rite.
2. A rite for the reconciliation of an individual penitent.
3. A rite for the reconciliation of many penitents with individual confession and individual absolution.
4. A rite for the reconciliation of many penitents with a general confession and a general absolution.
5. A rite in case of necessity or imminent danger of death.

Also included are biblical readings and prayers; special absolutions; penitential services for Advent and Lent and particular groups, e.g. children and the sick; and forms of examination of conscience.[65] The theological ideals put forward in this reform are expressed in the first place in the choice of the name "reconciliation." This promotes the document's aim to underline the social nature of sin and the ecclesial/communal aspects of the sacrament. Importance is also given to the presence of the Word in the sacrament and the role of the sacrament in the dynamic of conversion.[66] The new rite became available in the United States in Advent 1975.

As a reform, the rite for the reconciliation of an individual, according to theologian James Dallen, "presupposes that the goal of the sacrament of penance is not forgiveness of sins but reconciliation with church and God and

---

62. Dallen, *The Reconciling Community,* p. 209.
63. Dallen, *The Reconciling Community,* p. 211.
64. *Documents on the Liturgy* (Collegeville, Minn.: Liturgical Press, 1982), pp. 936-43.
65. Kenan B. Osborne, *Reconciliation and Justification* (New York: Paulist, 1990), p. 204.
66. Osborne, *Reconciliation and Justification,* pp. 205-12.

that conversion is first lived out in community by the penitent, with celebration being the prayerful though private reliving of what has been taking place."[67] The second and third rites are liturgies of communal reconciliation, the one containing also opportunity for private penance and the second being entirely a communal rite with general absolution. This latter has been the cause of most dissention concerning the reform. Conservatives are eager to deny to a general absolution any legitimate sacramental character. More liberal Catholics tend to see forgiveness as forgiveness and allow divine wisdom to settle the question of authenticity. The second rite — corporate and individual — is much esteemed but is often impractical because it requires a number of priests. The public liturgical opportunities of the new rite have been attractive to many in the face of waning participation in private penance and the felt need to practice church as a more vital community.

> The communal celebration is normative: it best expresses the nature and effect of the sacrament and thus the ideal form of the sacramental liturgy. Sacrament is more action than thing, the action of a community, and this action generates and organizes space. Since liturgical space houses the activity of a community that welcomes and reconciles, the proper environment for the celebration is one where the local church can assemble, hear God's Word, respond in the prayer of faith and praise, and express itself as a reconciled and reconciling community.[68]

There are, of course, not a few who view such a perspective as subversive of ancient and particularly Tridentine ideals, and moreover as too Protestant. Protestants can disabuse Catholics of the notion that a corporate approach will necessarily lead to the longed-for spiritual health.

Since the Reformation, corporate confession and reconciliation have been almost exclusively the Protestant manner of hearing confession of sin and declaring forgiveness. No matter, the ministry of Christ's blessing of healing forgiveness is to a large extent moribund in Protestantism.

For a mix of theological, historical, and cultural reasons Christianity faces serious challenges in the way of hearing and doing the mandate of Jesus: "The time is fulfilled, the kingdom of God is at hand; repent and believe in the gospel" (Mark 1:15). The Catholic theologian Julia Upton puts well the urgency of the church's reconciling ministry.

---

67. Dallen, *The Reconciling Community,* p. 234.
68. Dallen, *The Reconciling Community,* p. 313.

The Church's ritual approach to reconciliation underwent massive shifts over time. At no time however, did that affect the sacrament itself — God's merciful embrace of the repentant sinner. God does not need sacraments in order to forgive the sinner, but the Church needs them in order to express and effect that reconciliation, and as Church, we need sacraments to experience the enduring presence of God-with-us, covenanted in Jesus' death and resurrection.[69]

69. Julia Upton, *A Time for Embracing* (Collegeville, Minn.: Liturgical Press, 1999), pp. 78f.

Forgiveness and Reconciliation through Moral Development in Families, Churches, Schools, and Communities

A s we discovered in our study of local congregations, there were two directions suggested regarding forgiveness and reconciliation. One direction had to do with moral failure and human sin and how to help people deal honestly with their deep need for repentance. Second, there was concern about how to help persons develop stronger moral fiber, greater awareness of moral issues, and increased ability to confront and deal constructively with moral and ethical problems.

In this chapter we shall seek to understand the high potential of the second direction: *how we can enhance the possibility of forgiveness and reconciliation through the strategies of moral development in our families (the most powerful center of moral development), churches, schools, and communities.* The two directions are of course interrelated.

A Brief History concerning the Relation of Moral Education and Religious Education and Liturgical Celebrations to Public Education in the United States

Moral development, often couched in terms of Protestant assumptions, was a central concern in the education of the public from the earliest days in America. The New England Primer of 1690, written by Benjamin Harris, was widely used for many years in school and home settings. It was solidly anchored in Congregationalist theology, with moral lessons and aids to reading, spelling, and pronunciation. A Westminster Shorter Catechism along with prayers and Bible-based couplets (to teach the alphabet) were included.

This primer was in print for one hundred fifty years and sold around three million copies.[1]

The emphasis on moral development was present from the very beginning in the founding of the public school movement in the United States. Horace Mann, recognized as the major early leader of the movement, promoted the common school with great zeal out of Enlightenment principles wedded with Christian commitment. First serving as an attorney and state legislator in Massachusetts, he became the secretary of the newly created state board of education in 1837. In this position he sought to lead a movement for public education of all children and youth, supported by public funding. His goal was to develop responsible and moral members of a democratic society. He did this with the inclusion of nondenominational Christian values as his norm. His work became a model for public education across the nation.

Moral education, based on largely Presbyterian theology but seen as nonsectarian, was at the core of the first four Eclectic Readers published in 1836-37 by William Holmes McGuffey, a professor of moral philosophy at Miami University in Ohio and an ordained Presbyterian minister. The six editions of the McGuffey Reader were very widely used throughout the country with the exception of Northeastern states. The Reader started at the elementary level and progressed to the high school level in the sixth Reader. Alexander McGuffey, William's brother, is credited with writing the fifth and sixth Readers with 1857 and 1879 editions. In all of the Readers, moral admonitions and stories were integrated into the text, along with sermonic reflections, prayer and the Ten Commandments in the Second Reader, and the Sermon on the Mount in the Fourth Reader. McGuffey included moral lessons with stories, such as one about a man who purchased a boy's birds and then set them free, because he had spent some years as a prisoner of war; and another story about the proverbial "boy who cried wolf."[2] The various editions were in use well into the twentieth century. A study of the concepts of morality reflected in them is a good mirror of the progression of thought about the sources and outcomes of moral thinking and activity. In the earlier editions morals came from God and were centered in God's will. McGuffey even used the threat of hell in the Third Reader to motivate his young readers. In the same Reader he says, "If you are wise, study virtue and condemn everything that can come in competition with it. . . . Secure this and you secure every-

---

1. See Lloyd Duck, "Moral Education: Hard Choices on the Way to a New Consensus," *Religion and Education* 23, no. 1 (Fall 1996): 39.

2. See Benjamin Franklin Crawford, *William Holmes McGuffey: The Schoolmaster to the Nation* (Delaware, Ohio: Carnegie Church Press, 1963), p. 36.

thing. Lose this and all is lost."[3] By the 1879 edition, moral living was valuable in and of itself. Also, moral living was the pathway to success economically and socially and was more pragmatic. Such was the case even though the Readers' ethos was still quasi-Protestant and engendered personal piety and responsibility.[4]

John Westerhoff, in his excellent study of the influence of McGuffey's Readers on American education, states that by 1879 ". . . the theistic, Calvinistic worldview so dominant in the first editions had disappeared, and the prominent values of salvation, righteousness, and piety were entirely missing. All that remained were lessons offering the morality and life-styles of the emerging middle class and those cultural beliefs, attitudes and values that under-gird America and religion. . . . While a few continuations of the concerns dominant in the 1836-38 editions remain (such as kindness and patriotism), the contents of the 1879 edition have been severely secularized."[5]

As diversity increased, the linking of religion to morals became more and more difficult. With the increase of religious pluralism in the late twentieth century, we have returned to the separation of religion and morals seen in eighteenth-century Deists such as Thomas Jefferson. Noah Webster's Speller (first edition 1789) reflects such a view. The Speller included a "Federal Catechism" on the benefits of a republic and a "Moral Catechism" that projected the notion that moral behavior is virtuous not because God wills it but because it is its own reward. One should not expect reward for being good.[6]

Thomas Jefferson was deeply concerned about moral development and quality education for all citizens. In his attempt to inaugurate the University of Virginia he proposed no professor of religion. Rather, he drew up plans that made possible the establishment of denominational schools of theological study adjacent to the campus. He believed a professor of ethics should be sought who could teach a "common core" of religious beliefs essential to ethics. Jefferson believed that all people were created by God with a moral sense that could and should be sharpened and focused through education. He also believed that this common core of belief undergirding morality and law could be taught in the public schools. Interference from institutional

---

3. William H. McGuffey, *The Eclectic Third Reader* (Cincinnati: Truman and Smith, 1837), p. 30.

4. See Lloyd Duck's fine study of that progression in *Religion and Education* 23, no. 2 (Fall 1996).

5. John H. Westerhoff III, *McGuffey and His Readers: Piety, Morality, and Education in Nineteenth Century America* (Nashville: Abingdon, 1978), p. 19.

6. Duck, "Moral Education," p. 42.

churches should be avoided, because to have their sectarian doctrines taught in a tax-supported university or school would be in violation of the Constitution and the First Amendment of the Bill of Rights (1791). The First Amendment, of course, states that "Congress shall make no law respecting an establishment of religion, or prohibiting the free exercise thereof. . . ." The Fourteenth Amendment later reinforced this concept by stating that "No state shall make or enforce any law which shall abridge the privilege or immunities of citizens of the United States." These two amendments, along with Jefferson's admonitions, have become the basis of what Jefferson called "the wall of separation between church and state."

As pluralism increased in the twentieth century, these amendments along with the presence of Jeffersonian thinking in our history caused citizens to begin legally contesting the teaching of morals based on religious beliefs in our public schools. The flagging of a few Supreme Court decisions will serve to illustrate this trend.

The McCollum case in 1948 is one of the first Supreme Court decisions to result from the contesting of the teaching of a quasi-Protestant Christian religion as the basis of moral development. The court decided that religious groups do not have the right to teach religious education classes *inside* school buildings. This decision reinforced the popularity of released-time religious education patterns, already started in Gary, Indiana, in 1913. The Zorach case in 1952 strengthened and clarified this pattern. The court affirmed the right of children to be released, with parents' consent, for religious instruction held outside of school property in nearby churches or centers. These two decisions evoked several experiments that maintained the separation of church and state but made possible cooperation between the two. These experiments included released time, shared time between public and religious schools or groups, and dual school enrollment (where students were enrolled in two schools and attended each for "secular" courses and "religious" courses respectively). The motive for such sharing was often cited as the drive to build a strong moral sense and behavior among the nation's children and youth.

A series of other Supreme Court decisions has further moved sectarian religious instruction and liturgical celebrations out of the public school setting. In *Engel v. Vitale* in 1962 the courts held that the New York Regents prayer, prescribed for all students, was unconstitutional precisely because it was prescribed. Justice Black stated the opinion of the Court when he wrote that the prayer breached the wall of separation between church and state and that it was not the ". . . business of government to compose official prayers for any group of the American people to recite as a part of a religious program carried on by the government."[7] This decision was followed by the *Abingdon School District v. Schempp* and *Murry v. Curlett* (both in 1963) where the Court held (8 to 1) that devotional reading of the Bible and school-sponsored prayers (the Lord's Prayer in these cases) were violations of the establishment clause of the First Amendment. The Court maintained that the use of the state to promote even a minor breach of neutrality cannot be done, because "a trickling stream may all too soon become a raging torrent." The Court took a narrow view of the relation of church and state, but made it very clear that the study *about* religion and the Bible and other sacred texts was *not* prohibited in public schools. Rather, it was strongly affirmed. Justice Clark stated it well when he said ". . . one's education is not complete without a study of comparative religions or of the history of religion and the relation to the advancement of civilization. . . . Nothing we have said here indicates that such study, the Bible or of religion, where presented objectively as a part of a secular program of education, may not be effected consistently with the First Amendment."[8] Justice Goldberg used language that has been quoted often to delineate what the schools can do legally. He said, ". . . it seems to me . . . that the Court would recognize the propriety of . . . teaching about religion, as distinguished from the teaching of religion, in the public schools."[9] Justice Stewart dissented, emphasizing that a truly neutral position would be to allow prayer and Bible reading for those who wish them and to protect the right of others not to participate. Such a position has reappeared in more recent challenges to Supreme Court decisions. The major issue seems to be the *prescription* of religious prayers, baccalaureates, or sectarian teachings in public schools. It is the prescribing of certain religious activities that violates the First Amendment.

Instead of religious education and practices becoming the foundation for moral development and the creation of a caring and responsible community life, the efforts to instill such beliefs and patterns have often become the occasion for conflict. Instead of fostering forgiving attitudes and reconciliation, such efforts have sometimes done the opposite.

A second trend in Supreme Court decisions beyond their emphasis on the wall of separation between church and state has been a spirit of cooperation for the general welfare of our children, their families, and society. This trend can be seen in the *Everson v. Board of Education* (of Erving, N.J.) in 1947

---

7. See Richard C. McMillan, *Education, Religion, and the Supreme Court* (Danville, Va.: Association of Baptist Professors of Religion, 1979), p. 29.

8. McMillan, *Education, Religion, and the Supreme Court*, p. 225.

9. McMillan, *Education, Religion, and the Supreme Court*, p. 306.

where the Court (5 to 4) affirmed the use of public funds for bus transportation of nonprofit sectarian school children or the reimbursement of their parents for such expenses. The rubric for approving such a cooperative attitude was social welfare and traffic safety. The Court saw this cooperation as a service to the children rather than to the religious schools. Such legal precedents are now being lifted up in battles to get state legislatures to approve voucher plans for parents who wish to send their children to private or parochial schools. Many who defend the cooperative stance cite Justice Douglas, when he states in 1952 that "We are a religious people whose institutions presuppose a Supreme Being. We guarantee the freedom to worship as one chooses. . . . We sponsor an attitude on the part of government that shows no partiality to any one group. . . . When the state encourages religious instruction or cooperation with religious authorities by adjusting the schedule of public events to sectarian needs, it follows the best of our traditions. For it then respects the religious nature of our people and accommodates the public service to their spiritual needs: to hold that it may not would be to find in the Constitution a requirement that the government show a callous indifference to religious groups. That could be preferring those who believe in no religion over those who do believe."[10]

In more recent struggles many groups and persons of varying religious affiliations have sought to maximize this more cooperative approach. Some have done so autonomously with teachers and coaches leading prayers and bringing their own religious beliefs into their curriculum — in essence seeking to deny the separation of church and state. Others maintain they want to honor the separation but ask for much more cooperation in the form of tax-supported vouchers for religious schools that perform specialized services not readily available in public school programs.

Without citing all of the more recent Supreme Court decisions, we will cite from *Religion in the Public Schools: A Joint Statement of Current Laws,* April 1995, which has been endorsed by 26 national churches or interfaith groups including mainline Christian, Jewish, Muslim, Unitarian, Christian Science, etc. The National Association of Evangelicals was on the drafting committee but did not endorse the statement. The following agreements are the result of the effort on the part of the Clinton administration to find common ground concerning religion and public education. The statement deals with eighteen areas of concern. In general, there was agreement that public schools cannot prescribe prayer or sponsor religious celebrations such as baccalaureates. Schools cannot teach religion for commitment. However, reli-

10. McMillan, *Education, Religion, and the Supreme Court,* p. 25.

gious freedom mandates openness to student expression of their religious faith. They may read their Bibles or other scriptures, say grace before meals, and pray quietly except when engaged in school activities. Religious clubs should have the same right to assemble as other noncurricular groups. Students may distribute religious literature or express religious views in class discussion where germane to the issues being studied. Public school may and should teach *about* religion via courses on comparative religion, the Bible or other scriptures as literature, and the role of religion in American or world history. Particular sectarian views, such as creationism, may be discussed in class settings but may not be taught as science in science courses. Religious holidays may be studied but not celebrated as religious events. Religious garb may be worn and persons may not be forced to wear gym clothes they regard as immodest, on religious grounds. An individual student may be excused from lessons objectionable on the basis of his or her religion. The new guidelines were distributed to the nation's public schools in 2000. One of the six publications from the Department of Education is titled, "Public Schools and Religious Communities: A First Amendment Guide."

In respect to moral development, "Schools may teach civic values, including honesty, good citizenship, sportsmanship, courage, respect for the rights and freedoms of others, respect for persons and their property, civility, the dual virtues of morality and tolerance, and hard work. . . . However, these may not be taught as religious tenets. The mere fact that most, if not all, religions also teach these values does not make it unlawful to teach them."[11] This final agreement, of course, is a strong foundation for moral and character education programs which have proliferated greatly in the 1990s and early 2000s in public school programs, often in cooperation with religious and community leaders and parents.

The teaching of moral and ethical values has been a major emphasis in church religious education programs that have had a strong influence on children, youth, and their families all along the paths taken in the above history. Starting with the founding of the Sunday School movement by Robert Raikes in England in 1780, the Sunday School movement caught on and thrived in the United States from 1790 on, adopted by most Protestant denominations and adapted by Roman Catholics and Jews in their own distinctive ways. Moral living was a strong focus of early Sunday School lessons, often aimed at poor and uneducated children who worked during the week and studied reading, writ-

---

11. "Religion in the Public Schools: A Joint Statement of Current Law, April 1995," *Religion and Education* 22, no. 1 (Fall 1995): 17. See also "New Church-School Guidelines," *Christian Century,* January 5-12, 2000, p. 10.

ing, and arithmetic as well as religion on Sunday. Many refinements and developments followed the Sunday School movement, such as the Religious Education movement (starting in 1903 in the United States and emphasizing growth of human potential and a problem-solving methodology often centered in a Social Gospel), the Christian Education movement (starting around 1940 in response to the crises brought on by the world wars and the call to reassess the nature of evil in persons and in society), and various more recent expressions based on biblical theology, education "for the church to be the church in the world," the social science approach, sacramental theology, Christian religious education, etc. All of these forms of church education have had significant emphases on moral and ethical development and a call for persons to be forgiving, reconciling persons in their families, communities, and the world. We shall return to this central issue when we address the first of the four-pronged approaches to follow. Sometimes Christian education activities were interrelated with public school activities, especially in the period up through the mid-1900s. Later church education activities have been largely separated from public school learning due to a redefinition of the relationship between church and state appropriate in a highly pluralistic society.

The Emergence of Moral Education Models: Largely Independent of Religious Sanctions

During the long period of confusion about what can be done legally in respect to moral education based on religious sources, many public school leaders moved away from any references to religion and also away from moral education as well. With the significant increase in family dysfunction and social disorientation, schools have sought to move toward some form of moral and ethical education. Three major movements can be identified: (1) Values Clarification, (2) Moral Development Models, and (3) Character Education Models. While these three movements were appropriated primarily in public school settings they were also influential, in varying degrees, in religious education (in terms of curricular designs, teacher preparation, and parent education).

Values Clarification

Because of the fear of violating the norm of separation of church and state, Values Clarification was adopted by many schools as a way for the schools not to present any particular set of values. Rather, public school teachers were trained to use the values clarification process to help learners explore and find their own values. Louis Raths, Merrill Harmin, and Sidney Simon and others were to be found in school district after district holding workshops with teachers and parents, employing their books and strategies.[12] As students were guided through a process of exploring ethical problems, each person was invited to say what he or she thought should be done. Each person would then be asked to identify the particular values chosen and why they were cherished. Then, each was asked to identify the consequences of his or her choice for the self, for others, and society in general. In this process the school system took no stand on particular values. Critics, of course, said that the process itself had assumptions in it that implied that relativism in ethical life was the not-so-hidden norm. Supporters of the program said that it did stand for commitment to the democratic process and the freeing of the intelligence of the learners to solve personal and social ethical problems.

Moral Development

Moral Development theory and practice then became the most exciting approach to be adopted by various schools. The various moral development models are based on the structural-developmental thinkers such as Jean Piaget, Lawrence Kohlberg, Elliott Turiel, Carol Gilligan, and many others, all of whom opted for a commitment to universal justice (and/or mercy) as the moral norm to be taught in public schools and in society in general. These models were also consistent with the views of John Dewey, John Childs, and George Counts, and their strong pragmatic approach to value definition and formation in a democratic society. Dewey, for instance, believed that morals and values should be taught. These values, however, should be those that were democratically selected and proven to be humanizing for persons and health-giving for society. The values should be able to survive scientific scrutiny and should never be promulgated merely because they were a part of a traditional religious belief system or any philosophy of life anchored in metaphysics. However, corroboration of values from such sources should be explored and confirmed in the public schools. Moral living had to do with freeing the intel-

---

12. Louis E. Raths, Merrill Harmin, and Sidney B. Simon, *Values and Teaching* (Columbus, Ohio: Charles Merrill Co., 1978); and Sidney B. Simon, Leland Home, and Howard Kirchenbaum, *Values Clarification: A Handbook of Practical Strategies* (New York: Hall Publishing, 1972).

ligence of all persons (students, teachers, leaders in society). Dewey's problem-solving approach to learning would then equip persons to use their rational powers to define common problems and together seek solutions that would fulfill the potentialities of all people, bringing maximum justice into being. The attempt to meet the needs of all persons and to develop a healthy democratic society would not happen without a common faith that could unify all members of society in the quest for the common good. Such outgoing caring and self-giving, when realized, would have a religious quality to it but would not be based explicitly on any particular religious doctrine or be controlled by any religious institution.[13]

There is a faith in the ability of persons in a democratic society to develop moral strength that underlies the moral development approach to moral education. Grounded in the principles of Jean Piaget's genetic epistemology and his early theory of moral development,[14] Lawrence Kohlberg at Harvard did extensive research on the specific stages of moral development related to the processes of mental growth identified by Piaget and others. Kohlberg's problem-solving approach is similar to Dewey's. Instead of maintaining neutrality concerning moral stances, as values clarification approaches tend to do, Kohlberg's six stages move from narrow self-interest to universal justice for all persons and groups. Kohlberg has created problem-solving situations that challenge children, youth, and adults at the various stages of their development to think through and make decisions in an effort to be morally just. What happens in the discussions and decision-making process is somewhat predictable in relation to the stages of mental development identified by Piaget, moving from intuitive pre-operational thinking of young children who are egocentric by nature, to the concrete-operational stage of children, to the various stages of formal operational thinking of youth and adults. His six stages are refinements of three major phases of moral development: pre-conventional, conventional, and post-conventional moral thinking and acting. Using moral dilemmas, teachers help students face the contradictions in their thinking or actions. This process follows Piaget's emphases on equilibrium, disequilibrium, accommodation, and assimilation. When the learners face the contradictions in their thinking they fall out of the comfortable equilibrium they bring to the dilemma and go into a state of disequilibrium. It is in this state of disequilibrium that they are open to making internal accommodations so that they can assimilate new informa-

13. John Dewey, *A Common Faith* and *Democracy and Education*.

14. Jean Piaget, *The Moral Development of the Child* (London: Routledge and Kegan Paul, 1932).

tion and wider experience and thereby find a new internal equilibrium on a higher level of moral thinking and acting.

Kohlberg holds that growth from stage to stage ". . . is not dependent upon holding the beliefs of a particular religion, or upon holding any religious belief at all: No significant differences appear in the development of moral thinking among Catholics, Protestants, Jews, Buddhists, Muslims, and atheist children. Moral values in the religious area seem to go through the same stages as their general moral values. For instance, a stage 2 child is likely to say, 'Be good to God and he'll be good to you.'"[15] Kohlberg later saw the correlation between higher forms of moral thinking and higher forms of religious beliefs, even pointing to a possible seventh stage where religion and moral thinking were clearly related. However, he saw this as a phenomenon of growth mentally and morally, not as a result of moral instruction per se in higher forms of religious thinking. Kohlberg is often criticized for too much emphasis on cognitive dimensions of moral education. There is considerable truth in such a critique. There are several other dimensions to moral development, such as modeling from parents, teachers, folk heroes, older peers. There is the emotional dimension, symbolized by psychoanalytic theories of identification and transference via loving relationships. There are family socialization models and behavioral reinforcement and reward models. Kohlberg counters such criticism with his firm call for "just community" schools in which students have ample chances to participate in the decision-making necessary in a democratic school environment. In such a school equal value is placed on the views of students, teachers, and administrators. This ethos is designed to establish norms of fairness and justice for all participants. Such a perspective supplements the "moral dilemma" approach Kohlberg has designed to help students grow morally. Students are not left on their own. Teachers play important roles in such democratic decision-making. They are responsible for setting the direction and promoting and reinforcing the process of arguments about rules and norms, with a clear concern for justice and community. Student actions are evaluated along with their growth in moral thinking.[16]

A related but unique form of moral education comes from Elliott Turiel, who worked with Kohlberg's theories and practices over several years in an effort to find their validity. He discovered that Kohlberg placed too

15. Lawrence Kohlberg and Elliott Turiel, "Moral Development and Moral Education," in *Psychology and Educational Practice*, ed. Gerald Lesser (Glenview, Ill.: Scott Foresman, 1971), p. 438.

16. See E. C. Powers, A. Higgins, and L. Kohlberg, *Lawrence Kohlberg's Approach to Moral Education* (New York: Columbia University Press, 1989).

much emphasis on the moral thinking and growth process and not enough on a second dimension that he called the *domain of social knowledge or convention.* He found that morality and convention are different and parallel developmental frameworks, rather than a single pathway. For instance, in some societies it is conventional morality to line up to get tickets. Anyone who tries to break in is violating the unstated agreement. In other cultures, lining up is not practiced in the same way. These cultural and conventional patterns are multifarious and are in interaction with moral and ethical decision-making. Turiel developed Domain Theory, which recognizes much more inconsistency in the judgment of children and allows for the possibility of moral decisions based on fairness and welfare of others, from children younger than Kohlberg found.[17]

A penetrating critique of Kohlberg was done by another colleague, Carol Gilligan. She maintained that Kohlberg's theories were somewhat biased against women, because only men were used in his research. Gilligan found that women tend to think more about the morality of care, of relationships, of meeting human needs than the morality of justice or fairness promulgated by Kohlberg. While distinct, the two moralities are interrelated. As noted before, this same discovery was made by Robert Enright of the University of Wisconsin in his Institute of Forgiveness. (See Chapter 2.) Focusing on gender differences in moral education and growth, Gilligan found that men and women ". . . speak different languages that they assume are the same. . . . Because these languages share an overlapping moral vocabulary, they contain a propensity for systematic mistranslation, creating misunderstandings that impede communications and limit the potential for cooperation and care in relationships."[18] Gilligan's contribution is clearly one of providing more dimension as well as more balance to moral development than Kohlberg. She summarizes her findings when she states, "While an ethic of justice proceeds from the premise of equality that everyone should be treated the same — an ethic of care rests on the premise of nonviolence — that no one should be hurt. In the representation of maturity, both perspectives converge in the realization that just as inequality adversely affects both parties in an unequal relationship, so too violence is destructive for everyone involved. This dialogue between fairness and care not only provides a better understanding of relations between the sexes but also gives rise to a more comprehensive portrayal

---

17. Elliot Turiel, *The Culture of Morality: Social Development, Context, and Conflict* (New York: Cambridge University Press, 2002), pp. 107-15.

18. Carol Gilligan, *In a Different Voice: Psychological Theory and Women's Development* (Cambridge, Mass.: Harvard University Press, 1982), p. 173.

of adult work and family relationships."[19] It is also true that there are many clues to be found in Gilligan's work for moral education, especially with girls and women. These insights can then be integrated into moral education strategies for the young.

Johannes A. van der Ven has added significant depth to the discussion of alternate approaches to moral education in his book, *The Formation of the Moral Self* (1998). He engages his readers in an internal dialogue concerning seven basic strategies for the moral education of the child (1) through *discipline* that moves from external sources of moral norms to self-discipline achieved in commitments to the good life for all; (2) through *socialization* wherein the child appropriates moral behavior through experiences within the family and the wider society and then moves on to induction into the moral principles and values that guide his or her actions; (3) through *transmission* of specific moral values or norms in the family, church, and school, done in an intentional way; (4) through *development* in which there is an effort to resolve the dilemma between indoctrination and relativism by identifying the moral processes (stages) that naturally take place in every child and help the child grow morally at each stage, moving toward universal justice for all; (5) through the *clarification of values* during which the child identifies moral dilemmas and explores honestly his or her moral response, assessing what value is prized, what the consequences of choosing the particular value might be, and then making a choice to guide actions; (6) through *emotional formation* in which the domain of feelings is recognized as a powerful element in internalization of moral values, for example, when the child learns to love the good and fear behavior that hurts others and causes shame and guilt; (7) through *education for character* in which certain virtues are taught in a way that integrates reason, emotion, and will in relation to concrete situations in which a moral judgment is required in order to act.

In all of the seven approaches van der Ven addresses key philosophical, theological, psychological, sociological, and educational issues and analyzes insights from Plato and Aristotle to contemporary theorists such as Paul Ricoeur, John Rawls, Jean Piaget, A. MacIntyre, J. Habermas, John Dewey, Lawrence Kohlberg, A. Etzioni, and many more.[20] He recognizes that each of the seven approaches is important and that all seven in their varying forms can and should be integrated always in reference to the way the self perceives

---

19. Gilligan, *In a Different Voice*, p. 174.

20. Johannes A. van der Ven, *Formation of the Moral Self* (Grand Rapids: Eerdmans, 1998).

itself as growing toward the good. He believes that moral communication is the common denominator of all seven modes, a communication through social interaction and narrative that helps form the moral self.

Character Education

Rejecting Kohlberg's criticism of "the bag of virtues" approach to character building, leaders in character education believe that there are central qualities of character and citizenship essential for participants in a democratic society to internalize and act upon. These qualities of character should be affirmed by consensus and taught and celebrated in all aspects of school, family, and community life. Character education has emerged primarily as a grassroots movement with several distinct innovations developing consensus around qualities of character along with curricular and training designs for teachers, parents, and community leaders. Character educators recognize that specific qualities of character such as responsibility, respect, honesty, and integrity can be incorporated through problem-solving dilemmas and other indirect methods. However, they believe their experimentation and research has shown that a more direct owning of such values by the total learning community has significant power and is more convincing than indirect approaches.

The movement has grown rapidly across the United States and around the world, especially in countries such as Canada, England, Australia, New Zealand, etc. Recent studies of the attitudes of U.S. citizens have found that 39 percent see morals to be very weak and another 39 percent see morals as somewhat weak. A recent survey commissioned by *U.S. News and World Report* and reported by the Institute for Global Ethics found that "teaching children values and discipline in the schools" ranked as the most important issue in education today.[21] The global ethics staff interviewed two top researchers, Daniel Yankelovich and George Gallup, Jr., both of whom confirmed the general perception of moral decline. However, they flagged the great social increase of problems not faced before by parents, children, and our civic institutions (deadlier weapons on the street, diseases such as AIDS, exotic drugs, the divorce epidemic, violence on TV and the perpetuation of copycat violence on the street and in schools, the fear of children to go to school [25 percent], the continuing abuse of alcohol, too much individualism and not enough sense of social responsibility, etc.). On the positive side both Gallup

---

21. Patricia Born, "Ethics and Public Opinion," in *Insights on Global Ethics* 8, no. 3 (Box 563, Camden, Maine 04843): 1.

and Yankelovich identified a growing spirituality in the United States and a reaffirmation that we are very religious as a people. Gallup says, ". . . it is the faith factor that determines, to a great degree, our happiness, our ethical behavior, our having goals in life, or doing well in school, or keeping out of trouble. There is an intensified search for spiritual meanings and for having deeper relationships with other people."[22]

One of the greatest indicators of hope in this research was the public's overwhelming desire to teach moral values in the schools, including specific values such as responsibility and respect.

Several other studies have identified a great sense of urgency about moral and ethical reform in American society and the call for collective action among our civic institutions, higher education, government, law, religion, and family. A 1998 report from the Council on Civil Society, a joint project of the Institute for American Values and the University of Chicago Divinity School, agrees with the above report from Gallup and Yankelovich, saying that 67 percent of the public believes that "the U.S. is in a long-term moral decline" (a Chilton Research Services Poll). Ninety percent of the public believes that the problem of incivility is a serious national problem (lack of respect for others, lack of common courtesy, indifference, being treated like a number, children disrespecting adults, rejection of legitimate authority). Eighty percent think the problem has gotten worse during the last ten years.[23]

After analyzing the needs and challenges of many of our civic institutions, the Council called for the emergence of a "shared civic faith and a common civic purpose, undergirded by a strong public moral philosophy. Regarding public moral philosophy, our main challenge is to rediscover the existence of transmittable truth."[24] The Council made many recommendations, including one urging character education in U.S. public schools, while pointing to the many grassroots nonprofit organizations developing character education strategies, resources, and training.

One of the first grassroots groups was the Character Education Institute of San Antonio, Texas. Created in 1969, the Institute published a comprehensive instructional program designed to develop critical thinking skills and instill twelve universal values needed to function in a democratic society: honor, honesty, truthfulness, kindness, generosity, helpfulness, courage, convictions, justice, respect, freedom, and equality.

22. Born, "Ethics and Public Opinion," p. 5.

23. *A Call to Civil Society: Why Democracy Needs Moral Truths* (New York: Institute for American Values, 1998), p. 5.

24. *A Call to Civil Society*, p. 18.

Some grassroots efforts started in the 1980s, for example the Baltimore County school values education program, the result of a community-wide study begun in 1982. After wide survey and dialogue, the task force on values education decided that the major source of a "common core of values" was the U.S. Constitution. The community agreed on the values of honesty, human worth, and dignity, justice, due process, and equality of opportunity reflected in the Constitution. A program for Baltimore County's 148 schools was the result.

Many other grassroots experiments have taken place. One of the most exciting, productive, and reconciliation-oriented is the Allen School project in Dayton, Ohio. In 1989 this elementary school of 537 students was rated at the bottom in terms of student achievement and behavior. It was one of the worst schools in terms of fighting and suspensions. It was at that time that Rudolph S. Bernardo was appointed principal. When he arrived ten students a day were referred to his office for undesirable behavior. After a major transformation of the school through a character education program designed by Bernardo, teachers, and parents, students were referred to the principal's office to be recognized for their good performance, students' test scores improved by 49 percent, suspensions were reduced 93 percent, and parent involvement increased thirtyfold. This radical change in attitude and performance came about as the result of a process of open dialogue, brainstorming, team-building, and consensus/decision-making. During the process it was decided to emphasize the inherent goodness in each student rather than his or her defects. Guilt feelings were not cultivated on the part of students, teachers, or parents. The goal was to transform the school culture so that the best could be elicited from all participants, with maximum support from the wider community, media, churches, and other social agencies.

The character education program was built around 36 qualities of character the community of teachers, parents, community leaders, and students selected as crucial to improving the quality of life in the school and beyond. Character traits included punctuality, responsibility, respectfulness, honesty, joyfulness, cooperation, resourcefulness, loyalty, courage, fairness, and thankfulness. A "word of the week" program was designed in which the quality of character being studied and lived was introduced to the whole school on Monday, then discussed in homerooms, integrated into the curriculum during the week, and integrated into the total life of the school and of the family. Each Friday the word was highlighted in a ten-minute assembly led by one of the homerooms. Each grade level adopted a service project that put the particular quality of character to work. As a result of the success of the Allen

School character education effort, the entire Dayton school district adopted the Word of the Week Character Education program.[25]

Countless character education leaders and organizations emerged during the 1990s. Some of the strongest are as follows:

- *The Josephson Institute of Ethics and Its Character Counts Coalition.* In 1991 the founder, Michael Josephson, called a meeting of 30 top leaders in moral education to explore what should be done in character education together. The Aspen Declaration on Character Education was the result of their deliberations. These leaders agreed that ". . . character education is based on core ethical values which form the foundation of democratic society, in particular, respect, responsibility, trustworthiness, caring, justice and fairness and civic virtue and citizenship. . . . These core ethical values transcend cultural, religious, and socio-economic differences. . . . Character education is, first and foremost, an obligation of families; it is also an important obligation of faith communities, schools, youth and other human service organizations. . . . These obligations to develop character are best fulfilled when these groups work together in concert. . . ."[26] The Character Counts Coalition grew out of this meeting (1993). Many of the nation's youth-serving institutions belong to the Coalition and have worked together to design curricular programs, training designs, and video interpretations of these efforts. Many school systems across the country have adopted the Character Counts program and have sought to bring the whole community into the process.

  Albuquerque, New Mexico, is a good illustration. Even Congress has affirmed the program and has designated the third week in October as Character Counts Week.

  Each year parades, video premières (employing the Coalition's first two kids' videos, "Kids for Character" [1996] and "Choices Count" [1997]), contests, community forums, etc. are scheduled during this special week. The Coalition also sponsors a nationwide contest for drawings, poems, and songs that reflect ethical concerns and the importance of character. American Youth Character Awards are also given each year to recognize young people whose lives personify the Six Pillars of Character. For more online information see www.Character Counts.org.

---

25. Philip Fitch Vincent, *Promising Practice in Character Education: Nine Success Stories from Around the Country* (Chapel Hill, N.C.: Character Development Groups, 1996), pp. 95-104.

26. Michael Josephson, *Ethical Values, Attitudes, and Behavior in American Schools* (Marina del Rey, Calif.: Josephson Institute of Ethics, 1992), Appendix D.

- *The Center for the Fourth and Fifth R's* in Cortland, New York, is one of the central character education resource centers in the country. One of the reasons this is so is the leadership of the founder and director, Dr. Thomas Lickona, a professor at SUNY. His book, *Educating for Character,* is one of the most widely used resources by local leaders of the character education movement.[27] The Center offers a resource library, an annual summer institute, a newsletter, consultation, and a network of schools and communities following the Fourth and Fifth R Comprehensive Program (e-mail: c4rs5rs@cortland.edu).

- *Character Education Partnerships,* founded by Sanford N. McDonnell of the McDonnell Douglas Corporation in St. Louis, is one of the most significant national organizations promoting a total community approach to character education. The partnership has published *Building Community Consensus for Character Education; Character Education in the U.S. Schools: A New Consensus; A Primer for Evaluating a Character Education Initiative;* and other helpful guides.

  CEP holds national conferences of high quality, emphasizing their holistic approach. A major CEP program was started in the St. Louis, Missouri, school district with over 200,000 students involved. Esther F. Schaeffer, executive director at that time, said that CEP has a "strong conviction that character development is enhanced when schools involve the wider community — parents, businesses, religious institutions, youth organizations, government and the media — in promoting core ethical values" (www.character.org).

  The Communitarian Network, anchored at George Washington University in Washington, D.C., with Dr. Amitai Etzioni as director. The network has brought together local and national leaders at White House/Congressional Conferences on Character Building. The Network develops position papers that are widely read and critiqued and involves top academics, leaders in government, public educators, and family life and youth leaders. Task forces on specific issues study a wide range of issues and make their recommendations for change.[28] Etzioni's work emphasizes two central moral virtues, empathy and self-discipline, under which he groups other universal ethical virtues. He

27. Thomas Lickona, *Educating for Character: How Our Schools Can Teach Respect and Responsibility* (New York: Bantam, 1991). See also Anne C. Dotson and Karin D. Wisont, *The Character Education Handbook: Establishing a Character Education Program for Your School* (Cleveland: Character Press, 2001).

28. See *Character Building for a Democratic, Civil Society* (Washington D.C.: Communication Network, 1997).

and the Network emphasize the importance of a total societal approach to the implementation of the Golden Rule.[29]

The Center for the Advancement of Ethics and Character of Boston University founded by Dr. Kevin Ryan. The Center focuses on the public school curriculum as the primary vehicle for transmitting moral values to children and youth. The Center holds teacher academies for elementary and secondary teachers and administrators, and has a program for college and university faculty. It is also doing research and developing curricular materials. (For more information call: 617-343-3262.)

The Jefferson Center for Character Education, formed in 1953, publishes and promotes character education in schools. (Call 818-792-8130 for more information.)

Phi Delta Kappa's League of Values-Driven Schools, with Dr. Jack Frymier as director. The league made a very important study of the values on which we as a society agree and built its character education program around those agreements.[30] The study also identified values on which we do not agree. The League works with participating schools via newsletters and resources, and an annual summer camp for youth. (For more information call 1-800-766-1156.)

The above are only a fraction of the number of national programs that are promulgating character education. A quick check of the World Wide Web on character education programs produces 2,685,172 matches. That alone should tell the story about the explosion of interest in character education.

National and International Programs in Character Education and/or Global Ethics

The national character education movement has been greatly stimulated by the federal government through *Title X (Part A, Section 10103,* under the *Fund for Improvement of Education).* This fund made possible grants for pilot projects in character education up to $1,000,000 to qualifying states over a four-year period. As of this writing 48 states and the District of Columbia have received grants, and many pilot projects have been funded. External evaluators must be identified so that the outcome in terms of student behavior and atti-

---

29. Amitai Etzioni, *The New Golden Rule* (New York: Basic Books, 1996).

30. Jack Frymier, Luvern Cunningham, et al., *Values on Which We Agree* (Bloomington, Ind.: Phi Delta Kappa International, 1995).

tudinal changes or academic achievement can be measured and the overall results assessed. The program is being coordinated by the Federal Department of Education. Pilot projects often engage not only schools but parents, local governmental officials, business leaders, and religious institutions (Protestant, Catholic, Jewish, Muslim, Buddhist, etc.). The core values being affirmed nationally are the same as those established by the Aspen Declaration.

The Bush administration is extending and deepening the program.

The national, state, and local character education efforts are being stimulated by a strong quest for a global ethic that can guide the decision-making of leaders in all sectors of life from educators to business to governmental agencies. The work of Rushmore Kidder, president of the Institute for Global Ethics, has moved us to seek a global ethic that will transcend national, cultural, racial, and religious boundaries. Kidder interviewed 242 leading persons representing 50 faith groups in many fields across the world concerning their views about the values central to a global ethic for the twenty-first century. He found consensus on the following eight universal values: love, truthfulness (honesty, integrity), freedom, fairness, unity, tolerance, responsibility (accountability), and respect for life. In a follow-up study of five thousand persons in various seminars he found the degree of consensus in the following order (from highest to lowest): truth, compassion, responsibility, freedom, reverence for life, fairness, self-respect, tolerance, generosity, humility, and honor. He also found dilemma paradigms as follows: trust vs. loyalty; individual vs. community; short term vs. long term; justice vs. mercy.[31]

The Institute for Global Ethics is working on the implementation of such universal ethical values in many areas of national and international life, including character education in schools and communities across the world.

Another study, done by Dr. William D. Hitt of the Battelle Memorial Institute, inspires us to become global citizens with genuine commitment to finding and living a global ethic for the "Temple of Humanity" in which we now all live. His universal ethical values come out of and correlate with philosophy, religion, science, and daily life under what he calls "humanities, our framework for a global ethic." His five core values are:

1. Integrity: living by a set of moral principles.
2. Contribution: making a difference, adding value to the human enterprise.
3. Communication: engaging in genuine dialogue.

31. From his address at the Communitarian Network Conference on Character Building, George Washington University, June 1998.

4. Compassion: demonstrating an active concern for the well-being of others.
5. Cooperation: working with others to achieve a common goal.

These core values hold true for any culture, for any ethnic group, and for any religion.[32]

An inspiring international meeting was held in Chicago in 1993 where the 100th Anniversary of the Parliament of the World Religions was celebrated. Over six thousand representatives from the many world religions discussed countless issues of substance. One of these issues — the quest for a global ethic — was led by Dr. Hans Küng, internationally known Roman Catholic scholar. In his central thesis, "No new global order without a new global ethic," Küng maintained that "Every human being must be treated humanely" — a principle that has persisted in many religious and ethical traditions for thousands of years. It is some form of the Golden Rule: "Do unto others as you wish others to do unto you." This principle can be found in Buddhism, Christianity, Confucianism, Hinduism, Islam, Judaism, Zoroastrianism, and others.[33] A detailed statement of a global ethic to guide decisions (personal, social, political, scientific, etc.) was agreed upon and signed by over three hundred key religious leaders representing the world religions. These agreements fall under the following four irrevocable directives:

1. Commitment to a culture of nonviolence and a just economic order.
2. Commitment to a culture of solidarity and a life of truthfulness.
3. Commitment to a culture of tolerance and a life of trust.
4. Commitment to a culture of equal rights and a partnership between men and women.

Each directive can be stated negatively: i.e., You shall not kill; You shall not steal or deceive, etc.

In respect to our quest for forgiveness and reconciliation, Küng believes that there can be no ongoing human society without a world ethic for all nations. Also, he believes that there can be no peace or reconciliation among nations without peace and cooperation among the religions of the world. Finally, he believes that there can be no peace among the religions without dialogue between the world religions in an effort to find common ground and

---

32. William Hitt, *A Global Ethic: The Leadership Challenge* (Columbus, Ohio: Battelle Press, 1996), p. 106.

33. Hitt, *A Global Ethic*, p. 111.

mutual respect. Küng challenges the world religions to get beyond platitudes and be willing to face "any pernicious self-righteousness, intolerance, and rivalry" and find concrete theological sources for cooperative work; analyze the structure of thought and conduct that have crept in and have separated people; be willing to be self-critical and self-corrective and get beyond only showing loyalty to tradition and the status quo.[34] This quest will not be for a unitary religion but for all religions to work together to find consensus about ethical behavior that transcends any one religion and will become the basis of the reconciliation of individuals and of political, religious, ethnic, and gender groups.[35]

Such a goal is profoundly needed in our highly divided world, with its abundance of religious conflicts complicated by socio-economic and political factors. The critical need for agreement on a global ethic that will actually guide our decisions has never been more important.

---

34. Hans Küng, *Global Responsibility: In Search of a New World Ethic* (New York: Crossroad, 1990), p. 131.

35. Hans Küng and Karl-Joseph Kuschel, *A Global Ethic: The Declaration of the Parliament on the World Religions* (New York: Continuum, 1994).

CHAPTER 6

A Four-Pronged Approach to Increasing
Forgiveness, Reconciliation, and Moral Courage

It is self-evident that the church's strategy in respect to forgiveness and reconciliation should include both (1) moral development of children, youth, and adults; and (2) educational, liturgical, pastoral, and sacramental life oriented toward personal and social moral failure and spiritual separation from God and others. In order to take a holistic approach to these two dimensions we are proposing a four-pronged strategy: (1) a strong, focused moral and spiritual education and sacramental/liturgical life in our congregations; (2) the church's cooperative role in community-based moral or character education and service learning; (3) the church's active advocacy for the legal and necessary study *about* religion and ethics in our public schools; and (4) a strategy for the development of *public* churches that will take the lead in addressing public issues that often divide us, causing the need for forgiveness and reconciliation.

A Strong, Focused Christian Moral Education and
Sacramental Life for the Entire Congregation in Ministry

Too often leaders in religious education and sacramental life have approached ethical issues in a somewhat moralistic way. In designing a learning experience we have sought to end with "a moral lesson." These lessons sometimes add up to "be good and you will be Christian." The fact that children and youth at different ages have differing capacities and abilities to understand what it means to be and do good and what it means to be authentically Christian in increasingly more subtle ways may be overlooked. Christian ethical education should be attentive to the research on the stages of moral development as articulated by Piaget, Kohlberg, and their followers and critics. The emphasis on sharing of moral dilemmas, tailored to the learners' life experience at various stages, can be constructive. Such is the case in the normal stages of development: moving from the more egocentric decisions of young children, to the "I'll scratch your back if you scratch mine" to "let's follow the rules" to "let's follow only the laws or rules that bring justice for all" to a radical commitment to the principle of universal justice for all people in all situations. A Christian religious education can be designed that is sensitive to an ethic of justice (Kohlberg) combined with an ethic of nonviolence and care (Gilligan) and an ethic of mercy, forgiveness, and reconciliation (Enright et al.). The dynamics of personal equilibrium, disequilibrium, accommodation, and assimilation are very important to the process of growth both in terms of cognitive development and the affective domain.

Also, it is important to integrate what we have learned about *moral intelligence* with *emotional intelligence*. Both Amitai Etzioni and Daniel Goleman emphasize the quality of empathy as the root of ethical behavior. Goleman affirms the research findings of Martin Hoffman, who sees a natural progression in empathy from infancy onward. Hoffman finds empathy in even a one-year-old who sees another child fall and begins to cry: ". . . her rapport is so strong and immediate that she puts her thumb in her mouth and buries her head in her mother's lap, as if she herself were hurt. . . ."[1] Hoffman identifies stages of growth in empathy through early childhood to late childhood, when children have a capacity to "feel for the plight of an entire group, such as the poor, the outcast. That understanding in adolescence, can buttress moral conviction centered on wanting to alleviate misfortune and injustice." Goleman goes on to say that without empathy a person can have the morals of a molester or a sociopath.

Research findings on mental, moral, and emotional intelligence and growth can and should be integrated into faith development and as a central dynamic of religious education.

Faith Development

Faith Development as a movement was founded by James W. Fowler, formerly at Harvard Divinity School and now at Emory University. In his classic book, *The Stages of Faith*, he reported on his research (involving 359 persons

---

1. David Goleman, *Emotional Intelligence* (New York: Bantam, 1995), p. 105.

aged from 3.5 to 84 years) during which he distilled a six-stage theory of the natural structures and stages of faith. Fowler sees faith generically. Every person has some form of faith revealed in his or her behavior. Faith has to do with the values we make most important or ultimate. Often faith has been seen as a reality beyond reason, possibly having more to do with our feelings. Fowler sees faith as ". . . a way of knowing and seeing the conditions of our lives in relation to more or less conscious images . . ." we have of the ultimate meaning of life. People have quite different contents for their faith. Some put possessions, power, position, or a philosophical system at the center of their lives and beliefs rather than a religious content for their faith. The content of faith is very important in order for faith to be genuinely life-giving, creative, growing, and helpful to the self, others, and the environment. Fowler, himself a Christian, sees the Christian content of faith to be central in his own flowering of faith. He recognizes, however, that other religious and nonreligious content can perform similar functions in terms of organizing the self and giving it a sense of direction and meaning. The humanizing and transcendent qualities of the content of faith determine the goodness of the faith commitment. Fowler's continuing research and writing have focused more clearly on the Christian content of faith within the church as the body of Christ in our pluralistic society.[2] Fowler was more interested in defining the structures or basic elements involved in any faith orientation. He found that faith and belief are different realities, though related. Faith involves some form of logic (Piaget), some ability to get inside the lives of others in terms of perspective (Selman), some form of moral judgment (Kohlberg), some reference beyond the self in social awareness, some locus of authority in order to give the self confidence, some form of world coherence, and some pattern of dealing with symbols (from magical to symbols separated from the symbolized to the evocative power of symbols to give deep meaning, etc.).

For our purposes Faith Development already integrates several elements we have identified: namely, moral development, cognitive development, empathy or ability to relate deeply to others and their life situations, ability to expand social relations, etc. Fowler sees faith as triadic. It includes the way we *think, feel,* and *will* ourselves to act. Fowler sees the importance of emotions, and emotional intelligence by implication, but not as explicitly as Goleman. He sees the importance of integrating the conscious and unconscious elements of faithful living.

2. See James W. Fowler, *Becoming Adult, Becoming Christian: Adult Development and Christian Faith* (San Francisco: Harper & Row, 1984); and *Weaving the New Creation: Stages of Faith and the Public Church* (San Francisco: HarperCollins, 1991).

Fowler's most visible and celebrated work has to do with his view that faith formation starts at birth and should continue throughout life. His six-stage theory emphasizes the fact that faith can and *should* continue to grow and develop at each of the stages of life from birth to death. He found, however, that faith's form and expression may fixate at earlier stages rather than continue to grow. Such a discovery is one of the most important fruits of faith development research. In terms of the Christian belief in the importance of forgiveness, reconciliation, and moral courage, faith expressions can get fixated at the stage where we find it very difficult to *want* to relate to people of other beliefs than our own. We may be able to forgive and be reconciled to members of our own family or our own church but find it difficult to believe that God is calling us to forgive and be reconciled with persons of other political or religious loyalties, and even more difficult to believe that God may be acting in the lives of those who have alienated us, calling them to forgive and be reconciled with us. Fowler found that when all of the structures of faith are reviewed in any person's life, the person's stage of faith development can be identified in a way that can be helpful for the person as well as for those to whom he or she is related.

A brief review of the six stages follows:

Primal Faith (Infancy)

Fowler sees the first two years of life to be very crucial to planting the seeds of trust, love, and courage in the infant's life. Trust is the fundamental issue and need of the infant. Trust becomes the heartbeat of faith as a reality that gives the infant the grounding of trust in self, others, and the environment. It becomes the internal reality that makes trust in God a possibility later. At first, Fowler saw this stage as undifferentiated in terms of the elements of faith. More recently he has included the seminal research of Daniel N. Stern in his *The Interpersonal World of the Infant*. Stern has discovered the beginning of the emergent self, the core self, the subjective self, and the verbal self within the stage Fowler now calls *Primal Faith*. All of these selves are interrelated but all depend on a loving, caring, stable environment that the parents or their surrogates provide: an environment that nurtures what Erik Erikson calls a *numinous* quality (an indwelling force that animates or guides — evoking awe or reverence, a sense of seeing and being seen by an affirming presence which is the mother or parent). Such is the ground for higher forms of the rituals of religious faith. This is a relationship in which the child sees the meaning of life as he or she looks into the loving eyes of the parent and is prepared to later look into the face of the loving God. These qualities of love, trust, and self-affirmation are communicated via the simple rituals of feeding, changing, bathing, playing, etc. The possible danger of this period, of course, is the lack of such an environment, or its presence in a way that the experience of being central continues to dominate the child's way of relating. We now know that the first two years of life include the period of moving away from the parent toward autonomy and the sometimes unwelcome period of "no" when the child is separating the self from the parents. This is also the stage of the rituals of *right* and *wrong* behavioral distinctions. The child begins to identify himself or herself as good or bad in relation to the interaction with parents. This struggle is often over toilet training especially. Erikson sees this struggle as the ontological origin of not only shame and doubt but also of the *divided self* and the *divided species.* "The self-doubt and hidden shame," says Erikson, "attached to the necessity of 'eliminating' part of himself create in the human being a certain subdued rage which eventually must either rebel against the condemning authority or turn to righteous condemnation against others."[3] Not only does the child have to struggle to make the good self win over the bad self but also to ensure that he or she will not end up as a member of a lesser group of people. The child, therefore, has a "constant need for new everyday ritualization of moral discrimination in words and sounds truly corresponding to a shared moral climate which the child can comprehend and experiment with."[4] Moral life starts quite early. Remember this dynamic when we address issues of shame and guilt, moral strength and failure, forgiveness and reconciliation later in this study.

Stage 1 — Intuitive Projective Faith — seen in children ages 3 to 7 especially but also in persons older. In this stage the child thinks intuitively and projects his or her intuition out to the wider world — sometimes with amazing grasp of life's essential meanings and often in a way that is fragmented and distorted by "egocentric" perception. The child thinks pre-operationally (Piaget) with his or her perceptions and imagination rather than logically. The visual and active faith of primary adults can be caught and lived. "A little child shall lead them" is sometimes true. Erikson sees this period as the time to deal with the life issues of initiative vs. guilt and shame. The child is trying to move out and has the physical and verbal mobility to do so. The child is also trying to identify himself or herself as a boy or a girl and to do this in relation to mother and father with sexual overtones and fantasies. Such a sense

---

3. Erik Erikson, *Toys and Reasons: Stages in the Ritualization of Experience* (New York: W. W. Norton, 1977), p. 95.

4. Erikson, *Toys and Reasons*, p. 95.

of personal initiative is crucial for moving on with purpose in life, but it is also the source of tension, anxiety, and feelings of guilt or shame again. The child cannot easily distinguish fact from fantasy. Images about God are more general than Fowler expected (God is everywhere). As the child moves out on his or her own experimentally, a feeling of being "found out" can emerge. That is why Erikson says that "the great governor of initiative is conscience," which in time is the ontogenetic cornerstone of morality.[5] Positive exposure to the stories and rituals of the faith community are very important to nurturing a sense of self in relation to others and God.

Stage 2 — Mythic — Literal Faith — appropriate for children from 7 to 11 or 12 but often found much later in life. The stage correlates with the concrete operational stage of mental development (Piaget) in which the child can think logically but in relation to concrete experience — not abstractly. Here, the child tends to take everything at face value or literally. Therefore, the great myths of the faith community are taken literally. Only later in the stage of formal operational thinking can the deeper meaning of the symbols or stories be comprehended and put into words. Children, nevertheless, are very interested in learning the stories, beliefs, and practices of the faith community. They are also interested in the moral rules and attitudes but are not interested in contesting these to discern their adequacy generally but only in relation to themselves in terms of elemental fairness. Images about God are more anthropomorphic than in Stage 1. Stories about God or Jesus are important to them but they do not try to get behind their meaning or connect them to propositions of truth. The danger of this stage is the tendency to remain at the literal level and demand all religious truth in the scriptures and the creeds to be taken literally — even though such beliefs may conflict with many other areas of their lives, often centered in science. When children recognize the contradictions present in differing faith stories they are beginning to be ready for more rigorous thinking appropriate for adolescents in the next stage.

Stage 3 — Synthetic — Conventional Faith — 12 through 19+. This stage starts in adolescence but is the most commonly appropriated stage for adults in many churches. Adolescents are moving into formal operational thinking where they can think more abstractly, have the ability to critique their faith, to "think about their thinking." They also begin to discern the crucial importance of interpersonal relations in defining who they are and what others see to be their strengths and needs. They are also questing for an identity and a sense of direction. Fowler agrees with Erikson that adolescents want and need to find a great fidelity, someone or something to which the person can give

---

5. Erik Erikson, *Identity: Youth and Crisis* (New York: W. W. Norton, 1968), p. 119.

himself or herself in order to find a center of meaning for the self and to see a vision of the future. Fowler finds that adolescents tend to critique the faith that they have inherited from their parents and the faith community but in a limited way. While they have the mental ability to critique and own their faith they have limited life experiences and a high need for acceptance from peers and others. These other elements in their lives tend to make their final faith stances to be quite conventional. Their critique, according to Fowler, is at the personal level, having to do with their identity, rather than a critique of their faith "as a system." Stage 3 is synthetic in that it brings things together from various sources (views of peers, parents, leaders, pastors, educators, scriptures, history, science, etc.) and it is often conformist and conventional (in that the adolescent seems unable to get outside of the prevailing systems of values, beliefs, and practices in order to do genuinely autonomous reflections and assessment). This is an important stage because persons can and do find a faith commitment that brings meaning and direction to life, however synthetic and conventional. It is crucial, also, for adolescents to find a set of moral values to guide their daily decisions concerning honesty, truthfulness, integrity, responsibility, and respect for others. Many live out their faithfulness and their sense of ministry from this perspective. Fowler affirms what takes place in Stage 3 but has opened the door to much greater growth in faith during adult years. He identifies three stages of growth that are uniquely adult. Such a perspective has given great impetus to adult religious education with a view to much higher expectations for growth in faith and in the ministries of reconciliation and moral courage.

Stage 4 — Individuation — Reflective Faith — Young adult +. In this stage young adults and others have lived life in wider ways through college, work, travel, and the Internet to the point that they are ready to question earlier assumptions and commitments. They are ready to critique their beliefs and faith statements in ways that transcend the conventional thinking of their adolescent years. They are ready to risk critiquing their faith as a total system of belief, values, and practices in the light of their wider life experience. They are seeking to interrelate their faith with all other aspects of their lives — with family, work, community, governmental and legal structures, with scientific revelations. They have the interest and ability to seek to develop a unified philosophy of life, as Erikson says, and also to find a sense of intimacy and love both on the human and divine levels. Stage 4 persons can get behind the symbols of the faith; they can demythologize the stories in order to see why the stories arose and what their deeper meanings may be. They also want to own their faith in an honest way and relate it authentically to their abilities and sense of vocation. This is a great time for recommitment focused on the universal priesthood of all believers and the clear decision to be in some creative form of ministry employing those talents and gifts.

What is needed is a third-person perspective. Fowler sees the capacity for third-person reflection emerging out of the awareness of conflicting voices of external and internal authorities. Fowler asserts, "With its transcendental view of one's self-other relations, this third-person perspective allows one a standpoint from which conflicting expectations can be adjudicated and one's own inner authorization can be strengthened."[6]

One of the dangers of the period is too great a focus of energy on conscious processes of critique and reassessment and too little awareness of the importance of the unconscious and affective dimensions of life. Head and heart balance is needed but often does not come until more living has taken place. Thus midlife growth in faith is needed.

Stage 5 — Conjunctive Faith — Early midlife and beyond. Here we see the need for a rejoining or a union of things that may have been separated before. We have lived long enough to have recognized that our earlier clear commitments have become less clear, that there is evidence for and against certain beliefs, that persons of other religious commitments or no religion may have said and done things that both inspire us and make us question the depth of our own faith. We may begin to seek a wider spirituality that brings together both conscious and unconscious dimensions of our inner life.

In terms of moral development Stage 5 persons can see the flawed nature of many of our laws and social norms (Kohlberg) and are concerned to purify our laws and norms to be more profoundly just and equitable for all races and classes of people. There is more willingness to affirm civil disobedience in order for change to take place.

Stage 5 persons begin to see the interconnectedness of all of life. They are willing to let the symbols they critiqued and rationalized in Stage 4 speak with fresh power. They can see the authenticity of Paul Ricoeur's call for a "second naïveté" in which they can ". . . believe in the organic unity of all things and become able to resubmit to the initiative of the symbolic. Interestingly, such persons begin to distrust the separation of symbol and symbolized, sensing that when we neutralize the initiation of the symbolic we make a pale idol of any meaning we honor."[7] Stage 5 persons are seeking a deeper spiritual unity with God and others who come from quite different backgrounds, employing faith stories and belief systems quite unique. They are

---

6. James W. Fowler, *Faithful Change: The Personal and Public Challenges of Postmodern Life* (Nashville: Abingdon, 1996), p. 63.

7. Fowler, *Weaving the New Creation,* p. 177.

seeking integrity and honesty in their affirmation and in their moral life. They deeply want forgiveness and reconciliation among all people but are profoundly aware of their own limitations and failures to meet their own higher standards and calling.

Stage 6 — Universalizing Faith — Midlife and older adulthood. As Fowler says, this stage ". . . involves persons moving beyond the paradoxical awareness and embrace of polar opposites that are the hallmarks of the conjunctive stage."[8] It involves a widening of social perspective taking. The press to move beyond the boundaries of social class, race, nation, gender, ideology, or religious affinity comes to "a kind of completion. . . . This Universalizing stage moves beyond usual forms of defensiveness and exhibits an openness based on groundedness in the being, love, and regard of God."[9] Fowler reminds us that persons in Stage 6 are rare indeed. However, when found they are focused and committed in authentic but not perfectionistic ways. They liberate others and help them find wholeness and love rather than making them dependent. "Similarly, the authentic spirituality of the Universalizing stage avoids polarizing the world between the 'saved' and the 'damned.' Persons of this stage are as concerned with the transformation of those they oppose as with the bringing about of justice and reform."[10] Fowler points to examples such as Martin Luther King, Jr., and Mother Teresa: persons who lived in a radical way the Golden Rule (which may be learned by children but is seldom lived fully until later adulthood if at all).

We have paused to unpack Fowler's views concerning the nature, structures, and stages of faith in order to suggest the following: Stage theory may be used as a framework into which contemporary views of cognitive, moral, and emotional intelligence may be woven. Fowler is increasingly aware of findings from studies of moral development, emotional intelligence, and character education, along with the more focused approaches to Christian education and sacramental and liturgical renewal found in various churches. Of course, he is also very generic in his views about the nature and dynamics of faith so that his framework is helpful for strategies coming from other world religions. Faith development, therefore, not only highlights the importance of reconciliation with God, others, and the self, but presents guidelines for education, worship, and action.

The above sensitivity to the patterns of mental, moral, and emotional faith development and a philosophy of Christian religious education need to

8. Fowler, *Faithful Change*, p. 66.
9. Fowler, *Faithful Change*, p. 67.
10. Fowler, *Faithful Change*, p. 67.

be related to the intuitive aspects of participation in caring, committed community which is the body of Christ. Craig Dykstra has called for a *visional* ethic that is the by-product of children, youth, and adults being part of a moral and ethical body of believers in a God of justice and love revealed and lived out by Christ. Children well in advance of their specific stage of mental development can appropriate and internalize intuitively caring, moral behavior. Participants, Dykstra says, can connect religious faith and moral behavior by being in families or in the faith community where persons see themselves as extensions of Christ's love within and beyond the church family. Persons can grow morally because as members of the faith community they can ". . . see why worship and prayer, confession and repentance, biblical and theological study and interpretation, fellowship and discipleship, are important for moral growth and in moral education. . . ."[11] Such an ethos is a rich, more adequate representation of what the moral life is like.

Our Strategy

It is our belief that the interrelating of moral education with a rich sacramental and liturgical life is the direction with most potential for the future. We will explore how various congregations have given children, youth, and families excellent preparation for sacramental/liturgical life and how such sacramental/liturgical experiences have profound power to educate and ground children, youth, and adults at the various stages of life in an internalized ethic of justice and love, of empathy and personal responsibility before God and the community. We will explore patterns of sacramental education and participation in the Sacrament of Reconciliation in Roman Catholic congregations and the Sacrament of Confession and Repentance in the Orthodox community. We will assess various approaches to moral development and sacramental and liturgical life in Protestant churches, assessing how the matter of moral and spiritual growth can take place, following paths unique to the expressions of faith found in the communities chosen. The latter will be done in dialogue with the congregations studied in Chapter 1. Educational and liturgical resources will also be highlighted. See Chapter 7 for much more concerning the first prong.

---

11. Craig Dykstra, *Vision and Character: A Christian Educator's Alternative to Kohlberg* (New York: Paulist, 1981), p. 3.

A Cooperative Character-Building Strategy for the Total Community, with Strong Leadership Coming from Churches

There is much potential in the Character Education Movement that is gaining strength in the United States and across the world. It is increasingly clear that the best approach to character education and development is one in which the total community is involved and committed. Such a generalization can be made because reports and studies of character education efforts across the nation and the world highlight the crucial nature of community support, cooperation, and participation. It is not enough for teachers and parents to insist on the teaching of basic moral values in the schools. Children and youth are more deeply influenced when leaders and participants in city government, businesses, labor, media, entertainment, community organizations, and churches are celebrating the same qualities of character in their lives and work. A study of ten thousand educators, noneducators, and students was conducted by Phi Delta Kappa, a national professional educators' organization, concerning core values on which most people agree. It became very clear that there is high agreement that parents, schools, and churches should work together to teach, reinforce, reward, and recognize the many values on which we as members of a democratic society agree. For instance, in ranking the ten purposes of education, *character* was second, right after teaching basic skills. In community after community there was agreement that "The educated person is honest, responsible, dependable, loyal, and a person of integrity." Moreover, it was agreed that schools, parents, and churches should cooperate in teaching such qualities of character without apology. The Phi Delta Kappa study found that the home had the primary responsibility in a society for teaching moral values; schools and churches had important secondary and tertiary responsibilities. For instance, one of the qualities we are especially concerned about in this book, "Forgiving, willing to pardon others," was seen as a primary responsibility of the home, but a secondary responsibility of the church and a tertiary responsibility of the school.[12] Other qualities of character on which persons agreed were ". . . courageous, stand up for beliefs, honest, truthful, loving, affectionate, tender, . . . accepting of others, nonprejudicial, kind, altruistic, peaceful, compassionate, committed, honorable, principled, benevolent, generous. . . ." The Phi Delta Kappa study identifies many moral and ethical problems in our society that must be addressed. But, more importantly, the study discovered much agreement on core values to be

12. Jack Frymier et al., *Values on Which We Agree* (Bloomington, Ind.: Phi Delta Kappa International, 1995), p. 33.

taught and rewarded. The study concludes that ". . . Americans are clear in their own minds about what is good and what is bad, and they want to steer toward the good. But they want their hands on the tiller as well as on the oar. They intend to pull, but they intend to chart their own course too. And the tiller aims them in the direction of honesty, civility, equality, learning, freedom, and responsibility. These are the core values on which most Americans agree."[13]

There are many models emerging concerning how to make character education a total community effort. Many of these models are the result of school systems recognizing serious moral problems in the schools and the community and deciding to inaugurate character education in the schools, followed by clear involvement of the total community in order to support the effort based in the schools. Other models *start* with the needs of the total community for education for character and citizenship, with the schools as one important context for the total community effort. Churches, synagogues, mosques, etc. have been involved creatively in both approaches. Religious leaders have taken more initiative, probably in the total community model than the one starting in the schools.

An illustration of the model that starts in the school district and involves the total community as a support system is Cumberland County Schools in Fayette, North Carolina. "The local school system has encouraged religious leaders, elected officials, parents, law enforcement officers, military corps, media personalities, youth organizations and others to join in a unified campaign. This initiative began as a response to serious problems facing the community." The school district was experiencing the second-worst violent youth crime rate in North Carolina, along with other serious evidence of ethical disintegration. The school leaders decided to try to intervene by integrating character education into the ongoing goals of the school. But, what qualities of character and citizenship were going to be taught and celebrated? A consensus process was established that brought together summits for adults and for youth in order to listen to what the qualities of character should be. Thousands of people were involved in the consensus building. Outside resource leaders gave assistance. Eight qualities of character were agreed upon: respect, responsibility, integrity, caring, self-discipline, trustworthiness, fairness, and citizenship. Another summit was held with 350 community members attending in order to get total community participation. A kickoff event was held to promote the program, with 750 participants. The "concept of the month" campaign was introduced to involve the

13. Frymier et al., *Values on Which We Agree*, p. 37.

total community. All of the different aspects of the community — from religious congregations to businesses to media, etc. designed their own strategies for cooperation. For instance, 75 local ministers and leaders agreed on ways to cooperate with the schools. It was agreed to dedicate a sermon each month to the designated character quality, as well as to focus on the same quality of character in the church education programs. The ministers also funded a motivational speaker for assemblies at the eight high schools in the county.[14]

The second model starts with the community and involves the schools as an important partner along with all other aspects of the community, including churches, businesses, media, government, social agencies, parents, etc.

A concrete illustration of the second model is what has been initiated by Partners for Citizenship and Character in Worthington, Ohio, a community in which one of the authors of this book lives and was involved in the process described below. Worthington is a suburban community but with deep roots as one of the early villages founded in Ohio in 1803. It has a reputation for fine schools, intelligent and engaged citizens, racial diversity, and strong communities of faith. The school district is much larger than the city. As numerical growth has accelerated, demanding several new schools including a second high school, social and ethical problems have increased. A peer mediation program was initiated and was successful. As funding for the peer mediation program was sought, community leaders brought persons from the schools and community along with student mediators together to discuss the needs of the program. In the process it was decided to get below the surface: to intervene before destructive behavior emerged. In short, it was decided to explore the possibility of engaging the whole community into adopting, practicing, and celebrating important qualities of character and citizenship. It was the early feeling of these leaders that the approach should be wide. It should involve all aspects of the Worthington community including the schools, but only as one of the partners. In 1995 Partners in Citizenship and Character was established as a nonprofit organization with Dr. Paul Minus as president. Minus brought his expertise as the former president of the Council on Ethics in Economics.

The Board of Trustees decided to seek total community involvement in

14. Carol Leslie-Hudson, "Celebrating Character in Cumberland County Schools Engenders Positive Community Support," in Philip F. Vincent, ed., *Promising Character Education: Nine Stories from Around the County* (Chapel Hill, N.C.: Character Development Group, 1996), pp. 41-51.

identifying the qualities of citizenship and character the community would affirm and incorporate as guides to moral decision-making in businesses, media, athletics, families, governmental agencies, churches, etc. A year-long process of *listening* to people from various arenas of community life was commenced. Teams of dialogue leaders were recruited and trained in preparation for 30 dialogue groups for 316 participants who were invited to brainstorm, list, and prioritize the qualities of citizenship and character the community could unite around to strengthen the moral fiber of the persons at all levels of community life. A *Dialogue Group Process Guide*[15] was prepared to be used in all dialogue groups in order to have consistency between groups. In addition, 714 other persons filled out survey forms, indicating their top qualities. Over three hundred qualities of character were listed but with the highest agreement on responsibility, respect, honesty, compassion, integrity, spirituality, moral courage, and self-discipline. You will notice that these qualities are similar to those identified in other settings. The key factor is: the total community was involved in discussing the issues/needs and deciding and owning the qualities to affirm and incorporate into family life, schools, businesses, community organizations, churches, etc.

Seven teams of community leaders planned specific ways to complement the cooperative program. The teams are: city government, business, schools, congregations, resources, preschools, and senior citizens.

A kickoff was held on the Village Green with youth from the two high schools doing dramatic vignettes on each of the eight qualities of character, with bands, food, speakers from the media and from the Ohio State football team who told their own stories about the importance of commitment to strong moral values.

Worthington received much cooperation and assistance from statewide and national leaders. Mrs. Jenny Smucker, initiator of a strong community-oriented character education program in Orrville, Ohio, spoke to Worthington community leaders twice about ways to engage the community. Orrville organized the Heartland Education Community in 1991 and proceeded to train discussion leaders who led 24 other seminars in order to come to consensus on the nine core qualities of character that guide the efforts of the Orrville school district. Then, the Word of the Month program was written; professional development of teachers took place; parental, business, church, and community organization participants were engaged in cooperative efforts. The Orrville City Schools officially adopted the program. While their

15. *The Dialogue Group Process Guide* is available from Partners for Citizenship and Character. Web Page: www.Worthington.org/civic/pccbuild.htm. Jan Elliott, Executive Director.

program centered more heavily in the schools, total community involvement and ownership is emphasized.[16]

Great help has also come from Sandy McDonnell, former CEO of the McDonnell Douglas Company in St. Louis. McDonnell is the national chairperson of Character Education Partnership with headquarters in Washington, D.C. A strong advocate of character education, Mr. McDonnell was invited to Worthington to inspire the community to move ahead. (Information concerning Character Education Partnership is to be found earlier in this book.)

Pastors and congregational leaders participated in the dialogue group process and made up one of the seven teams planning creative ways to involve churches and religious communities in cooperative work in the total community effort. While specific definition of the qualities of character has been developed and agreed upon for the schools, businesses, governmental agencies, etc., congregations can find biblical and theological sources that help put the stories of the faith community to work in ways possibly inappropriate for public school settings but important for the faith development of children, youth, and adults in the cooperating congregations. This more specific form of character development, coming out of the beliefs, traditions, and experiences of the faith community, has great potential. Specific curricular ramifications have been identified and designed by creative teams in several congregations, focused specifically on particular age groups but also on the total liturgical and service life of the congregations.

Enhancing Reconciliation through the Legal Study of Religion in the Public Schools

Our world is at a crossroad concerning conflicts that appear, on the surface at least, to be coming from religious and ethnic groups with differing beliefs, histories, cultural expressions, practices, and political alignments. The most obvious illustration, of course, is the attempt to deal with international terrorism and our effort to sort out varying religious and political dynamics. It is now known that many of these apparent conflicts between religious groups are actually conflicts over political and economic issues that tap into religious symbolism and passions.

Children and youth who have been educated in American public

16. See *In Orrville Character Counts: Words of the Month*. Heartland Character and Citizenship Education Committee. Jenny Smucker, Chair, P.O. Box 280, Orrville, Ohio 44667, Telephone (216) 684-3010, FAX (216) 684-3428.

schools were largely unprepared to understand the recent events in world history: the conflict between Muslims, Roman Catholics, and Orthodox in Bosnia, the conflict between Jews and Arabs with their Christian and Muslim backgrounds, the troubles in Northern Ireland between Protestants and Catholics, the attacks of Christians by Hindus in India, and the incredible complexity of religious and political issues involved in the war on terrorism. We agree with Hans Küng's statement that there can be no peace or reconciliation in our world today without peace and reconciliation between the great world religions. Such a movement toward reconciliation among the world's religions calls for *understanding* the nature and roles of these religions in our contemporary world. Our public schools must get past their hesitancy to study these religions for fear of violating the separation of church and state position as enunciated by the Supreme Court.

Moreover, children and youth cannot even understand American history without being free to study the role of religion in the founding and development of our democratic form of government. Many recent critiques of public school textbooks and curricular designs have identified the serious lack of attention to religious motivations and personalities in U.S. history. The same is true of our lack of adequate inclusion of religious elements in the total curriculum, including literature, languages, the sciences, music, and the arts.[17]

During the Schempp case in 1963 the Supreme Court declared it to be unconstitutional to prescribe prayer or to imply commitment to a particular religion in public schools. Schools should be neutral in religion, neither promoting it nor inhibiting its free expression (the First Amendment). Such neutrality, Justice Goldberg said, does not mean that religion shouldn't be studied in public schools. ". . . [I]t seems to me that from the opinions in the present and past cases that the Court would recognize the propriety . . . of teaching about religion, as distinguished from the teaching of religion, in the public schools."

Since 1963 several states have taken Justice Goldberg seriously and have developed policies and curricular designs for teaching *about* religion within the basic course patterns as well as initiating elective courses: The Bible as Literature or Comparative Religion; and the two courses prepared by Pennsylvania — Religious Literature of the West (1967) and Religious Literature of the East (1975). Florida moved ahead with the cooperation of Florida State University in creating the Religion-Social Studies Curriculum Project, followed by the training of teachers to include the study about religion within social studies courses. Other creative efforts were made in Nebraska, Iowa, Indiana, New York, and

17. Warren Nord, "Religious Literacy, Textbooks, and Religious Neutrality," *Religion and Public Education* 16, no. 1 (Winter 1989): 111-21.

Massachusetts. By 1971 Wisconsin, Michigan, Vermont, and California had established certification programs in religion studies for public schools.[18] By 1990 22 states had some form of a policy on the teaching about religion in public schools, according to Charles Kniker, a leader in the movement.[19] During the 1990s much more effort has been made to integrate the study of religion authentically into textbooks, into course objectives and processes, and into the ethos of schools. The Williamsburg Charter Foundation has published a curriculum that examines the impact of the First Amendment on individual and communal liberty in America. The curriculum has been endorsed by Catholic, Protestant, Jewish, Mormon, Muslim, and Orthodox leaders. Lessons in the curriculum are designed for upper elementary, junior high, and senior high. The curriculum, *Living with Our Deepest Differences: Religious Liberty in a Pluralistic Society,* by Charles C. Haynes et al. (Boulder, Colorado: Learning Connections Publishers, 1988), uses primary sources for every major period of American history, seeking to focus on the student's appreciation of the importance of religious liberty for persons of all religious faiths or none.

Many other resources have been developed for teacher education programs in order to strengthen the ability and confidence of public school teachers to address the content and issues related to the inclusion of the study about religion in their classrooms.[20] Today it is commonly agreed that "knowledge about religion is not only a characteristic of an educated person, it is also absolutely necessary for understanding and living in a world of diversity." The position of the National Council for the Social Studies continues, "Since the purpose of the social studies is to provide students knowledge of the world that has been, the world that is, and the world of the future, studying about religions should be an essential part of the social studies curriculum."[21] Such an attitude has led teachers increasingly to realize that they have a responsibility and an opportunity to help students not only understand better the impact of religion in our past but understand one another and gain more trust in one another today.

18. Nicholas Piediscalzi, "Public Education-Religious Studies Since the Schempp Decision (1963)," in Marvin J. Taylor, ed., *Foundations for Christian Education in an Area of Change* (Nashville: Abingdon, 1976), pp. 186-97.

19. Jim Castelli, "Schools Take Up Religion as an Academic Study," *USA Today,* November 6, 1990, p. 4D.

20. See Charles Kniker, "Teacher Education and Religion: The Role of Foundation Courses in Preparing Students to Teach about Religion," *Religion and Public Education* 17, no. 1 (1990): 203-22.

21. *Rationale and Guidelines for Teaching about Religion* (Boston: Houghton Mifflin, 1991), p. 1.

Leaders from religious communities need to take the initiative to support these efforts in public education to bring understanding and reconciliation alive in our highly pluralistic society. Today many school systems not only have students, teachers, and parents coming from Catholic, Jewish, and multifarious Protestant backgrounds, but also Buddhist, Muslim, Hindu, Sikh, and many other religions. Such a reality can be the occasion for tension and mistrust or it can be the occasion for authentic study, dialogue, and the engendering of peace and reconciliation among friends who not only study together but play together, share information about their beliefs and rituals with one another, and work together for the improvement of our common life.

One of the more promising new developments is the publication of a series of 17 volumes on *Religions in American Life,* edited by Jon Butler and Harry S. Stout, for Oxford University Press. The series is designed for youth in a public school setting in order to engage them in understanding the significant role religion has played and still plays in American life. The authors have sought to focus on "teaching about religion," as the Supreme Court has underscored, rather than teaching for commitment to any particular religious tradition. The series is comprehensive. Early book titles are *Church and State in America, Religions in 19th Century America, Religions in Twentieth-Century America, Alternative American Religions,* and *Native American Religions.* Volumes on more specific aspects of American religious experiences are on Jews, Mormons, Orthodox, Roman Catholics, Protestants, Muslims, Buddhists, Hindus, and Sikhs. Finally, books on immigration and religion, African American religious issues, and women and American religion address special contemporary concerns. The complete set costs $374.00, or $22.00 each.

What is needed, along with these volumes, are teachers who are educated and oriented not only in the subjects of religion in American life but in an open, dialogical way of engaging students. Meeting such a need for professional development will demand a reassessment of the responsibilities of college and university departments of education and religious studies as well as schools of theology.

A Strategy for the Development of Public Churches That Will Address and Act On Controversial Public Issues, Courageously Seeking Understanding, Forgiveness, and Reconciliation

Martin Marty called for mainline, evangelical, and Catholic churches to reclaim a vision of a church that is committed to the well-being of all people — the public, not just their own constituents. Marty, in 1981, recognized a tendency toward incivility in our country. He observed ahead of his time, "The decline of civility has not reached crisis proportions in North America, but there is a disturbing decline of faith in the value of civility."[22] Marty believed that the public church must be turned out to all peoples who are suffering, trapped in social or political boxes that hurt or abuse. He also maintained that the public church should be concerned about the authenticity of the gospel of love and justice for individuals but be against primitivism, tribalism, and totalism. Faith that is genuine and deep must be personal but not insensitive to societal issues of civil rights for all, especially minority groups. The Christian faith in order to be authentic must be social but not in an ingrown tribalistic way where only "our people are in or saved." The Christian faith needs to be open and enjoying of the total scene but not totalistic in the sense that there is only one way for all people to believe or act. Marty reminds us that Christian leaders in early America had a vision that saw the country with a manifest destiny, on a mission to the wider world. Such a vision had certain unrealities within it, but some aspects of the passion for civic welfare must be recaptured. Civil righteousness was emphasized by Augustine, Calvin, Luther, and others who preached about a God who calls us to produce good for all, even for people who do not know God in Christian terms. This theme is also solidly biblical.[23]

The need for forgiveness, reconciliation, and moral courage in society is extremely great today. We *are now* in a crisis of civility. On every hand we see extreme examples of incivility, especially in public education with the series of shootings, deaths, and injuries in our schools climaxing in Columbine High School in Littleton, Colorado. Issues such as homelessness, malnutrition in many parts of the world, the ignoring of basic civil rights between various religious groups around the world, and between Christians, Muslims, and Jews in the United States where efforts have taken place to protect civil rights and at the same time to deal with the threat of terrorism — all call for churches to get involved in action, and in study informed by action.

In our survey of the four congregational groups we found considerable confusion about the church's involvement in social problems and especially about the issue of forgiveness and reconciliation (i.e., the amnesty offered by the Truth and Reconciliation Commission in South Africa, President Clinton's request for forgiveness of the U.S. government for not caring for

22. Martin Marty, *The Public Church: Mainline-Evangelical-Catholic* (New York: Crossroad, 1981), p. xi.
23. Marty, *The Public Church*, p. 168.

black men who died because they were involved in a syphilis experiment, etc.). Many people agreed that the major source of forgiveness and reconciliation is the individual's faith in Christ's death and resurrection, given to all of us as a gift from God. Most also saw that it is a positive thing to work with non-Christians to strengthen the moral fiber of society. Several affirmed the importance of moral education and development along with parent education. There was also awareness that there are good, moral people who are not Christian. Such views, however, were often in conflict with the tendency to make commitment to Christ as the central source of reconciliation or even the only source of forgiveness and reconciliation.

One person in the Pentecostal church expressed the conflict well when she said, "When you try to bring all kinds of people together without Christ it is a social gospel. It is a lifeless thing. . . . When you bring true believers together with people of other religions you do not have reconciliation: because it is only in Jesus Christ that we find reconciliation with God. We cannot compromise on anything."

Our position is: faithful members of the public church can celebrate God's greatest gift of forgiveness and reconciliation on a personal basis while at the same time accepting the call to servanthood to the outcasts, the hungry, the dispossessed, those in need of health care, education, moral and spiritual development, and especially interpersonal and intergroup forgiveness and reconciliation. The public church enables the members of the body of Christ to become "Christ" to their neighbors, near and far.

For instance, after a student in Heath High School in Paducah, Kentucky, went on a shooting spree that killed three and wounded five of his classmates, a Christian group of youth, called Chrysalis, decided to seek forgiveness and reconciliation among their classmates and in the community. They taped posters in the halls saying, "We forgive you, Mike." The group, normally about 35 students, swelled to some two hundred the day after the shooting. One of the wounded girls, paralyzed by a bullet, sent a message to the group expressing her forgiveness for the assailant. Ministers and church members volunteered to serve on a crisis ministry team to help counsel students and parents, and to minister to the families of those killed or injured. The church through its youth and others moved out to serve and care in Christ's name.[24]

Following Martin Marty's lead, religious educators have called for a refocusing of the task of religious education. The early leaders of the

---

24. Cynthia B. Astle, "Students Return Forgiveness for Shooting," *United Methodist Review*, December 26, 1997, p. 3.

Sunday School movement in England and the United States were concerned deeply about the education of the poor and dispossessed children and youth in society. The Sunday Schools were formed in order to improve the education, health, and general welfare of children who worked long hours in factories and shops and were not in school. The concern was to improve the quality of life of the public. By mid-1800s the Sunday Schools were adopted by the churches and became wings of denominational ministries. The domestication of religious education started and accelerated over the years until the original purpose to improve society has largely been lost today. Christian religious education (even with the Religious Education Movement with its emphasis on child-centered learning, graded curriculum, and the social gospel [1903+], Christian education with its attempt to deal biblically and theologically with human sin and failure [1940+], or the focus on a biblical theology that recaptured the importance of education of all members of the body of Christ to be prepared for ministry [1950+], and more recent expressions of Christian religious education) still tends to be concerned heavily with internal nurture and building up the church rather than external extensions of God's love and truth into the very fabric of our public life.

Something of the vision of early Sunday School leaders such as Robert Raikes needs to be recaptured, say Jack Seymour, Robert O'Gorman, and Charles Foster in their 1981 book about the importance of a church education for a public church. They agreed with Marty: "The church and the public cannot be separated. They are not substances to be dichotomized. The church and religion are rather part of the public, always influencing the public and it is necessary for the church to understand this participation and claim it. Our thesis is that faith communities are the only intentional agencies within the public that have primary responsibility for the religious. For the church to restrict its educational ministry to itself ignores this crucial responsibility."[25]

The task of church education is to shape a public character, a consciousness of the necessity of reconciling the world to God, as Horace Bushnell said, and to heal divisions — ethnic, cultural, racial, sexual, the "haves and have-nots," and the religious (the most generous source of divisiveness often clouded by political and economic factors). The church needs to recover its prophetic voice and its world-shaping responsibility. Such an undertaking must be done in cooperation with the family, schools, media, community, and governmental agencies so that a comprehensive and coordinated pro-

---

25. Jack L. Seymour, Robert T. O'Gorman, and Charles R. Foster, *The Church in the Education of the Public: Refocusing the Task of Religious Education* (Nashville: Abingdon, 1981), p. 21.

gram of education for the whole person and the whole community can take place.[26] Seymour, O'Gorman, and Foster see church education of the public church to include the following: (1) a mediation of a sense of transcendence in public life; (2) a development of religious imagination which is sacramental in nature, one that sees all reality in terms of the presence of God even as God became flesh in Jesus Christ; (3) a nourishing of our quest for universal justice by infusing the world with sacramental imagination; (4) being responsible in the public arena "for gathering people into and shaping the common life of both the nation and the global community. This calls for a new kind of consciousness and relationship of each agency to the whole, an awareness of a new learning system in which the church plays a central and crucial role."[27] Such a stance has slowly but surely influenced the actions and attitudes of the contemporary church.

One of the most convincing proponents of the public church is James Fowler. Starting in the 1980s he and his colleagues sought to define the characteristics of a congregation that genuinely is both deeply nurturing of a committed inward faith journey and a covenanted commitment to an outward journey to meet common human needs and change dehumanizing social and political structures. Fowler's team of researchers identified seven characteristics of what they called a public church and invited civic and church leaders to nominate congregations that met their guidelines. From the 17 congregations nominated they chose three for in-depth study. The three churches were Cornerstone African Methodist Episcopal Church, Saint Stephen's Episcopal Church, and Covenant Baptist Church. All three are located in Atlanta, Georgia.

The seven characteristics of a public church the Fowler team defined are (as paraphrased):

1. The public church fosters a clear sense of Christian identity and commitment. The congregation has certain clear boundaries and criteria for being a faithful member. Membership preparation and formation are very important. There are expectations that covenants and agreements to be in specific forms of ministry will be made, meeting certain standards of accountability.
2. Public churches have a diverse membership. The policies, programs, and personnel of the church make it clear that diversity (racial, ethnic, class, theological differences, etc.) is valued. Members can be in minis-

---

26. Seymour, O'Gorman, and Foster, *The Church in the Education of the Public*, p. 117.
27. Seymour, O'Gorman, and Foster, *The Church in the Education of the Public*, p. 144.

try with other persons or groups from varying religions or no religious backgrounds because they are well grounded enough to be open. They are prepared to deal with controversial issues in a nondefensive and nondestructive way.

3. A public church consciously prepares and supports members for a sense of vocation and witness in a pluralistic society. Faithful members can share the good news of Christ's love through their attitudes and actions as they work with a variety of Christians and non-Christians. They recognize that persons other than Christians experience the presence and power of God. They are trained to embrace a dialogue in the public arena as they address controversial issues in a civil manner. They are trained in approaches to conflict mediation and skills of persuasion rather than coercion. Public churches are communities where the stranger is welcome and where there is a safe space (a campus) where persons can struggle over issues that matter the most for the common good of society.

4. A public church balances nurture and group solidarity within the congregation with accountability in one's vocation in work and public life beyond the walls of the church.

   A sense of vocation is essential for all Christians from children to "retired" persons. It is not related only to work (important!) but to one's response to the call to be in partnership with God in all of life. It includes our leisure, our work, our roles as citizens, as members of family, social, political, and religious groups. Public churches especially support members to be in ministry around the problems that occur in large-scale economic, political, commercial, and religious structures that make life full or cause deep wounds (oppression, poverty, inadequate food, housing, education, jobs, opportunities for growth, etc.). Instead of membership meaning the maintenance of the church's internal program, membership also means to equip people for their vocation in the wider world of the marketplace, the legislative halls, the hospitals, the schools, the efforts of peacemaking and ecological renewal.

5. The public church evolves a way for pastoral and lay leadership to be in fruitful balance. The public church's governance pattern avoids personalizing issues and tries to develop skills in leadership that invite diverse voices in the dialogue prior to decision-making. Consensus is sought. Serious attempts to forgive and reconcile are made when divisions occur. Pastors risk vulnerability in order to enable the empowerment of lay ministry and the meeting of common goals within and beyond the congregation.

6. The public church offers its witness in publicly visible and intelligible ways.

The commitment to the gospel of love and justice for all is seen in the budget of the congregation and in the ministry of the members through their witness, service, advocacy, lobbying, and at times, protest. The goal is to live *publicly* the congregation's version of the gospel story.

7. The public church shapes a pattern of *paideia* for all — children, youth, adults — that combines individual commitment with vocation in the world.

The congregation is committed to the disciplines of prayer, common worship and sacramental life, study of scriptures and the issues of the day. *Paideia* is much more than instruction or education in the schooling sense. It involves a wide-ranging participation in the total life of the faith community in its proclamation, spiritual life, community discernment, apprenticeship engagement in mission, ongoing development in faith, and personal and social transformation.[28]

The seven characteristics were used by Fowler and his team to analyze the strengths of the three churches mentioned above. Rather than describing the details of those three excellent public churches, we will recommend Fowler's 1991 book, *Weaving the New Creation: Stages of Faith and the Public Church*.[29] In order to see how he has deepened his work on the stages of faith in the life cycle and how he has related his stages to an analysis of major social/political/theological movements of our time, we also recommend his 1996 book, *Faithful Change: The Personal and Public Challenges of Postmodern Life*.[30] James Fowler is continuing his work on the public church as the Candler Professor and director of the Center for Ethics in Public Policy and the Professions at Emory University.

With Fowler's characteristics of the public church in the background, we will present two other illustrations of effective public churches. One is an outgrowth of the well-known Church of the Saviour in Washington, D.C., the Seekers Church. The second is *The Church in the City* project of the Catholic Diocese of Cleveland, Ohio, involving all the congregations in the diocese along with many churches of other Christian denominations and congregations from other world religions. The Cleveland diocese is seriously working to encourage all local congregations to address the central problems

28. Fowler, *Weaving the New Creation*, pp. 155-62.
29. Fowler, *Weaving the New Creation*, pp. 155-62.
30. Cited in full in n. 6 above.

of the city as extensions of Christ's love and justice for all humankind and nature.

First, the Seekers Church is the result of the recognition by the pastor of the Church of the Saviour, Gordon Cosby, that the church had grown too large (140 members) to command the same level of commitment and covenant that it had. So, the Church of the Saviour was disbanded in order that nine smaller, more focused churches could be born, centered around specific needed public ministries in Washington, D.C. The Seekers Church is one of the nine. The focus of the church's ministry is on child advocacy. There are now 24 members of the church. Each member brings particular gifts and sees his or her ministry as a total commitment. Becoming a member in the Church of the Saviour has been seen essentially as an ordination. Prospective members are required to take a two-year course of study. The courses are: Old Testament, New Testament, Christian Growth, and Christian Doctrine. Classes are kept small and personal in order for genuine integration to take place. Members meet weekly. Attendance is mandatory except for certain circumstances. The group meetings include creative liturgical life, sharing, prayer, and work on the group's mission. An advance agreement is that the church will disband when the mission is considered complete and will reformulate around another public ministry. Children of the members are invited to be participants in the liturgical celebrations and in the mission where feasible. Members tithe, at least. Fifty percent of the annual budget of $190,000 goes to outside child advocacy groups and agencies in which particular Seekers members are involved as a part of their ministry. Approximately four times as many people attend Sunday services as are members. Membership requirements are not lowered to gain more people. If people continue to attend services but do not agree to make a covenanted commitment it is suggested that they may want to find another church that correlates better with their needs. If participants do make a commitment they agree to be in a specific form of ministry and write a weekly report of what is going on in their lives and share it with a spiritual companion, seen as a "faithful friend." Members not only take leadership roles in their public ministry, they lead worship — including preaching; some members are lawyers who advocate for children and families at HUD (Housing and Urban Development); others operate Hope and a Home, a 17-unit building that houses poor families with children and helps them become self-sufficient; others work with issues around child welfare and education. The church recently decided to make an offer on a building where they can open a coffeehouse/bookstore in order to involve Capitol Hill workers who might participate in lunchtime policy discussions about children.

Seekers feel that their church is "their life," "their spiritual home," "their family." One Seeker captured the main thrusts of the ministry when she said, ". . . [W]e need to help mothers and kids with a place to thrive; we need to change public policy; we need to educate our own children about what it means to live out the gospel mandate."[31]

Other public churches that emerged from the original Church of the Saviour are organized similarly around such public ministries as housing, jobs, health, addiction, homelessness, etc. The total community still relates to the Potter's House, the School for Christian Living, For Love of Children (for unwanted or abandoned children), a retreat center, and a Sunday ecumenical service where Gordon Cosby preaches the gospel for both the inner journey of each soul and the outer journey of ministries in the public arena.

The second illustration is quite different. It has to do with a large Catholic diocese, seeking to interrelate all of the congregations as partners in confronting the real issues of people in the Cleveland diocese in an attempt to bring the reign of God's love and justice alive for the common good.

Anthony M. Pilla, bishop of the diocese, has provided strong and sensitive leadership in the initiation and implementation of *The Church in the City* effort. Aware of the destructive results of outward migration to suburbs that have taken place over the past 40 years, the diocese has tried to bring parishioners from suburb and inner-city churches together as partners — as equals — in order to study the issues; to increase communication and a sense of Christian community; to identify changes that need to be made in church and governmental policies; to work with other Christian and interfaith groups to advocate changes that will make life wholesome for all. Outmigration and urban sprawl have caused a shift in the tax base so that resources for education, jobs, social services, housing, and governmental agencies have gone down in the cities of Cleveland, Akron, Lorain, and Elyria while resources in the suburbs have gone up. Sprawl has moved jobs needed by inner-city persons to the suburbs; transportation and housing needs in order to get people and jobs together are often not met. More recently, suburbs are experiencing similar problems to the inner cities as migration continues to move farther out to exurbia, leaving the suburbs underfunded. The outmigration is also eating up farmland and harming rural life. Churches in the central cities are experiencing severe losses in membership and leadership while the problems of poverty, drug and alcohol abuse among youth and adults, marital and family disintegration, etc. are increasing.

31. Paul Wilkes, *Excellent Protestant Congregations* (Louisville, London, Leiden: Westminster/John Knox, 2001), p. 24.

Bishop Pilla's pastoral letter, introducing *The Church in the City* strategy, bases the program on five principles.

1. *Social justice:* Going beyond charity to changing the underlying causes of the problems, focusing on policies and practices of federal, state, and local government.

2. *Redevelopment:* Changing governmental policies that favor development of new suburbs (not negative per se) but neglecting the redevelopment of central cities. Likewise, church development is out of balance, with too much emphasis on building larger and larger suburban parishes as central city parishes decline markedly.

3. *Interdependence:* Cities and suburbs are linked by a single economy. Also, suburban and city churches are linked with a common mission. Suburban and city churches are called to create partnerships around particular issues of justice and care.

4. *Restructuring:* Both suburban and city churches need to be restructured in order for needs to be met and for the churches to work together. Special attention is given to factors of cultural diversity.

5. *Preferential love for the poor:* With recognition that suburbs also have poor people, "... we must still admit that more and more the results of outmigration have contributed to the existence of two societies: one poor and living in the older cities, the other affluent and living in the outer suburbs. The love of Christ compels us to turn our attention to the needs of our poorer sisters and brothers, who have been most hurt by present policies."[32]

Since 1993 churches in suburbs and the central city have responded to the call to be in partnership in order to learn from one another concerning strengths and needs and in order to develop specific ministries that deal with regional planning and revitalization. A carefully planned handbook was created to assist parish leaders. *Partnering: An Experience in Unity — for Beginners and the Experienced* is a marvelous guide for any faith community seeking to be a public church.[33] The handbook includes grounding in Scripture and Vatican II foundations along with specific suggestions on how to build partnerships not only with rural, suburban, and city parishes but with other

32. Bishop Anthony M. Pilla, *The Church in the City* (Diocese of Cleveland, 1027 Superior Avenue, Cleveland, Ohio 44114), pp. 5 and 6.

33. *Partnering: An Experience in Unity — for Beginners and the Experienced* (Diocese of Cleveland, 1031 Superior Avenue, Cleveland, Ohio 44114).

non-Catholic Christian congregations and with those of other world religions. There is a strong focus on building relationships that transcend racial, socio-economic status or geographic area and recognize the unique gifts each person brings. Bishop Pilla has said wisely, "More can happen among friends than any of us can imagine. Not much, if anything, happens among strangers."[34] Each partnership, then, moves on to create a common vision as a basis for the agreement on a specific plan of action on an issue of crucial importance in the community.

The handbook presents stories concerning several creative partnerships and their projects. The partnerships range from three Catholic parishes (rural, suburban, and city) working together on the issue of outmigration, to a Catholic parish and a Baptist church working together on juvenile justice, to religious leaders and judicatory staff of Christian, Jewish, and Muslim faith communities in northeast Ohio working together on poverty and welfare reform issues. Such a cooperative history establishes the foundation for the understanding of the varying faith traditions so crucial in international relations in our difficult time.

The Church in the City project reveals that churches of varying sizes, locations, and resources can be public churches. It is true that smaller more closely knit teams must emerge, with committed agreements to care for one another and to serve a common cause. The matter of high commitment and standards of membership have been addressed in much more detail, from our perspective, in an earlier publication.[35]

The handbook has a rich resources section with liturgies, prayers, readings, and poetry. One liturgy says,

> . . . We have been silent too long.
> *God forgive us.*
> We have failed to act
> *Sister and brother, forgive us.*
> The time has come to act.
> *Together we seek to discern what to do. . . .*
> We call upon ourselves
>> to join in prayer, to break the silence; to speak the truth,
>> to reach out in friendship,

---

34. *Partnering: An Experience in Unity*, ch. 1, p. 2.

35. Robert L. Browning, "Belonging: A Sacramental Approach to Inclusion and Depth of Commitment," in C. Ellis Nelson, ed., *Congregations: Their Power to Form and Transform* (Atlanta: John Knox, 1988), pp. 166-92.

to break down walls of hate and division;
to appreciate the diversity God creates;
to seek to live together in love. . . .[36]

An Educational and Liturgical Effort

An illustration in which the authors were involved is the educational and liturgical efforts of the Ohio West Conference of the United Methodist Church. After careful study and serious thought concerning the United Methodist Church's history of involvement in slavery and its aftermath of racism, subtle and blatant, a decision was made to call the conference to confession, repentance, forgiveness, and reconciliation. The result of these efforts was a liturgy titled "To Act on Our Apology and to Celebrate Our Vision of a United Future." In a service designed by Dr. Robert Simmons of Centenary United Methodist Church, Columbus, Ohio, clergy and lay members of the conference praised God for eternal love and forgiveness, giving them courage to confess their sins of slavery and racism of the past and the present. The three thousand plus delegates prayed the prayer of confession: "Let the sound of your requirement of justice, O God, waken us from the slumber of denial, indifference, and complacency. We confess that fear limits us, personal agendas burden us, and denial undermines our capacity to accept responsibility for slavery, racism, and discrimination. Help us to confess the racial sins of those before us and to accept responsibility for the racism and discrimination of today. Forgive our failure to follow Christ and our deafness to hear the trumpets sound for justice."[37] Following the confession, pardon and forgiveness were offered and celebrated. While the confession, repentance, forgiveness, and the call for reconciliation took place publicly, it was still internally oriented toward members of the annual conference, but because it was a public act it received much attention from the press, a fact that influenced the general society in a powerful, authentic way. More important than these efforts at education and liturgy, however, are the actual acts of healing and repair that can and should follow — the true fruits of a genuine public church.

36. *Partnering: An Experience in Unity,* ch. 10, p. 4.
37. *A Service of Word: To Act on Our Apology and to Celebrate Our Vision of a United Future* (West Ohio Annual Conference, United Methodist Church, June 8, 1999).

CHAPTER 7

Moral and Spiritual Education
Linked to Sacramental/Liturgical Life

Moral and spiritual education has often been linked with sacramental and liturgical celebrations in the church. In Chapter 4 we have shared the history of the quest to deal with moral failure and sin through catechetical and sacramental/liturgical celebrations. The need to help members of the faith community deal with their sins of separation from others, God, and themselves is perennial. Roman Catholics and Orthodox have developed and refined the Sacrament of Penance or Confession to meet the need for confession, forgiveness, and reconciliation. Later, the refinement of Penance to be the Sacrament of Reconciliation invited a fresh dialogue with Protestants and Orthodox.

In this chapter we will explore ways to learn from one another. We shall examine how the changes within Catholicism and the Orthodox community resonate with Protestant views and expressed needs. We shall explore patterns and resources in Catholic and Orthodox educational and liturgical life and their transfer potential for Protestant churches. We shall present a case study of a Roman Catholic church's educational and liturgical designs for the celebration of the Sacrament of Reconciliation with children, youth, parents, and whole congregations. We shall also highlight a Protestant pattern with potential for Catholic and Orthodox communities. Finally, we shall identify several important clues for moral and spiritual education that come from our study of the four churches. Specific resources will be highlighted for each clue in order that experimentation can take place and we can move closer and closer in our understanding of mutual ministry.

As you read these suggestions, keep dialoguing with yourself or others about what we can learn from one another and what changes in our present educational, liturgical, or sacramental life are possible and desirable.

In an earlier book, *The Sacraments in Religious Education and Liturgy: An Ecumenical Model* (1985), we rejoiced in a movement within Protestantism to be more open to some form of individual confession and reconciliation to accompany the already affirmed forms of general confession in corporate worship. We cited the movement to reform the Sacrament of Penance within the Roman Catholic Church, a movement away from a legalistic and substantialistic confession/absolution, given by the priest, to a relational and personal/corporate interpretation. The latter resulted in the changing of the name to the Sacrament of Reconciliation with its emphasis on the importance of the total congregation as the community of faith in which confessions are heard, and in which forgiveness and reconciliation come from God through the priest, who represents the forgiving and renewing congregation. The emphasis on the forgiveness that comes from God through the priest and the congregation opened the door to a dialogue with Protestant and Orthodox churches on possible fresh agreements in respect to sacramental theology, religious education, and liturgy. The dialogue has continued, especially in our theological schools with students who have experimented on their own in their parishes. Some constructive study and reformulation have taken place in formal ecumenical commissions or study groups within denominations, especially the Episcopal, Lutheran, Roman Catholic, and Orthodox communities.

We also highlighted the corporate nature of the ministry of confession, forgiveness, restitution, and reconciliation. The Catholic and Orthodox liturgies provide a communal celebration with opportunity for individual confession during and after corporate worship. While both faith communities offer individual confession and absolution, the Catholic Church's new rituals emphasize the representative nature of the priest's role within the whole body of Christ, and the Orthodox liturgy in style and substance has been generally open, interactive, and personal. The Catholic Sacrament of Reconciliation also provides for communal reconciliation without individual confession and absolution. The communal option represents a move toward the general confession found in many Protestant liturgies.[1] The major change in the thinking over the past fifteen or twenty years has been the emphasis on the loving nature of God who calls us to be a loving, supportive, honest, open, forgiving, and reconciling community of faith, whether Protestant, Catholic, or Ortho-

---

1. Robert L. Browning and Roy A. Reed, *The Sacraments in Religious Education and Liturgy: An Ecumenical Model* (Birmingham, Ala.: Religious Education Press, 1985), pp. 254-59.

dox. The call for confession is a call from the God of love and justice revealed in Christ, whose loving, caring community invites all of us to be transparent, to share our love, faith, and hope, and to face honestly when and how we may have failed to live out in practice such a Christ-centered life. Such a focus on the love of God creates an environment where we can open our inner lives to God, to one another, and even to ourselves; share our honest pilgrimages with God and others in our families and in the church family; share our joys, which have come from being channels of God's love to others; and share our fears, which have kept us centered in ourselves in self-protection rather than trusting God, others, and ourselves (our sin). This more positive attitude about the sacramental aspects of confession, forgiveness, and reconciliation can be seen in both new religious education designs and in fresh liturgical forms. The approach is often undergirded by a careful program of faith and moral development with parents, teachers, and leaders at all age levels.

There has not been a groundswell for an ecumenical Sacrament of Reconciliation since our earlier suggestions concerning its high potential in our society. However, at the very moment of the writing of this chapter the *Christian Century* has an article titled "Bring Back Confession, Urges Reformed Pastor." J. J. Weij, from the Netherlands, is quoted as favoring a return of the sacrament of confession within Protestantism. His point is that people in our society need more opportunities to articulate their mistakes, share their sense of guilt, and make fresh starts. He states, "Many know the experience of guilt and need to speak out. That requires people who are able to listen and accept people where they are." The chairperson of the Reformed Churches in the Netherlands agreed that such a move could be very helpful as a form of pastoral care.[2] It is our belief that there are many more pastors and members of Protestant churches who share Pastor Weij's view. Such a trend is seen in the inclusion of services of individual and corporate confession, forgiveness, and reconciliation in the Lutheran Book of Worship, the Book of Common Prayer in the Episcopal Church, and in alternative books of worship in the United Methodist Church (in *From Ashes to Fire*), and in other faith communities.

2. "Bring Back Confession, Urges Reformed Pastor," *Christian Century,* August 11-18, 1999, p. 772.

Religious Education and Liturgical Life in the Roman Catholic and Greek Orthodox Churches with Transfer Potential for Protestant Churches

Since Vatican II the Roman Catholic Church has made a significant contribution to all of Christendom in its creative, positive approach to religious education and liturgy in respect to the Sacrament of Reconciliation. Church leaders recognized the negative reactions many otherwise faithful members had to the legalisms and unhealthy guilt sometimes accompanying the former Sacrament of Penance. As already mentioned, a concerted effort was made to change not only the basic concept of the sacrament but to change the expectations of participants and the ethos in which the sacrament is celebrated.

One way to change these realities was through a program of catechesis for children in relation to their participation in the other sacraments of the church, especially the Eucharist and Confirmation. This movement grew out of research on the catechism of the early church and the discovery of the power of the unified initiation found there: initiation into the body of Christ through careful preparation over a one- to three-year period followed by Baptism, Eucharist, and Confirmation, a pattern never abandoned in the eastern church. In the western church after Vatican II there have emerged several patterns of education and liturgical celebrations with an effort to interrelate the three sacraments of initiation either in a total unified way, as is the case in the Rite of Christian Initiation of Adults and its four-phase program of catechesis, or in a sequential but integrative way in which the child is baptized as an infant, is prepared for and celebrates communion at about age 7, and is confirmed either in the eighth grade or later in high school (depending on the diocese). In many dioceses bishops are now recommending the inclusion of the Sacrament of Reconciliation *before* the celebration of first Eucharist. This emerging pattern is designed to help children and their parents look more honestly and deeply into their inner lives to assess why they are in need of God's loving presence, affirmation, and forgiveness in every aspect of their lives, including their failures to love God, others, and themselves in honest and healthy ways.

Several curriculum designs have been published in order to help children in the second grade be prepared for participation in the Sacrament of Reconciliation. One of the best, from our perspective, is *We Celebrate Reconciliation: The Lord Forgives* by Christiane Brusselmans and Brian Haggerty, with the assistance of Jacquelyn Mallory (Morristown, N.J.: Silver Burdett & Ginn, 1990), with Catechist's Guide, Family Guide, and Student's Book. This curriculum is a very sensitive, affirming, caring approach to the experience of forgiveness and reconciliation. It culminates in joyous participation in the Sacrament of Reconciliation, usually on a corporate basis with opportunity for individual dialogue with the priest, during which the child can share actions or attitudes that are not in harmony with God's love as revealed in Christ (Confession), talk about the child's need for forgiveness and renewal through acts of restitution, and acts that bring spiritual growth, finally receiving absolution through the priest symbolizing absolution from God and the congregation.

The series reveals a relational interpretation of God's love and the importance of love from and for family, peers, and other human relations in the wider community. There is a strong recognition of the gifts God has given us, and a call to share those gifts with others. Sin is identified as the centering of life in the self too much and not being willing to share our gifts, our love, and our forgiveness with others. Children are invited to center their lives in Christ, as the branches are fruitful when they remain connected to the vine. The catechetical experience moves on to celebrate human freedom and the opportunity to make choices. Interactive learning is assisted through writing and discussions concerning choices made in the family, on the playground, in the classroom at school, or in the neighborhood. Persons who have revealed God's grace and love are used as models to guide the children in ways to make sound decisions and to share their lives with others: César Chávez, Sharon Christa McAuliffe, Francis of Assisi, Jesus and his parables and teachings.

The unit goes on to explore God's forgiving ways and God's call for us to forgive others and therefore to be willing to ask for forgiveness. Finally, the learners explore the church's invitation to participate in the Sacrament of Reconciliation. The graphics show a smiling priest helping a child share her love of God, share the result of her examination of her conscience, express where and how she has not loved or forgiven others, make her act of contrition either in her own words or following the act of contrition in the Rite of Reconciliation. The experience concludes with the priest making the sign of the cross and laying his hand on her head and saying, "God, the Father of Mercies, through the death and resurrection of his Son has reconciled the world to himself and sent the Holy Spirit among us for the forgiveness of sins; through the ministry of the church may God give you pardon and peace, and I absolve you from your sins in the name of the Father, and of the Son, and of the Holy Spirit."[3] Usually a penance is also agreed upon, identifying specific acts of kindness.

3. Christiane Brusselmans and Brian A. Haggerty, *We Celebrate Reconciliation: The Lord Forgives* (Morristown, N.J.: Silver Burdett & Ginn, 1990), p. 54.

Another curriculum that is positive and sensitive to theological and developmental issues is *First Reconciliation* (New York: William H. Sadlier Inc., 1997) by Dr. Gerald Baumbach et al. with Dr. Thomas Groome of Boston College. The Guide for Catechist and the study book again celebrate God's great love and mercy along with an emphasis on the sacrament as a healing gift of peace with a joyous invitation. Children are called to acknowledge that peace begins with each one of them in their relationships with God, others, and themselves. The curriculum resource is strong in its focus on full participation of the congregation as well as the families. It starts with a liturgy that is celebrated within the congregation at the time children, parents, and others begin a preparation process that culminates in the celebration of the Sacrament of Reconciliation.

The steps in the preparation process are clearly defined and explored: from the examination of conscience to sharing with the priest one's sins as unloving actions and attitudes, to the act of contrition and agreement concerning penance, to the joyous reception of absolution. This series helps children and families rejoice in being within the Catholic sacramental family, and it is less didactic and more relational than some other series such as *First Reconciliation: A Catechesis for Primary Grades* (Woodland Hills, Calif.: Benziger Publishing Co., 1996).

The Benziger series *is* affirming of the sacredness of all of life, of the child's life, of the church, and of the sacraments. While the student's book is interactive and colorful it is not as relational or as engagingly honest about a child's life as the Brusselmans and Haggerty approach or the Silver Burdett unit described above. The Benziger series gives much more attention to the nature of the Roman Catholic sacramental system. Starting with the Baptism of the Child, the sessions move quickly to Reconciliation and the roles of the priest, parents, and the catechists in the church's catechetical and liturgical celebration. There is much more concern to help the child learn right beliefs and right rules, to make correct choices, to examine his or her conscience, to confess, be contrite, seek forgiveness, do penance, and receive absolution. Each session has a reinforcing section titled "We Catholics Believe." The inclusion of such a section symbolizes the purpose of the series: to educate the child into the beliefs and practices of a good, faithful Catholic. The series also includes preparation for First Eucharist (primary and middle grades). The family is involved at all levels. Because of the strong emphasis on Catholic beliefs and practices rather than on more universally experiential issues of human strengths and failures related to the child's life, the series probably has less transfer values for most Protestant churches.

Sadlier has published another resource that emphasizes Roman Catholic basic doctrines while keeping its relational and positive approach: *Coming to Jesus* (New York: William H. Sadlier Inc., 1997), again with Dr. Thomas H. Groome as consultant. The curriculum resource includes an explanation of Catholic understandings concerning God, Christ, the Holy Spirit, the Catholic Church, and the local parish, with dialogue at all points. A section called "Faith Alive at Home and in the Parish" includes family Scripture moments. A unit addresses the Sacrament of Reconciliation, following the preparation themes in the earlier Sadlier series above. Two additional units study the nature of the Eucharist and preparation to celebrate the Eucharist. The series concludes with a summary review and a very brief test that looks back at core ideas in language that children can absorb. The series can be useful to those seeking to interrelate preparation for Reconciliation prior to First Eucharist preparation and celebration.

It must be said that Benziger publishes additional resources to help a congregation achieve its goals in the preparation for the Sacrament of Reconciliation. The two resources are for primary grades and middle grades. They are quite specific in nature with worksheets for preparatory meetings with parents, forms for use in instruction, bulletin inserts, invitation letters, mini-retreat patterns, handouts, bibliography of books and tapes, a Family Activity Day to bring together the children, their families, the catechists, and the parish staff to reflect on the formation of conscience and the parts of the Sacrament of Reconciliation.[4]

Another resource that takes a positive stance about the nature of God's love, sin, and reconciliation is *In the Lord's Peace,* published by Our Sunday Visitor. The series prepares children for their first Reconciliation. An effort is made to help families and children deal with any possible negative feelings they may bring to the sacrament. The catechists are helped to understand the moral thinking of children ages 7 to 9, as well as Catholic moral thinking. The religious potential of children is underscored. The series addresses well children's inner world, their feelings about doing wrong, seeking forgiveness, and peace within themselves and in their daily lives in the wider world. *A Family Prayer* included in the series captures the tone of the curriculum:

The Response: *Father, forgive us.*

Leader: Father, you give us this family. You give us each other to love. But we are not always loving.

---

4. *Resources for Primary-Grade Sacramental Preparation: Eucharist and Reconciliation* (Mission Hills, Calif.: Benziger, 1989), and *Resources for Middle-Grade Sacramental Preparation: Eucharist and Reconciliation* (Mission Hills, Calif.: Benziger, 1989).

> Someone wants a hug, and we hold it back,
> Someone wants us to listen, and we close our ears,
> Someone wants us to talk, and we are silent,
> Someone needs quiet, and we are noisy,
> Someone wants us to share, and we are selfish,
> Someone wants our forgiveness, and we say no,
> Someone wants the truth, and we tell lies,
> Someone gets more than we do, and we are jealous,
> Someone hurts us, and we get even,
> Someone says no to what we want, and we pout,
>
> All: Father, for our sins, we are sorry. Help us to forgive one another as you forgive us. Reconcile us. Help us to be more loving and peaceful.
> Amen.[5]

This prayer transfers with power to all faith communities — Protestant, Orthodox, and even other world religions. The series then continues with preparation concerning a relational approach to participation of children, families, and the congregation in the Sacrament of Reconciliation.

Greek Orthodox Preparation of Children for the Sacrament of Confession

As would be expected, the Greek Orthodox curriculum unit having to do with the Sacrament of Confession employs icons and biblical and other stories that apply well to the world of young children (second grade). There is no special curriculum or programs for the Sacrament of Confession as the Catholic Church has developed. Rather, the unit is built into the regular curricular design. The timing of first confession is the same as Catholic designs, the second grade. A unit inside of a course written by Theodore Kaltsounis, professor of education, University of Washington, well illustrates several of the Orthodox themes and ways of preparing children for their first Confession. The series, *Loving God*, is very positive about life and its fullness. The unit on Confession starts with the joy of God's love for us and our love for God and others. There is a use of icons (pictures) showing God's love coming to us through Jesus, our parents, marriage (Sacrament of Love), Communion (an-

---

5. Patricia O'Brien Fischer, *In the Lord's Peace* (teacher and student books) (Huntington, Ind.: Our Sunday Visitor Publishing Division, 1996), p. 76.

other sacrament of God's love through Christ); through icons, which show our love for God; through the church, which is a community of love; through God's forgiveness and our response in the Sacrament of Confession; and through symbols that help us show our love for God and the saints. The unit ends with an emphasis on the meaning of love: to serve others in need, to respect others (our community leaders, church leaders, the saints, and our contemporary guides). Finally, love means obeying rules that help us live together at home and in the wider worlds of play and school.

Employing an icon concerning the prodigal son, the teaching plan helps children discuss the prodigal son's misuse of his father's resources; his "coming to himself" and recognizing his wrong, coming home to confess the error of his ways and seek forgiveness; his father's loving forgiveness; and his brother's jealous refusal to forgive. The child is asked to look at his or her own behavior and attitudes via a simple self-assessment instrument and a dialogue triggered by the use of three types of tape used to repair or mend broken things. These activities and a "Forgive me" game help the children bring the learning about forgiveness alive in their own settings.

The Sacrament of Confession is then seen as ". . . an important way to ask God to forgive us." The icons concerning the sacraments are quite straightforward and simple, in relation to which the child is invited to consider the following steps: (1) "You decide to tell God you are sorry. (2) You go and tell the priest what you did wrong. (3) The priest tells you how to be good. (4) The priest asks God to forgive you and blesses you."[6] Such a discussion within the context of church education apparently assumes considerable follow-up by priests and parents in order to help the children be prepared to participate actively in the Sacrament of Confession. The icons of the girl and the priest show a warm and open setting before an icon of Jesus, with the girl and the priest in a face-to-face dialogue concerning her sense of sin and the priest's accepting spirit, followed by the use of a stole over the child's head and the priest's words of absolution. The third step in the curriculum says that the priest ". . . tells you how to be good." This step, we hope, will be done in a dialogical way with the child and the priest talking about a sense of contrition and agreeing on some way (penance) that the child can make good on his or her sincere desire to correct a wrong. The lack of clarity about this step is one of the weakest parts of this particular unit. The open nature of the child and the priest meeting before the icon implies more equality of participation rather than a one-way confession behind a screen, followed by a peni-

---

6. Theodore Kaltsounis, *Loving God* (Brookline, Mass.: Department of Education, Greek Orthodox Archdiocese of North and South America, 1990), pp. 64, 65.

tential admonition and absolution by the priest (the more traditional pattern). The actual dynamics of this relationship obviously are determined not only by the theology behind the sacrament and the priest's understanding of the child before him, but also his personality within the context of the cultural expectations present in differing settings. Again we find considerable transfer.

How One Parish Prepares Families to Celebrate
the Sacrament of Reconciliation

It was our hope to illustrate concretely how a parish program of preparation and celebration actually takes place in a constructive and engaging way. The diocesan office of Christian Education recommended that we talk with a director of Christian Education who was doing a superior job of developing and coordinating a positive educational and liturgical approach to the celebration of the sacrament. Mary Fran Cassidy, director of religious education for St. Brigid of Kildare Parish in Dublin, Ohio, was recommended, and we visited her parish and interviewed her concerning the various phases of the St. Brigid program. Mary Fran has some strong feelings about the past misuses of the Sacrament of Penance and has committed herself to helping children and their parents find a positive, deeply meaningful, and relevant experience as they participate in the present forms of the Sacrament of Reconciliation. Her feelings were so strong that when the bishop was considering the policy of having children in the second grade be prepared for their first confession, she had said to herself, "If I am forced to have the sacrament for second graders, I will resign." When the bishop did make that recommendation she did not resign; rather, she pledged to herself to make the preparation and the celebration a natural and positive experience for children, their parents, and the whole parish. She was so anxious not only because many parents had expressed their fears about an early first confession, but because she brought many negative memories out of her own past experience. The bishop had decided to have the first celebration of the Sacrament of Reconciliation *before* the child's first Eucharist. At the time of her own preparation for First Communion and First Confession the two sacraments were linked. Mary Fran remembered her own fears when a nun had prepared her for her own confession prior to Eucharist by saying, "Be very careful and do not sin between now and tomorrow when you receive Communion."

She also shared another experience where she had gone to confession and had "poured out her soul" only to have the priest behind the screen not respond at all to her real hurts, only asking her to give the number of her sins so he could ask her to do so many acts of penance. That experience, taking place in college when she was studying theology, soured her on confession.

Mary Fran said, "I didn't want them to be taught sin. I want them to be taught love." In this light Mary Fran tried to prepare second graders and their parents by starting with God's love for us and our love for God. And, in the Sacrament of Reconciliation the focus should be on our nonloving choices. The concept of sin, then, is choosing to do what we already know to be wrong or hurtful to others. The feeling that children should have is, "Anytime we are sorry, we can tell God and know we are loved and will be forgiven."

With her positive views in mind, Mary Fran worked with parents, priests, catechists, and the total congregation to design the various phases of the Reconciliation program of preparation and celebration. While the sacrament is celebrated every week at St. Brigid Church, a special celebration for First Reconciliation takes place in early December. Preparation sessions for parents of second graders are scheduled for early October, followed by a session with parents of third and fourth graders and a final session with parents of second, third, and fourth graders in November. Many parents have not been regular participants in the weekly Reconciliation services and are in need of a fresh understanding of the sacrament and opportunities to share their experiences and raise questions about their own participation as well as their children. Children study about the meaning of the Sacrament of Reconciliation in their regular religious education classes or in their parochial school classes at St. Brigid, again employing a positive curriculum approved by the diocese. Fifth-, sixth-, and seventh-grade students in both settings study more deeply the nature of Reconciliation and also issues in moral development and decision-making. Eighth graders in their preparation for Confirmation again go more deeply into both moral development and the Sacrament of Reconciliation, participating in the sacrament along the way and especially prior to their Confirmation. High school students deepen their understanding in course patterns but especially during retreats where the sacrament is celebrated and individual and group confession, forgiveness, and absolution are experienced. Adults are prepared through adult education experiences, and through participation on teams of facilitation for parents' meetings, for a major Reconciliation Workshop for the whole congregation during Lent, and as sponsors in the preparation of catechumens who are moving toward adult Baptism, Confirmation, Reconciliation, and Eucharist, usually at the Easter vigil.

Special parent sessions include the following:

Parents of Second Graders: A discussion is held concerning ways in which families already practice reconciliation in their daily lives. They then share ways children are already dealing with issues of contrition and forgiveness. They move on to a discussion of the fresh emphases in the Sacrament of Reconciliation and why second-grade children are invited to experience these. Then, they explore the First Reconciliation celebration and their first Confession (whenever they look into their lives to see in what ways they may have made nonloving or hurtful choices). Careful discussion of the roles of parents, catechists, facilitators, and priests takes place in relation to the service of Reconciliation during Advent, at which time children may join their parents in the service of corporate confession and reconciliation but also participate in their first individual confession. Parents are helped to understand that the individual confession will take place in a side room where a priest will meet the child either face to face or behind a screen, in whichever way the child is most comfortable.

Parents of Third Graders: At this session issues of children's religious and moral development will be discussed. Guidelines from the Diocesan Plan for Reconciliation will be reviewed in relation to the child's readiness for individual confession and the examination of conscience that each child will be helped to understand in religious education classes. Mary Fran then outlines the educational and liturgical program at St. Brigid: How parents can participate at home and prior to the special Reconciliation services in Advent and Lent. Parents are also alerted to the Reconciliation Workshop for parents and children in Lent.

Parents of Fourth Graders: This session provides an opportunity for parents to ask questions to clarify their understanding of the Sacrament of Reconciliation and the ways to cooperate in the program at St. Brigid. In case few questions are raised, a list of "Commonly Asked Questions" based on the catechism and the patterns at St. Brigid Church will be discussed. Again, parents will be reminded that Reconciliation is a sacrament celebrated each week. Also, the Advent and Lenten special services will be reviewed with attention to parental values and how they may participate along with their children.

Parents of Second, Third, and Fourth Graders: A follow-up session in February for parents of children in all three grades will take place with a focus on "Reconciliation and Conscience Formation." Here the issue of conscience examination will be probed in more depth, with sensitivity to various levels and ways to proceed — from the very simple in the second grade to the more complex in older childhood or youth and adulthood. The latter will be stimulated through the use of a video prepared by the Diocesan Department of Religious Education concerning adult examination of conscience. Questions will be raised and discussed specific to the fourth-grade study of Reconciliation and the upcoming Family Reconciliation Workshop for all family members during Lent. Parents and their children will all be invited to receive the sacrament at the climax of the workshop.

Parents of Fifth, Sixth, and Seventh Graders: No special sessions are suggested for these parents. However, they are invited to the Family Workshop and other churchwide celebrations, especially Reconciliation Services for fifth graders in early March and a special celebration for sixth and seventh graders later in March. Participation in weekly reconciliation services is encouraged. However, attendance is still spotty. Parents and children tend to opt for designated churchwide special celebrations where eight to ten priests are present and have been especially prepared to be sensitive to the experiences and concerns of children and their families.

Eighth-Grade Students and Parents Preparing for Confirmation: One parent-student meeting is planned in preparation for Confirmation in September. Special attention is given to receiving the Sacrament of Reconciliation during the Day of Recollection prior to Confirmation. The Day of Recollection is usually for a full day in which confirmands meet with priests for a more intense discussion of Reconciliation and what it means for the lives of teenagers. The format is informal with icebreaker experiences shared in order to open communication between all the youth, their catechists, facilitators, priests, and any parents. Usually an inspirational speaker is invited to share the meaning of faith in his or her own life and dialogue honestly with the youth concerning life issues they are bringing with them. The last speaker was the star quarterback of the Ohio State University football team. Skits are designed by the youth concerning the real temptations they experience on a daily basis. Guided meditations are planned and experienced. A video such as the *Dead Poets Society* may be used, followed by small group discussions. A personalized "letter from God" is given to each youth as a stimulus to each person to write a letter *to* God during the Reconciliation service to follow later.

After lunch other group activities take place, such as a trust walk, or a small group prayer writing session during which personal intentions in each pilgrimage of faith are shared and lifted up in prayer — and finally placed in helium balloons that are then released into the sky.

Mass is celebrated during the day, and finally all share in the Sacrament of Reconciliation with both group and individual confession. The letters written to God are shared during this concluding liturgy at the time of the offering.

High School Youth and Parents: No special session for parents of high school youth is planned. However, parental cooperation in the total program of education and service is invited. Especially is this so for high school retreats, where issues of moral living (personal responsibility, caring relationships, respect, commitment to a life of truthfulness and integrity) are addressed in an informal setting. A celebration of the Sacrament of Reconciliation is always a part of the retreat and is seen as highly relevant and personally meaningful.

The Reconciliation Workshop for the Family

St. Brigid Church is in a growing suburb and is quite large. The director of religious education heads a large team of lay and religious leaders who play important, even crucial roles in many of the sacramental celebrations or preparatory sessions. As many as ten priests are invited to be celebrants. These priests are chosen for their openness and sensitivity to children, youth, and their families. They are given orientation concerning the various stations they will be in and how to function in the large sanctuary with its multiple Reconciliation rooms adjacent to the sanctuary. They are also invited to be a part of the Reconciliation Workshop so that parents, children, and youth will be able to relate to them comfortably and with trust.

In order to show how the director of religious education works with the several facilitators chosen, we shall present the *Facilitator's Guide* for the Reconciliation Workshop held on March 6, 1999. We hope this more detailed set of guidelines will have value to others who might wish to design a Reconciliation Workshop for families. See Appendix B. The guide was prepared by the Columbus Diocesan Office of Religious Education. We ourselves participated in the workshop, which was very well attended. Mothers and fathers and children met in family groups with other family units to share their joys and to acknowledge, in playful but genuine exercises, their unloving attitudes and actions. In so doing they were prepared for the Sacrament of Reconciliation in the sanctuary. The atmosphere was joyous and honest. After the service one father said to his son, "Now, that wasn't so bad, was it?" Such a statement acknowledges that there may have been some apprehension before. However, the actual experience was more of a celebration of God's love and forgiveness and of their love, forgiveness, and reconciliation in the family.

As a sample of the liturgical life of the St. Brigid parish we also share the order of worship for the Reconciliation Celebration for parents and children in the second grade. This service represents the effort of the St. Brigid leaders to make the service inviting and joyous for all worshipers, especially the children.

Reconciliation Celebration
Grade Two

Welcome

Opening Song

> God is rich in Mercy
> (Please echo)
> God is rich in mercy,
> full of compassion;
> our God has mercy on us.
>
> Jesus is forgiving,
> full of compassion;
> Jesus has mercy on us. We must be forgiving
> as we are forgiven;
> our God has mercy on us.

Opening Prayer

> Jesus, You are the Good Shepherd. You take care of us always and show
> us how much God loves us. We come together today to ask God's
> forgiveness for the times that we have turned away from You by hurting
> one another. We know that You are always ready to forgive and we
> thank You. We pray in Jesus' name.
> Amen.

Sing Alleluia!

Gospel: Luke 15:4-6

Homily

> (*The Runaway Bunny* by Margaret Wise Brown)

Examination of Conscience

> Have I listened and talked to God?
> Have I obeyed my parents?
> Have I obeyed my teachers?
> Have I been helpful at home and at school?

Have I shared with my brothers and sisters?
Have I told the truth?

Let us think of the times we have not been as good as we could be, and ask Jesus to help us be better.

* * * * * *

Jesus, You are our Good Shepherd who always takes care of us.
We thank you and say, Lord, have mercy. *Lord, have mercy.*

Jesus, God the Father sent You to show us God's love and forgiveness.
We thank you and say, Lord, have mercy. *Lord, have mercy.*

Jesus, You help us to make good choices.
We thank you and say Lord, have mercy. *Lord, have mercy.*

In the quiet of our hearts let us each tell Jesus we are sorry for anything we have done wrong. (Pause) We thank you and say, Lord, have mercy. *Lord, have mercy.*

Jesus, our Good Shepherd, we are sorry for the times we have turned away from You. We ask You to help us love God and other people always. In Jesus' name we pray. Amen.

Let us join together in praying the prayer Jesus taught us to pray:
Our Father . . .

Sign of Peace

Individual Confessions

Children: Please begin, "Bless me, Father, for I have sinned. This is my first confession."

Family: Please wait with your child in the pew until he/she is ready to go into the Reconciliation Room. Please pray quietly while the children go individually to the priests. Quiet music will be playing in the background.

As the St. Brigid program clearly illustrates, religious education and liturgical life are interrelated and mutually reinforcing and supportive. Many Protestant churches have units in their religious education curriculum on forgiveness and reconciliation both personal and social. Often these matters are lifted up in drama, films, vignettes from Scripture, history, or a contemporary life, or are included in corporate prayers of confession, forgiveness, and reconciliation in the smaller groups or in the total congregation. These efforts are very important and are to be extended and deepened. However, for the study and discussion to move on to the level of individual reflection and examination of conscience and to be lifted up in a liturgical celebration such as the Sacrament of Reconciliation is to strengthen the experience markedly. Protestant experimentation with liturgies of personal confession, contrition, forgiveness, and reconciliation has already taken place, especially in pastoral counseling sessions and in corporate liturgies in various denominations. More study is needed concerning the essential nature of sacramental theology, of specific sacraments beyond Baptism and Communion, including the Sacrament of Reconciliation.

More specific educational and liturgical designs for forgiveness and reconciliation coming from Protestant faith communities can make a significant contribution to the ecumenical effort to rethink how the Christian church responds to issues of moral growth and human failures and brokenness.

Healing Ministries

Many Protestant churches are now instituting healing ministries that include both educational and liturgical elements. The approach to healing is wide-ranging, including healing of relationships as well as physical and spiritual wholeness. In our own tradition the United Methodist Book of Worship includes two healing services. The introduction of the service makes clear the dimension of healing or spiritual wholeness. "Spiritual healing is God's work of offering persons balance, harmony, and wholeness of body, mind, spirit, and relationships through confession, forgiveness, and reconciliation. Through such healing God works to bring about reconciliation between God and humanity, among individuals and communities, within each person, and between humanity and the rest of creation. . . . All healing is of God. The church's healing ministry in no way detracts from the gifts that God gives through medicine and psychotherapy. It is no substitute for either medicine or the proper care of one's health. Rather, it adds to our total resources for wholeness."[7]

The movement to restore healing ministries and to link them to personal wholeness and interpersonal relationships opens the door to the linking

7. *The United Methodist Book of Worship* (Nashville: United Methodist Publishing House, 1992), p. 613.

of healing to the sacramental nature of life and a fresh view of the Sacrament of Reconciliation within Protestantism.

Clues for Religious Education from the Survey of the Churches

There were several clues for the future that emerged in the comparison of the focus groups (Chapter 1).

We noted several areas of religious education where all four churches were affirmative to very affirmative. These included: (a) strong approval of the need for parent education concerning moral and spiritual development. We shall return to this matter later in the chapter; (b) creative use of resources (curriculum material, tapes, videos) in the basic program of Christian education for all ages. Curriculum designs and resources come from denominational publishing houses as well as independent presses. In respect to forgiveness, reconciliation, and moral development it is possible to discover units at different places in the curriculum designs that are quite well conceived, with much potential for special attention and use; (c) significant Bible study groups, using denominational resources or special series such as the Disciple Bible Study series (for youth and adults) of the United Methodists, or the Kerygma Series of the Presbyterian Church USA, or an ecumenical series such as the Bethel Series. Each of these series calls for an extended period of time, commitment to do advance reading, research, and reflection, and participation in a smaller sharing and caring group where forgiveness, reconciliation, and moral courage can be probed and experienced. In order to address the latter issues directly we have included in our book Chapter 3, "Forgiveness and Reconciliation in the Bible." Reading, discussing, and relating this chapter to inner and outer spiritual journeys could be a positive way to initiate Bible study groups; (d) small support groups receive significant affirmation. Such groups can become communities of trust in which honest sharing about moral ambiguity or failure can take place and where forgiveness and reconciliation strategies can be explored. Such groups can be centered in a rich liturgical and sacramental life (as is demonstrated in Chapter 8). Many churches have offered support groups for those who have sustained a divorce or a death, or are suffering from drug, alcohol, or other abuses. Very often issues of moral failure and the need for forgiveness and reconciliation are at the heart of such discussions. Group therapy is available in some churches with experts in pastoral care. Such therapy can be deepened by being linked with spiritual and liturgical dimensions. Of course, individual counseling and pastoral care are often related creatively to group sessions.

The moral aspects of pastoral care have been identified and important strategies delineated.[8]

Other areas of religious education received mixed support from the focus groups. These included church school classes, marriage and family-life education, preparation of children and youth concerning sacramental life, youth groups, training in nonviolent methods of conflict resolution, work teams where people take action on a social problem, study of contemporary social and political issues, and direct training in forgiveness.

The first part of this chapter was a detailed response to the need to prepare children, youth, and their families to understand and participate in sacramental life. We have selected certain of the above aspects of religious education that have special potential in enhancing forgiveness, reconciliation, and moral development. As you read the discussions below, think about their power to enrich your own educational ministry.

Parent Education concerning Moral and Spiritual Development

As we stated in the summary, all four focus groups affirmed the need for such education. At several places in our discussion, especially in Chapters 5 and 6, we have identified the issues and leaders involved especially in moral and faith development. Many churches have designed programs for parents, often related to preparation of parents before or after infant baptism, using the works of James Fowler in faith development or Lawrence Kohlberg and others in moral developments. A previous book of ours, *Models of Confirmation and Baptismal Affirmation: Liturgical and Educational Issues and Designs* (1995), has several chapters that can be used as a basis for parent education in moral and spiritual development (all of Part III). The assumptions are that all of life is sacred and that parents as members of the body of Christ are preparing themselves for the priesthood of parenthood. Parents are part of the universal priesthood of all believers with a special focus on their parenting roles. It is also assumed that they commit themselves to this crucial ministry within the ecclesiola (the intimate body of Christ in the family) and extend their ministry on out to the world through the larger ecclesia which is the church, the body of Christ. In Part III parents are led through the major stages of life from infancy and childhood to adolescence, young adulthood, middle and older adulthood — from infant baptism to the honest affirmation of baptism

---

8. Don S. Browning, *The Moral Context of Pastoral Care* (Philadelphia: Westminster, 1976).

at the various times of growth and reassessment of one's self-understanding and deeper faith. Approaches to moral and faith development are addressed at each of the major stages.[9]

Ways the family can become a caring, loving, truth-seeking, worshiping community of faith are mapped out in a new series on Religion, Culture, and the Family, edited by Don S. Browning. The eleven books in the series probe the deepest questions of family life in our fast-moving and often conflicted culture. Among the several books in the series is one every family should have: *The Family Handbook*.[10] Besides sound biblical and theological guidance for the family there are many chapters on the practical, everyday issues in family life including worship within the family and within the larger community of faith. Many denominations have published helpful resources to guide parents in the moral and spiritual development of their children. These resources are most engaging when they are in dialogue with the major works that are classics or soon to become classics in moral and faith development. It would be good to have these basic books available for individual and group study.

These resources should start with Jean Piaget's study of *The Moral Judgment of the Child* (1932) and should include the research and insights of the following authors: Lewis Sherrill (1951), Erik Erikson (1968-1977), Edward Robinson (1977), Lawrence Kohlberg (1981-1984), Carol Gilligan (1982), James Fowler (1981-1996), Robert Coles (1986-1990), Sharon Parks (1986), Robert Kegan, (1984), Robert Enright (1998) [Ross and Martha Snyder (1986)], and Johannes A. van der Ven (1998).[11]

---

9. Robert L. Browning and Roy A. Reed, *Models of Confirmation and Baptismal Affirmation* (Birmingham, Ala.: Religious Education Press, 1995), pp. 111-95.

10. Hebert Anderson, Don Browning, Ian Evison, and G. Mary Stewart Van Leeuwen, eds., *The Family Handbook* (Louisville: Westminster/John Knox, 1998). Other books in series with particular insights for family ministry are K. Brynolf Lyon and Archie Smith, Jr., *Tending the Flock: Congregations and the Family Ministry* (Louisville: Westminster/John Knox, 1998), and Phyllis D. Airhart and Margaret Lamberts Bendroth, eds., *Faith Traditions and the Family* (Louisville: Westminster/John Knox, 1996).

11. See Jean Piaget, *The Moral Judgment of the Child* (1932) (New York: Free Press, 1965); Jean Piaget, *Six Psychological Studies* (New York: Random House, Vintage, 1967); Lewis J. Sherrill, *The Struggle of the Soul* (New York: Macmillan, 1951); Erik Erikson, *Identity: Youth and Crisis* (New York: W. W. Norton, 1968); Erik Erikson, *Toys and Reasons: Stages in the Ritualization of Experience* (New York: W. W. Norton, 1977); Lawrence Kohlberg, *Essays on Moral Development*, vol. 1: *The Philosophy of Moral Development*, vol. 2: *The Psychology of Moral Development* (San Francisco: Harper & Row, 1981, 1984); James W. Fowler, *Stages of Faith* (San Francisco: Harper & Row, 1981); James W. Fowler, *Becoming Adult, Becoming Christian* (San Francisco: Harper & Row, 1984); Edward Robinson, *The Original Vision* (Oxford: Religious Experience Research Unit, 1977); Robert Coles, *The Spiritual Life of Children* (Boston: Houghton Mifflin,

Many other persons have made important contributions, often presenting alternate views. The above authors have often either set the direction or have been centrally engaged in the conversation concerning moral and faith development of children, youth, *and* adults. The assumption is that many of the stages of human and faith development are primarily adult. This means that the study of moral and spiritual development can and should be profoundly personal for parents and other adult mentors as well as for children and youth.

Strong Youth Ministry Programs

Many of the above resources can help parents and youth leaders provide guidance in the moral and faith development of youth and young adults. There is a recognized need for engaging young people in exploring honestly their own faith but also in enlisting them in exciting ministries in their school and community life and in meeting "head on" serious social problems in society. Strong programs of confirmation education and commitment are needed. Such programs are more effective when nurturing and challenging mentors are present and when commitment is related to a sense of vocation and service. Several new confirmation curricular resources are emerging with such an emphasis.[12] In churches where infants are dedicated, similar educational efforts are needed, culminating in baptism and commitment to specific forms of ministry, using fully the talents and energy of young people.

1990); Robert Coles, *The Moral Life of Children* (Boston: Houghton Mifflin, 1986); Carol Gilligan, *In a Different Voice: Psychological Theory and Women's Development* (Cambridge, Mass.: Harvard University Press, 1982); Sharon Parks, *The Critical Years: The Young Adult Search for a Faith to Live By* (San Francisco: Harper & Row, 1986); Ross Snyder and Martha Snyder, *Theory and Documentation: How Meanings We Live Can Develop* (San Rafael, Calif.: Institute for Meaning Formation, 1986), a video series in which the Snyders model the sensitive process needed in helping persons share their stories of development in faith. Robert Kegan, *The Evolving Self* (Cambridge, Mass.: Harvard University Press, 1984); Robert Enright and Joanna North, *Exploring Forgiveness* (Madison: University of Wisconsin Press, 1998); Johannes A. van der Ven, *Formation of the Moral Self* (Grand Rapids: Eerdmans, 1998).

12. See *Claim the Name* (Nashville: General Board of Discipleship, United Methodist Church, published by Cokesbury, 2000); *Affirming Faith: A Congregational Guide to Confirmation* (Cleveland: United Church Press, 1996); and others. See Richard Robert Osmer, *Confirmation: Presbyterian Practices in Ecumenical Perspective* (Louisville: Geneva Press, 1996), for an alternate locally designed program.

Preparations for Marriage and Family Life

Parents in our survey of churches were quite concerned about their adolescents understanding and affirming their sexuality in healthy ways. They were concerned about the apparent split between commitment to Christ and the church and their sexual behavior. They were concerned about personal fidelity and preparation for marriage in a society that is seemingly filled with sexual irresponsibility and infidelity. Sex education should be a by-product of living in a family where the love of parents for each other, where their affirmations of their own sexuality, is deep-running and contagious. Having agreed on the premise, we can still want the church to help us more explicitly deal with the pressures on youth to engage in premature and unthoughtful sexual expressions. Denominational resources from our own tradition are illustrations of several available. They are: Don and Rhoda Preston, *Before They Ask: Talking about Sex from a Christian Perspective,* a Guide for Parents of Children from Birth through Age Twelve (Nashville: General Board of Discipleship, the United Methodist Church, 1989); Dorlis Brown Glass with James H. Ritche, Jr., *Created by God: About Human Sexuality for Older Girls and Boys* (Nashville: General Board of Discipleship, the United Methodist Church, 1989); for teens, *Let's Be Real: Honest Discussions about Faith and Sexuality* (Nashville: Abingdon, 1998); for young people preparing for marriage, Joan and Richard Hunt, *Growing Love in Christian Marriage,* 2nd edition, 2001. Two new books from the Religion, Marriage, and the Family series, edited by Don S. Browning and John Wall, are especially designed for premarital education. They are: Robert Cueni, *Great Start* (Grand Rapids: Eerdmans, forthcoming), and Charlene R. Kamper and Shana Kamper, *Making Marriage Meaningful: Marriage Education for Youth* (Grand Rapids: Eerdmans, forthcoming).

It is our belief that education concerning sexuality, the family, and marriage should be included in confirmation education, especially in the middle to late teen years.[13]

Study of Social Problems

An area that was not very highly affirmed was "study of social problems." This is somewhat strange, given the emphasis on social responsibility in the United Methodist and increasingly in the Roman Catholic traditions. Southern Baptists, with an emphasis on personal faith but with some history of social cri-

---

13. See outline in Browning and Reed, *Models of Confirmation and Baptism,* pp. 153-55.

tique, indicated higher interest. Again, Pentecostals focus on the presence of the Holy Spirit within but have some outreach ministries, such as the Prison Ministry team.

Most faith communities are addressing racism, poverty, sexism, civil rights, unequal distribution of food, shelter, education, and homosexuality. In our own tradition, the United Methodist Church has an Advance Specials Program that raises second-mile funds to extend the church's ministry beyond the local church to the world. Some of the high-priority advance ministries tell the story: the Bishops' Initiative on Children and Poverty, Communities of Shalom (to address social, economic, and spiritual development), Justice for Our Neighbors: An Immigration Response, Hope for Children of Africa, Global Refugee Response Programs, Native American Comprehensive Plan, Shared Mission Focus on Young People, Strengthening the Black Church for the 21st Century, Substance Abuse and Related Violence, World Hunger/Poverty, etc. These programs and many others are developed as study programs and are available through the *Partners in Missions: Catalog of General Advances Specials, 2001* (Cincinnati, Ohio: General Board of Global Ministries, U.M.C., 2001). A video called *So Great a Cloud of Witnesses* is also available, describing the creative engagement of local churches, such as John Street Church, New York; Community Church, Nome, Alaska; La Trinidad Church, San Antonio; etc.

Work Teams

The study of social problems can take place in the context of participation on a work team. The team can be recruited to take action by building a Habitat for Humanity house, serving in a homeless shelter, food pantry, or an early childhood center in a Settlement house, or a work camp in an area of the world suffering from a natural disaster. As the team does its service, studies naturally can be done concerning the social and political dynamics that are behind the needs being met. An action/reflection/action educational model can significantly deepen the learning and clearly relate them to the concept of the universal priesthood of all believers. The work team schedules time to serve; time to reflect on areas of strength, hurt, or conflict; and time to plan ways to bring healing, wholeness, and reconciliation. Those insights are then put back to work as the team moves ahead.

Study and action on social problems, of course, are central to the stance of the *public church*. See the strategies and their educational components in the illustrations of public churches in Chapter 5.

Christian Religious Education for a Culture of Nonviolence

All churches were challenged to join the United Nations General Assembly in its proclamation of the year 2000 as "the Year for the Culture of Peace" and the years 2001-2010 to be the "International Decade for a Culture of Peace and Nonviolence for the Children of the World."[14] The Assembly, in response to the groundwork done by the Fellowship of Reconciliation to get the signatures of every living Nobel Peace laureate, made the proclamation on November 19, 1998. The Nobel laureates were Mother Teresa, Elie Wiesel, Aung San Suu Kyi, Shimon Peres, Nelson Mandela, Bishop Desmond Tutu, the Dalai Lama, Mikhail Gorbachev, UNICEF, Norman Borlaug, Adolfo Esquivel, Oscar Arias Sanchez, Frederik Willem de Klerk, Joseph Rotblat, Betty Williams, Lech Walesa, José Ramos-Hortan, Mairead Corrigan-Maguire, Yasir Arafat, and Carlos Felipe Belo. A study of the lives of the Nobel Peace laureates would be a powerful stimulus to the peace process in itself.

The culture of nonviolence highlights the following:

> ". . . teaches conflict resolution and respect for human rights both in home and schools:
>
> ". . . promotes racial and economic justice including the equitable distribution of global resources;
>
> ". . . works for the abolition of nuclear weapons and war;
>
> ". . . nurtures the spiritual roots of nonviolence and compassion in all religions;
>
> ". . . supports diversity and encourages multicultures in all structures of society;
>
> ". . . embraces the sanctity of all living things and values the earth itself."[15]

Of course, since the above decision was made, the United Nations has a new international context in which to pursue a strategy of nonviolence. The quest to bring terrorists to justice and accountability, having taken a military direction, will test in a severe way the United Nations' goal of a nonviolent means to conflict resolution. However, the goal of a nonviolent culture is even more important in the years ahead. The significance of demonstrating and modeling nonviolent conflict resolution for the children of the world cannot be overemphasized.

14. *Decade for a Culture of Peace and Nonviolence for the Children of the World* (Nyack, N.Y.: Fellowship of Reconciliation, 1999).

15. *Decade for a Culture of Peace*, p. 4.

The Fellowship of Reconciliation (FOR) is the largest and oldest interfaith peace and justice organization in the U.S. and in the world. FOR is working with schools, communities, and congregations to achieve peace in our world. Reminding us that we live in a culture of violence (Columbine High School and many other evidences), FOR recommends the cooperative creation of a culture of nonviolence that ". . . values love, compassion and justice . . . rejects violence as a means of solving problems . . . embraces communication, cooperative decision-making, and nonviolent conflict resolution, . . . ensures freedom, security, and equitable relationships, . . . promotes inner peace, personal transformation, and disarmament."[16] Schools are called to teach nonviolence resolution workshops, study the lives and issues faced by the Nobel laureates, research the lives of Gandhi, Martin Luther King, Jr., Dorothy Day, César Chávez, and other peace leaders. Churches are called to start study circles to explore the issues related to nonviolence, racism, youth empowerment, the growth of economic disparity, or homophobia. Especially, churches can deepen the effort by studying the spiritual dimensions of nonviolence in each tradition, and sponsor conflict resolution training within the congregation.

FOR leaders such as Dr. Richard Deats, Dr. Walter Wink, Dorothy Cotton, Sister Mary Evelyn Jegen, Rabbi Michael Robinson, Robert Aitken of the Buddhist Peace Fellowship, etc. have conducted many workshops on nonviolence in the United States and around the world. Richard Deats, who is the former executive director of FOR (U.S.) and is now the editor of the FOR journal, *Fellowship,* has been invited to lead nonviolence workshops in many of the very troubled parts of the world (the Philippines and the Soviet Union prior to their respective bloodless revolutions, Latin America, Thailand, the Middle East, Korea, South Africa, etc.). He has developed a clear outline and a sensitive strategy for workshops in nonviolence that can be employed by local churches.[17]

A very profound and penetrating resource for local congregational study that puts together the issues of forgiveness, reconciliation, and nonviolent approaches to conflict is Walter Wink's *When the Powers Fall: Reconciliation in the Healing of Nations.* Wink explores the difference between true and false forgiveness and genuine and false reconciliation. He helps us discern the relationship between individual reconciliation and social reconciliation wherein hierarchies of domination must be changed structurally. Dr. Wink, Professor of Biblical Interpretation at Auburn Theological Seminary in New

---

16. *Decade for a Culture of Peace*, p. 2.

17. See Richard L. Deats, *Workshops in Active Nonviolence* (Fellowship of Reconciliation, Box 271, Nyack, NY 10960. E-mail: fellowship@forusa.org).

York City, has written a trilogy of excellent books on Jesus' ethic of nonviolence that can be employed in adult education and as resources for workshop participants.[18]

The above insights and approaches are consistent with a religious education for a *public church* stance so needed in our society.

One of the most powerful resources for children in helping them explore nonviolence and cope with their fears after the September 11, 2001, attack comes from the Southern Poverty Law Center. Their *Teaching Tolerance* curriculum issued a special report, "Hate Hits Home — Talking to Kids about Terrorism," a selection of tips and tools recommended by child psychiatrists. The *Teaching Tolerance* curriculum itself is excellent as a resource for general education, character education, and/or religious education. See www.tolerance.org. The center has a distinguished 30-year history seeking justice and reconciliation in the courts in the United States. Their publications focus on the countless threats to freedom and civil rights coming from hate groups within and without. Morris Dees, founder of the center, and his associates have been on the front line in efforts to celebrate freedom and tolerance and to intervene in the work of hate groups. Dees and the Center won the 1995 Academy Award for the documentary *A Time for Justice.* They also won the 2001 National Education Association Friend of Education Award and the 2001 Chapman University Albert Schweitzer Award for Excellence. These and other awards symbolize the integrity and public acceptance finally coming to the Center after many years of rejection, bomb threats, and legal battles. The many resources for youth and adults can be found online at www.splcenter.org.

Direct Training in Forgiveness

Our survey results revealed considerable interest in educational efforts to prepare persons to be able to forgive. The Pentecostals and the Southern Baptists both had over 50 percent interest while the Roman Catholics and United Methodists were well under 50 percent in interest. While there are units on the nature and importance of forgiveness in the Christian life in most curricular designs of the various denominations, there is little attention being given to specific training to enable persons to share openly and honestly their particular experiences of alienation and hurt and their specific difficulties in forgiving specific persons who have hurt them. The research of Dr. Robert

18. Walter Wink, *Naming the Powers* (Minneapolis: Fortress, 1984), *Unmasking the Powers* (Minneapolis: Fortress, 1986), and *Engaging the Powers* (Minneapolis: Fortress, 1992).

Enright and the International Forgiveness Institute at the University of Wisconsin–Madison has discovered that ". . . most people need to be taught about forgiveness to begin forgiving. . . ."[19] If this assumption is true, it is not enough for the educational, liturgical, and pastoral care life of our churches to admonish and offer forgiveness. Churches can and should be informed concerning the research findings about the nature and dynamics of forgiveness and reconciliation and especially the specific steps that have been found to be essential in the training of persons to forgive. Enright and his associates have identified 20 steps that must be taken in one form or another, in one sequence or another, in the process of forgiveness training that results in genuine (and not superficial or false) forgiveness. Researchers have found that forgiveness and reconciliation are quite different things. Reconciliation cannot take place interpersonally or corporately without forgiveness. However, persons can genuinely forgive others and not be able to be reconciled due to the lack of reciprocity from the offender or due to the lack of a desire on the part of the offended to be reconciled in terms of future ongoing relationships.

Enright and the members of his Human Development Study Group have done careful research concerning the outcome of forgiveness training for incest survivors, parentally love-deprived college students, and elderly persons with difficulties in forgiving. The results, in comparison to control groups, were quite significant. Participants gained statistically in levels of forgiveness, self-esteem, and hope, and they decreased markedly in levels of anxiety and depression. In follow-up studies the change patterns were maintained, with no washout effect.

The dynamics of forgiveness were discussed in Chapter 2. The steps in forgiveness training are important to discuss at this point. Enright found four phases emerging in the training design: (1) The Uncovering Phase, (2) The Decision Phase, (3) The Work Phase, and (4) The Deepening Phase.

The Uncovering Phase included an open examination of the psychological defenses persons bring with them to keep them in a state of unforgiveness and pain; confrontation of anger and the release of anger; the admittance of shame when appropriate; awareness of cathexis (energy used to hold fast to old feelings); awareness of internal rehearsal of the offense; insight into the real damage done by the offender; and insight concerning an altered "just world" view.

19. Robert D. Enright, Suzanne Freedman, and Julio Rique, "The Psychology of Interpersonal Forgiveness," in Robert D. Enright and Joanna North, eds., *Exploring Forgiveness* (Madison: University of Wisconsin Press, 1998), p. 52. See also Everett L. Worthington, Jr., *Five Steps to Forgiveness: The Art and Science of Forgiving* (Crown Publishing Group, 2000) for an alternate pattern of training — the pyramid model of forgiveness.

The Decision Phase involves the offended person coming to new insights that the old resolution strategies are not working, and a change of heart or conversion begins to take place so that the person is willing to consider forgiveness as a real option. This phase eventually ends with a sense of personal commitment to forgive the offender.

The Work Phase involves a very important step of reframing. The offended begins to perceive the reasons why the offender did what he or she did to hurt. Through role-taking the wrongdoer is led in his or her life situation back into his or her own childhood. Empathy and compassion then begin to develop for the offender. Yet, there is acceptance of the real pain involved. Avoid false forgiveness.

The Deepening Phase. The offender begins to discover meaning for the self and other people in the suffering and in the process of forgiveness. There is also a fresh realization that the offended person has also needed forgiveness in the past. There is awareness that he or she is not alone. The final two steps are: (a) the realization that the person has been strengthened by the crisis and that a new purpose in life has resulted from the process of forgiveness; and (b) there is an awareness of decreased negative affect and increased positive attitudes toward the offender and the self, including an awareness of internal emotional release. (See Appendix C.)

It seems that forgiveness training has the most potential in older youth and adult education in our faith communities. However, some versions of the above stages can surely be included in Christian education for children and families. The latter can be modeled after the various quite effective peace education and peer mediation programs that have been developed and are in wide use in many of our public school settings, starting in early childhood centers and going on through the twelfth grade. If public school teachers and students can learn to lead younger students and peers to assess the dynamics of conflict within their school settings and help members of the community find constructive ways to express their deep feelings about their life together and to forgive and be reconciled, the church should be able to design educational, liturgical, and pastoral ways to help children and youth gain insight concerning their patterns of conflict and its resolution. Many of our public and private schools do not have programs that train teachers and students in nonviolent approaches to conflict resolution. Churches can lead the way in such settings. Where peace education, nonviolence training, peer mediation, and character education approaches do exist churches can play a crucial role as supporters of such efforts. Churches, moreover, can deepen the reasons for such programs (the biblical and theological rationales undergirding these efforts to bring nonviolent mediation and conflict resolution approaches alive in our society).

While forgiveness, reconciliation, and love for the oppressor or enemy are the core principles of Christ's life and teaching, there are those who maintain that there are certain conditions where force or arms may be used (especially to protect the innocent, to prevent genocide, to counter violence coming from individuals or groups bent on the total destruction of families, nations, or a civilization). Such biblical and theological struggle has resulted in the Christian faith community's response to the September 11, 2001, attack on the United States and to the decision of the government to initiate a war on terrorism. Such a decision evoked formal statements from church bodies concerning the war effort. The range of responses was from the defense of the government under "just war" guidelines to statements of love, support, and caring for the victims and their families but with a strong stance against violence as a way to deal with the attack. The statement of the U.S. Conference of Catholic Bishops decried the violence but maintained that the United States has a moral right to pursue the war on terrorism under the circumstances — a just war response. Other, more peace-oriented churches called for police efforts in cooperation with the United Nations but did not support the war effort. Our own denomination is struggling internally because of pro and con responses to the Pastoral Letter coming from the United Methodist Council of Bishops, speaking words of peace and hope to people in 120 annual conferences in more than 50 countries. Sending their deep concern for all victims and strong support and recognition for all of the heroic caring evidenced, the bishops were clear in their stance: "We, your bishops, believe that violence in all of its forms and expressions is contrary to God's purpose for the world. Violence creates fear, desperation, hopelessness and instability. . . . It is only sacrificial love, not war, which can reconcile people to God and to each other. We call upon the church, leaders, nations and individuals around the world to make room for love so that the patterns of our common life might reveal God's justice. . . ."[20]

The fact that the positions of various official bodies have caused much negative and positive response is a solid call for the educational, worship, and service life of our churches to stimulate and increase dialogue and deeper understanding of the issues in an attempt to find consensus and guidelines for action. Forgiveness, reconciliation, and moral courage are qualities that must finally be related to the concrete challenges before us.

20. *The Worldwide News* (Dallas: United Methodist Reporter, December 14, 2001), p. 1. A serious dialogue concerning the stance of the church must continue, denominationally, ecumenically, and on an interreligious basis. Such dialogue and study must emphasize this search for truth concerning the roles of varying nations and religious bodies in creating the current worldwide culture of suspicion, fear, and violence.

CHAPTER 8

Dealing with Moral Failure: Forgiveness and Reconciliation in Christian Worship

The Contemporary Topography

Forgiveness has always had at least some place in the common liturgy of all the churches even if confined to its voice in the Lord's Prayer. The Orthodox *Divine Liturgy*, while not containing a public confession or forgiveness as such, is replete with prayers acknowledging common guilt and petitions for mercy including, of course, the *Kyrie eleison* and the Lord's Prayer as well as the prayer and hymn of the Thrice-Holy and litanies of supplication.[1]

In *A Time for Embracing*, Julia Upton points out how the motif of reconciliation is presented in the Catholic Mass.

> At the beginning of the celebration, turning our thoughts to whom we have pledged ourselves to be as followers of Christ, in either the Asperges or the penitential rite we admit our sinfulness and need for God's forgiveness.
>
> In the Lord's Prayer we plead "forgive us our sins as we forgive those who trespass against us."
>
> Before approaching the altar to receive Holy Communion, following that ritual deep in our ancestral past, we turn to one another in an embrace of reconciliation, restoring the peace that Jesus came on earth to effect.
>
> Then, together in one large chorus, we plead for mercy: "Lamb of God, you take away the sins of the world, have mercy on us."
>
> Finally, as the communion procession is about to form, we make a pas-

1. *The Orthodox Liturgy* (London: SPCK, 1964), pp. 32-104.

sionate plea: "Lord, I am not worthy to receive you. Speak but the word and my soul shall be healed."[2]

It is probably safe to say at this point in Protestant history that this public form of handling reconciliation is not very effective. One reason for this is that the existent forms are too perfunctory. We have tamed these to the point of dysfunction (more about this below). Another reason for the failure of Protestant corporate confession is the vast unpopularity of sin and guilt. They used to be in fashion. Not any more. "Woe is us" just doesn't play well today. There are several reasons for this. In the first place there is all the weight of the church's condemnation and threat in the past. Frightening people into heaven by scaring the hell out of them has been a long-term ecclesial strategy that most of the modern world finds contemptible. Children's Sunday School songbooks of the nineteenth century could dwell on the terrible fires of eternal punishment as a means of evangelism, but fear as a primary incentive to faith has been found wanting, and rightly so.

Letting up on this allows the pendulum to swing to another pole, and thereby create another reason for the erosion of reconciliation, namely, a revised anthropology. Original sin is out; original OK is in. We are created good, or at worst, ambivalent. Negative thinking is hurtful and self-destructive. Positive thinking is a power for health and success. Don't deal with the negative; let it go. Overwhelm it with positive.

A third reason for the shaky status of reconciliation is the failure of sin, and its subsequent replacement by sickness and addiction. Why let sin be just unpopular when you can get rid of it entirely?

In the fourth place there is the possibility of doing harm in even allowing the possibility of confession of sin. Self-esteem is vital for everybody, and if we begin to probe into bad deeds and failures we could damage someone. Moreover, there is such a thing as a guilt complex. Some people who feel guilty are not really particularly guilty, and opportunities for confession may just exacerbate someone's psychological problems. All told, sin is out; if I am OK and you are OK, who needs confession? We have dealt with the negative, negatively.

Any pastor who would establish a ministry of reconciliation within the service of worship has to deal with these cultural/ontological issues. The case for contrition, confession, and reconciliation needs to be made, we think, on scriptural, anthropological, and ecclesial grounds.

What does one make of a prophet whose opening message in his public ministry is "Repent!"? "Pay attention," would seem to be the answer, if the

---

2. Julia Upton, *A Time for Embracing* (Collegeville, Minn.: Liturgical Press, 1999), p. 84.

man's word and witness are compelling at all. And in this call to live in the values of God's coming kingdom, Jesus echoes John the Baptist and the whole roster of prophets, priests, and patriarchs who have preceded him. We trust we have already described the biblical witness clearly enough for anyone to see that we can ignore the ministry of repentance and reconciliation only by renouncing something essential to the faith. Reconciliation is one of the indispensable chapters in the story of faith into which our lives are seeking a place.

It seems to us that an anthropological argument can be just as persuasive as the scriptural. Human moral failure exhibits a remarkable consistency. To ignore this is simply to be dangerously hanging on the precipice of ignorance and incompetence. In fact, everyone betrays ideals. Some more; some less. Some of this betrayal we can be sure people will bring with them to worship. All have some thanksgiving; all have intercessions welling up in them; all are wounded; all are burdened. And all are guilty. We all come with our graces, glories, and assorted troubles and rubbish, and if the worship of God's people does not have room in it for garbage disposal, then in at least one respect it is seriously dysfunctional for the faithful.

The Liturgy of a Common Priesthood

And thus we come to the ecclesial issue. One of the ways to understand the church is as "the people of the forgiveness." We all came into the faith through baptism, and a primary and essential meaning of baptism, as Peter witnesses at Pentecost and as Jesus witnesses in going to John for baptism, is "for the forgiveness of your sins" (Acts 2:38). If this is not a moment of magic worked by words and water, what can it be? It can be a belonging and a becoming into the people of God's forgiveness, people whose common life is to receive this forgiveness, to proclaim it and share it.

Surely one of the problems Protestants have in achieving this identity is a failure to appreciate Luther's ideal of a universal priesthood. The gross perversion of this idea is the supposition that since we Protestants are relieved from the burden of priests, there need be no human intermediary between us and God. My morality and spirituality are a matter between me and God alone. There is a truth in this conclusion. It is the truth we noticed back at the end of the ninth century in Bishop Theodulf's reservations about tariff penance.[3] It is the conviction that repentance begins in contrition, and necessarily involves personal and private dimensions of conscience. We might settle for this were it

3. See above, p. 110.

not for "church"; were we not a people called to be reconciled and be reconcilers; were we not a fellowship rather than simply an aggregate of persons.

It is important to realize that Luther's "priesthood of all believers" is no less a priesthood, that we are all called in some sense to be priests to our neighbors, to hear their confessions and speak words of forgiveness. Of course, this sort of thing can be corrupted; one can imagine a congregation of busybodies nosing around for sins to forgive. But don't we already know that we can go to hell on all roads. There is nothing worthwhile that cannot be perverted.

What does it take for a church to become a people of the forgiveness? First of all, it takes insight and understanding. It takes an education in the Bible especially, and in the fundamentals of our identity as Christian people. Church is not really a do-it-yourself kit; there are maxims and borders, as arguable as those always are. Undertaken as indoctrination the project would no doubt fail. Such a living concept of church can best be achieved in a process of what some Christians call "formation,"[4] which means, more or less, "learning by doing." This will be a mixture of the life of prayer in worship, preaching, teaching, pastoral care, and the personal prayer exercise of individuals.

There are various programs that aim to assist congregations in the development of caring ministries. One such is *Stephen Ministries* of St. Louis.[5] Since 1975 they have served hundreds of congregations, offering courses and ministry systems to equip laypeople for meaningful ministry. One can contact them about this work and also compare Stephen's programs in local churches. Several churches indicate on websites that they are allied with Stephen ministries. Of course, individual congregations can develop their own program. Kenneth Hauch has written what is essentially a training program in *Christian Caregiving: A Way of Life.*[6] There is a *Leader's Guide,*[7] and these resources could help a congregation develop something analogous to *Stephen Ministries.* A program for a congregational identity as a priesthood of believers and a sense of what it might mean could also be evolved out of a study of Marva Dawn's book, *Truly the Community: Romans 12 and How to Be the Church.*[8]

---

4. "Formation" is not exactly a happy word in this connection. It has a military and indoctrinating ring to it for many. However, it has become a much-used term for a process of creating a Christian identity, so we use it here.

5. *Stephen Ministries,* 2045 Innerbelt Business Center Drive, St. Louis, MO 63114, telephone (314) 428-260, www.stephenministries.com.

6. Kenneth C. Hauch, *Christian Caregiving: A Way of Life* (Minneapolis: Augsburg, 1984).

7. Kenneth C. Hauch and William J. McKay, *Christian Caregiving: A Way of Life, Leader's Guide* (Minneapolis: Augsburg, 1994).

8. Marva Dawn, *Truly the Community: Romans 12 and How to Be the Church* (Grand Rapids: Eerdmans, 1992).

There are other Protestant resources to tap,[9] and Protestants should not ignore Catholic resources.[10] Protestants may lay claim (if falsely) to a universal priesthood, but we should recall that it is an ecumenical awareness of the social and corporate dimensions of penance that has driven reforms of the sacraments. Certainly one of the ways to become truly the reconciling community is through some self-conscious plan of study, training, testing, and evaluating, i.e., formation.

Reconciliation in the Common Liturgy

The primary means of achieving a reconciling identity for a church is the liturgy. The community itself at praise and prayer is the main educating and training function of the church. Forgiveness happens here, or certainly should happen here. Confession and forgiveness are one crucial dynamic in the rhythm of Word and response that happens in worship. In this case the rhythm is really Word-response-Word. That is, the Word of God ignites contrition and confession in us, and our repentance is met by God's Word of loving mercy. That sounds simple and boringly abstract. It is, of course, not simple at all and in no way abstract. The discovery of our place in the encounters of the kingdom of God with the "principalities and powers" of our world is complicated and troublesome. Finding the way to walk, the yes and no of things, the why and why not, is difficult and vexing. It is no easy matter to sort out our motivations. It is not something simple to be truthful and vulnerable enough to admit our faults and failures and voice our sorrow and repentance. And, moreover, it is not always a simple and easy matter to hear God's Word of forgiving acceptance. In repentance, confession, and forgiveness, nothing is abstract theology. It is intensely, even excruciatingly, personal and real.

9. L. William Countryman, *Forgiven and Forgiving* (Harrisburg, Pa.: Morehouse, 1998); Georgia Harkness, *The Ministry of Reconciliation* (Nashville: Abingdon, 1971); George W. Bowman, *The Dynamics of Confession* (Richmond: John Knox, 1969).

10. Paul B. Brown, *In and for the World* (Minneapolis: Fortress, 1992); Ruth Duck, *Finding Words for Worship* (Louisville: Westminster/John Knox, 1995); Walter Huffman, *The Prayer of the Faithful* (Minneapolis: Augsburg, 1986); Peggy Haymes, *Be Thou Present* (Macon, Ga.: Smyth & Helwys, 1994); Doris Rudy, ed., *Worship and Daily Life* (Nashville: Discipleship Resources, 1999); Hughes Oliphant Old, *Leadership in Prayer: A Workbook for Worship* (Grand Rapids: Eerdmans, 1995); Julia Upton, *A Time for Embracing* (Collegeville, Minn.: Liturgical Press, 1999); Tad Guzie and John McIlhon, *The Forgiveness of Sin* (Chicago: Thomas More Press, 1979); Bernard Cooke, *Reconciled Sinners* (Mystic, Conn.: 23rd Publishers, 1986); Joseph Nassal, *Premeditated Mercy* (Leavenworth, Kans.: Forest of Peace, 2000).

Certain things are required of liturgy for this dynamic of Word-response-Word to come to life: Preaching that illumines our lives and our world in the light of God's righteousness and God's mercy, and a liveliness of prayer in worship that can allow people's real praises, petitions, confessions, and intercessions to find an actual and not a symbolic voice. These two sides of liturgy naturally belong to one another, for good preaching is instruction in how to pray, and prayer in worship ought to be reflective of what has been heard of God's Word.

In most of Protestant worship prayer is offered by the clergy, and people participate, so to say, "vicariously." As the prayers of the people this doesn't work very well. We will explore some ways to create a more corporate prayer.

What needs to happen among us as prayer is multifold. Our understanding of prayer is shaped by Jesus in the prayer he gives his disciples (Matt. 6:9-13; Luke 11:2-4), and has at least these themes:

Our Father in heaven, *Hallowed be your name,*	We pray in the first place, for the Holy Presence — that God will in fact be God for us, and be real for us. This includes our thanksgiving and praise.
Your kingdom come, *your will be done,* *on earth as in heaven.*	Second, we pray that God's realm of truth, justice, and love can come to pass for us, that God's holy will shall prevail. This includes our petitions and intercessions.
Give us today our daily bread.	Third, we pray for manna, for bread today, and for that holy bread of God's kingdom that shall come. This includes prayers that none should hunger.
Forgive us our sins *as we forgive those* *who sin against us.*	Fourth, we pray for forgiveness for our sins and for the will and the way to forgive others. This includes confession and absolution.
Save us from the time *of trial, and deliver* *us from evil.*	Fifth, we pray that the Holy Presence may not fall away from us, that we will not descend into evil. This is the same prayer as the first petition, only stated in the negative.

It is imperative that every congregation have some lay liturgy group at work planning, creating and implementing the people's prayer. There are many resources that can be helpful to such a group,[11] but in some measure their work must be creative since, to echo what has been said about politics, all prayer is local. If the times and structures of prayers in worship are indeed to be people's prayer, then they must be created not only for but by the people. Such a creation will be a genuine cooperative effort of pastor, liturgy group, and a praying congregation.

Suppose such a liturgy group turned its attention to confession and forgiveness. What are some creative possibilities that involve greater participation?

Prayers of Confession in denominational worship books and other collections: The usual format here follows the general pattern introduced by Archbishop Cranmer in 1547: call to confession, prayer of confession, Scripture sentences, prayers for forgiveness, and absolution. Ordinarily liturgical reconciliation will include some or all of these. In the Service of Word and Table in the United Methodist Hymnal (1989), the corporate confession is in this pattern:

INVITATION

Christ our Lord invites to his table all who love him,
> who earnestly repent of their sin
> and seek to live in peace with one another.
Therefore, let us confess our sin before God and one another.

CONFESSION AND PARDON

Merciful God,
we confess that we have not loved you with our whole heart.
We have failed to be an obedient church.
We have not done your will,
> we have broken your law,
> we have rebelled against your love,
> we have not loved our neighbors,
> and we have not heard the cry of the needy.
Forgive us, we pray,
> through Jesus Christ our Lord.
Amen.

11. Gail Ramshaw, ed., *Intercessions for the Christian People* (New York: Pueblo, 1988), p. 92.

(All pray in silence.)

Leader to people:
Hear the good news:
   Christ has died for us while we were yet sinners;
   that proves God's love for us.
In the name of Jesus Christ, you are forgiven.

People to leader:
In the name of Jesus Christ, you are forgiven.

Leader and people:
Glory to God. Amen.

THE PEACE

Let us offer one another signs of reconciliation and love.

(All exchange signs and words of God's peace.)

What are the possibilities for greater involvement and participation in this penitential?

1. One simple change. It can be led by a layperson; this in itself creates a different perspective.
2. Instead of a corporate recitation, lines of the prayer can be read by different individuals, and if feasible, from different places. This still has a sense of "us," yet it is a way for those lines to be heard in a fresh way.
3. Silence can be left between the lines read as in (2) or read by some one individual. This adds contemplative prayer into the pattern.
4. The prayer is general. It is possible for the liturgy group to take individual lines or pairs of lines and get more specific about, for instance, how we "have not heard the cry of the needy." Care needs to be taken here; the specifics still need to have a certain "general" character. This is a prayer for all to pray, so we might not single out "the attention and care we have failed miserably to provide for Mrs. So and So," but we can single out the needs of certain groups or categories of persons in the church or community.

In the creation of confessions there is some temptation to "lay it on 'em," which ought not to be indulged. What is sometimes accurate is not always helpful. So the writing of prayers of confession or biddings to confession is a bit tricky. They have to be general, since one size needs to fit all, yet they should have sufficient specificity so that we can see ourselves in them. Ideally we should be able, so to say, to read ourselves into the general statement of the confession. The trouble is that we easily domesticate these phrases and they fail to have the impact intended. This is why it can be helpful to improvise on the prayers to enable us to exegete them and find our place in them. For instance, take the phrase we have singled out, "and we have not heard the cry of the needy." Suppose this were read, some silence allowed, and then some of the obvious needs at hand were first lifted up: "the homeless in our city — pause — the struggling food pantry downtown, etc., etc." Without beating people over the heads about these confessing petitions, it is possible to introduce images specific enough to give the petitions a reality. There are many ways to go about this sort of thing. Take, for instance, this prayer above from the United Methodist liturgy. One could "expand" the prayer, as we have suggested, within the service of Eucharist. This might not be such a good idea since it could lengthen a service already apt to be long — usually not a good idea. On the other hand, it is an often used prayer easily tamed and rendered inoperative. The prayer could form the basis of confessional prayers for several weeks in ways that help to make concrete the separate themes. People should be aware that there is an idea being worked out. The whole prayer should be printed in some appropriate artistic format and distributed so that people could post it up on the fridge or utilize it in whatever way they wish. This kind of attention given to our common corporate prayers can allow them to come off the page and into our lives.

1. *Bidding prayers* are prayers where a leader "bids" the congregation to pray for certain things. The leader does not pray, but rather states what are sometimes called "intentions" and leaves a time of silence for people to attend to that prayer. This technique can be used with confession. No text in bulletin or book is required, just the biddings of the leader allowing each person to do the work of prayer. There are some cautions to raise. A lifetime of seminary teaching indicates that no matter how often one might say, "The biddings are not prayer, they are invitation to pray," something like one-third of the assignment attempted will be prayers where the people are to come along vicariously as usual. That is decidedly not the idea. The biddings are invitations to pray; the prayers are those the people make in the time of silence. The leader frames a context for prayer; people pray. A second caution is to recognize that people are not generally used to this format. They are used to being left alone. This means that one cannot expect that this way of praying will be immediately successful. It means that initially one should not leave too much time of silence; people don't know quite what to do with it. They will know as they

become practiced at it. This means that the method needs to be used often enough in prayer for people to get used to doing their own praying.

The use of bidding prayers need by no means be limited to confession. The art of this style of praying is to find the images that can evoke prayer in the people. These kinds of images, for instance, help give meaning to the real plight of "victims":

> Let us pray for all victims of our rapacious social order:
> for those scarred by new and old wars,
> for refugees, and those hungry and in despair,
> for those harmed by lies and blighted by false values;
> for the poor and the homeless, and for those who
> have no access to the world's abundant resources.[12]

Most of us know personally people scarred by war and are aware enough about our society and our world to picture and have empathy for all those named in this call to prayer. And most of us can in some way do something about it.

2. A *liturgy group* with guidance from a pastor or other qualified person can create new prayers and prayer forms for use in worship. One barrier to this task is the lack of confidence people generally feel in their capacity to do this. One very good way to get people beyond this reluctance is to begin with little "exercises" in paraphrasing passages from the Psalter. The language of the Psalms has always been the primary building material of Christian liturgy. Taking sections of the text and paraphrasing them in a language that can communicate today is a useful method to free people up, to set their creativity working and gain confidence. Good, useful material can be generated this way.

3. *Public Confession.* We know of at least one pastor who occasionally introduces a type of truly public confession into worship. She uses a "fill in the blank" method. For instance, once on the first Sunday of Advent, relating to the "keep awake" (Mark 13:24-37) theme, she put a confession in the bulletin that concluded with the sentence, "I have been asleep, I have not . . . ," followed by the rubric, "Prayers of confession, silently and aloud." She reports that about half a dozen chose to confess aloud. Shades of the first centuries of the church! Happily the penalties, punishments, and admonitions are no longer so harsh. Of course one can still find Christian communities where exclu-

---

12. *The United Methodist Book of Worship* (Nashville: United Methodist Publishing House, 1992), p. 35.

sion and shunning are still practiced, and indeed, some do this although they are more or less unaware of it, or at least realize that it is not the Christian thing to do. The church, it has been said, is something like baseball: more attend than understand. Naturally this form of open confession has definite limitations. This pastor has found a way of doing this that works in a rather small and intimate fellowship. It is not impossible.

4. *Absolution.* One of the most troublesome aspects of reconciliation is the absolution, the forgiveness itself. The difficulty is twofold. First, we have trouble speaking it, or even knowing that we are able to speak it, or allowed to speak it. After all, it is not simply person forgiving person; it is God forgiving person or persons, with you, me, or someone else in between. Second, we have trouble hearing the divine word of forgiveness, trouble accepting the message that we are accepted.

The former is one of authority. Who can speak for God? Anyone who is in some way authorized and emboldened by the church to say, "in the name of Jesus Christ, you are forgiven!"[13] Anyone not seriously daunted by this responsibility is just not taking the whole matter seriously. It helps in the liturgical formulation quoted above from the United Methodist liturgy that the forgiveness phrase is spoken by the pastor to people and then by people to pastor. If our confidence in a universal priesthood is real, then this absolving dialogue needs to happen regularly and in some different ways and in various formulations and with an exchange of personnel taking leadership.

The empowering texts for authority in forgiveness we considered in our chapter on the Bible: Jesus gives authority to Peter, telling him that what he "binds and looses" on earth will be so bound and loosed in heaven (Matt. 16:15). He later gives the same authority to the disciples in a context specifically dealing with forgiveness of sins (Matt. 18:15-20). These empowerings are bestowed in the context of commissioning the disciples to extend the ministry of Christ into a wider world. The same is true about the empowering bestowed by the risen Christ in John 20:21-23.

> "As the Father has sent me, even so I send you." And when he had said this, he breathed on them, and said to them, "Receive the Holy Spirit. If you forgive the sins of any, they are forgiven, if you retain the sins of any they are retained."

There are three parts to this small scene: one, commissioning; two, Holy Spirit blessing; and three, bestowing of authority to forgive or to withhold the

---

13. Paul Tillich, *The Courage to Be* (New Haven: Yale University Press, 1952).

blessing of forgiveness. The first and third moments in this scene need to be understood in the light of the second. Jesus does not simply authorize, he sends the disciples out in the power of God's Holy Spirit. They are empowered and loosed into the world not simply with a plan, but with the inspiration of a holy presence.

Ultimately the warrant for forgiveness, even the divine forgiveness given in the name of Jesus Christ, rests not so much upon a verbal formula as upon the reality of the Holy Spirit moving in the lives of Christian people and in the wholeness of the church — a gift of the Father and the Son. It is to this inspiration that St. Paul witnesses when he extols the new creation gifted to the world by Jesus:

> All this is from God, who through Christ reconciled us to himself and gave us the ministry of reconciliation, that is, in Christ, God was reconciling the world to himself, not counting their trespasses against them, and entrusting to us the message of reconciliation. So we are ambassadors for Christ, God making his appeal through us. (2 Cor. 5:18-20)

It does not seem that the "us" here is something organized into a bureaucracy but a people of the Spirit whose reconciling ministry is a freedom of love, which can be stimulated but never finally organized.

We are aware of a pastoral situation where a young man whose transgressions had gotten him temporarily suspended from school was in trouble with the law and seriously alienated from his family. Come the first Sunday evening after this matter had been exposed the lad did not show up for Christian youth fellowship. The youth group took it upon themselves to go and get him and spent the evening with him in a caring exchange about him, his difficulties, and the bond of love that kept the fellowship together. In subsequent counseling sessions with the pastor it was obvious that the message of God's forgiveness was not getting through to this young man. Eventually the pastor asked the boy if he had experienced any forgiveness at all in this crisis. He immediately cited the meeting with the youth fellowship that Sunday night. The pastor then reminded the young man that these friends in faith were the people of the forgiveness, baptized for the forgiveness of sins, and that the blessing Spirit of Christ was in their words and actions with him that evening. Together, pastor and youth explored the speech of Peter at Pentecost in the second chapter of Acts. From an awareness of the dynamism of forgiveness alive in the church, this young man was able to accept the blessed comfort that he was forgiven by God.

We can find the forgiveness of God reading the Bible by ourselves, or in contemplation in church, or anywhere by multiple means, but more likely it is something we pass around in word, in deed, and in loving embrace.

Accepting that we are accepted was a theme prominent in the work of the theologian Paul Tillich. It becomes the climax of the journey on which he takes the reader in *The Courage to Be*.[14] He epitomizes the issue in his succinct prose: "In the center of the Protestant courage of confidence stands the courage to accept acceptance in spite of the consciousness of guilt."[15] And, "The courage to be in this respect is the courage to accept the forgiveness of sins, not as an abstract assertion but as the fundamental experience in the encounter with God. Self-affirmation in spite of the anxiety of guilt and condemnation presupposes participation in something which transcends the self."[16] Tillich understood that no theological formulations or liturgical declarations can of themselves accomplish this acceptance. "Acceptance by something which is less than personal could never overcome personal self-rejection. A wall to which I confess cannot forgive me. No self-acceptance is possible if one is not accepted in a person-to-person relation. But even if one is personally accepted it needs a self-transcending courage to accept this acceptance, it needs the courage of confidence. For being accepted does not mean that guilt is denied."[17] The ground of such a courage is faith. Faith alone is a "courage of confidence conditioned not by anything finite but solely by that which is unconditional itself and which we experience as unconditional in a person-to-person encounter."[18] Such faith is not an opinion; it is rather a state of being. "It is the state of being grasped by the power . . . which transcends everything that is and in which everything that is participates."

Paul Tillich frames quite well, we think, what is the bottom line in the rhythm of sin — sorrow and contrition — confession — forgiveness. It finally roots in faith. All along the line, in the personal awareness, the speaking and the hearing and the acceptance, the koinonia of the Christians is indispensable, but an end point is the courage of a trusting personal faith. One winces at the thought of the many superficial means we employ to attempt to arrive at this reality.

Because the responsibility is so great and the stakes are so high and our confidence in ourselves and even in God's Holy Spirit is so tenuous, many pastors and almost all laypeople are reluctant to risk the words, "In

14. Tillich, *The Courage to Be*, pp. 163f.
15. Tillich, *The Courage to Be*, p. 165.
16. Tillich, *The Courage to Be*, p. 166.
17. Tillich, *The Courage to Be*, p. 167.
18. Tillich, *The Courage to Be*, p. 173.

the name of Jesus Christ, you are forgiven!" Earthen vessels we may be, but these vessels are what the Holy Spirit comes to fill. Risk the audacity to be God's reconciler!

5. Liturgies for baptismal renewal have been created by many denominations, and these can be useful instruments of reconciliation. Forgiveness is only one meaning of baptism, but a primary and crucial one. For some occasions renewal of the baptismal covenant, for a congregation, particular group, or an individual can be a meaningful experience of rediscovery of the cleansing water bath of baptism. We are aware of one pastor who, in January at Epiphany recalled the baptism of Jesus in an invitation to the congregation to come forward and be marked with the sign of the cross on their foreheads with water to symbolize their own contrition and repentance and acceptance of Christ's blessing of forgiveness. Somewhat to his surprise many participated. Liturgies for baptism and the renewal or affirmation of baptism are in many worship books and can be used or adapted for reconciliation. One of our previous books, *Models of Confirmation and Baptismal Affirmation* (Birmingham: Religious Educators Press, 1995), contains a chapter on "Liturgies of Confirmation and Baptismal Affirmation throughout the Life Cycle."

Liturgy Resources

One means of discovering possible liturgical structures for reconciliation is to consult the texts created for this purpose in denominational worship books and other resources. Getting one's hands on such material used to be difficult and frustrating. Today, with so many libraries on the Internet and connected in networks of interlibrary loans, the task is increasingly simple, including the obtaining of out-of-print books. A walk down the street to borrow a book from a sister church is a good idea too.

Three kinds of reconciliation liturgies will be found in the resources to which we make reference: reconciliation within the context of general worship; second, services specifically for reconciliation; and third, penitential ritual with a single individual. Though separate formats, the materials in each can, of course, be used or adapted for various purposes.

The Lutheran Book of Worship[19] includes confessional liturgies intended as preparation for communion (pp. 56, 77, and 98). There are also forms for corporate confession and forgiveness (p. 193) and for an individual (p. 196).

19. *The Lutheran Book of Worship* (Minneapolis: Augsburg, 1978).

The Book of Worship[20] of the United Church of Christ contains an order for the reconciliation of a penitent person (p. 268) and for corporate reconciliation (p. 275). The Presbyterian Book of Common Worship[21] has liturgy appropriate for reconciliation under the heading of "A Service for Wholeness." There is one for a congregation (p. 1005) and one for an individual (p. 1018). As the title suggests, their use is inclusive of reconciliation, but broader. There is also a specific "Service of Repentance and Forgiveness for Use with a Penitent Individual" (p. 1023). These denominational resources have specific intentions but in the creation of the specifics of worship one can gather material from whatever source is available, using whatever is workable.

Other resources include the section on "Confession" in *The Wideness of God's Mercy,* vol. 1 (pp. 71-81).[22] There are chapters on liturgy that could be useful in the following volumes: *Personal Confession Reconsidered,* [23] by Mark Morton (pp. 23f.); *Confession and Absolution,*[24] chapter 11; "Rites of Penance and Reconciliation" (pp. 181-205), by Martin Dudley and Jill Pinnoch; *Reconciled Sinners,*[25] by Bernard Cooke, chapter 7; "Liturgies of Reconciliation" (pp. 71-82); and *Come, Let Us Celebrate!*[26] This latter is a volume of 16 communal reconciliation services with a section titled "Themes for Creating Your Own Services." The collection can be very useful. It does introduce, however, a category entirely unfamiliar to Protestants, namely, "Examination of Conscience." All of these liturgies contain a segment so named. Almost all Protestants will find such an exercise in worship something new and different. This is not, of course, because all Protestants are sinless and their consciences are clear. It is because of two basic Protestant principles: total depravity and salvation by grace through faith. *Total depravity:* Well, nobody understands that anymore (see above, p. 113) but there is at least a residue of the idea lingering in a sense that sin is general, not specific. So one is excused from enumerating sins. *Salvation by grace through faith:* This means that good works are always suspect as a means to the discovery of God's grace, and confessing specific

20. *Book of Worship: United Church of Christ* (New York: United Church of Christ Office for Church Life and Leadership, 1986).

21. *Book of Common Worship* (Louisville: Westminster/John Knox, 1993).

22. Jeffery W. Rowthorn, ed., *The Wideness of God's Mercy: Litanies to Enlarge Our Prayer* (Minneapolis: Seabury, 1985).

23. Mark Morton, *Personal Confession Reconsidered* (Nottingham, U.K.: Grove, 1994).

24. M. Dudley and Geoffrey Rowell, eds., *Confession and Absolution* (Collegeville, Minn.: Liturgical Press, 1990).

25. Bernard Cooke, *Reconciled Sinners* (Mystic, Conn.: 23rd Publishers, 1986).

26. Sarah O'Malley and Robert Eimer, *Come, Let Us Celebrate! Creative Celebrations of Reconciliation* (San Jose, Calif.: Resource Publishers, 1986).

sins and being forgiven by some present person or persons seems all too much like a good work worked, i.e., something we do to obtain God's grace. The matter is not that simple, but that is about it. If these explanations of Protestant reluctance seem to lampoon Protestant understanding and practice, well, they do.

There is a liturgy of reconciliation in *Confession*[27] by Taizé theologian Max Thurian (pp. 130-41). It begins with a long and excruciating self-examination. A bit much, to be sure, but it can be a fruitful stimulus to create a more useful instrument. The notion of reaching down into our consciences to provoke personal awareness of our own transgressions is a useful exercise, and it can be done in a way appropriate to Protestant sensibilities. There is a collection of *Penitential Services*[28] edited by Olive Crilly, which can be very useful. The book is intended for a variety of purposes: for parish liturgy in different seasons, small groups, youth, children, and for ecumenical services.

The books we have referenced do not exhaust the possibilities. They are some of what we would consider most helpful. Most will not be found at your local bookstore or at Amazon.com. Some are available through denominational outlets. But to repeat, in this day of the Internet, all of these volumes can be obtained, especially from the libraries of the theological schools.

Private Confession

As anyone knows who has done it, a considerable part of a pastor's work of "pastoral care" is the hearing of confession. Conducted in a pastor's study, or some special space for counseling, it is possible and generally desirable to have a liturgical aspect to this experience. Elaine Ramshaw, in *Ritual and Pastoral Care*, suggests some ways in which liturgy may be appropriate:

> There are all sorts of ritual variations possible in confession and absolution, formal and casual, old and new. Sometimes a conversation about grace is most appropriate. Sometimes a definite symbolic gesture or word is more reassuring and effective than talk alone. The pastor might suggest saying the formula for absolution used on Sundays, or she/he might improvise the words but ritually underscore them with a gesture, such as the laying on of hands or the greeting of peace. She/he might use gestures that recall the connection between forgiveness and baptism — for exam-

27. Max Thurian, *Confession* (London: SCM Press, 1958).
28. Olive Crilly, *Penitential Services* (Dublin: Columba, 1986).

ple, making the sign of the cross on the person's forehead. One pastor takes people from his office to the font when the time comes for the absolution and pours the water over their hands or uses it to mark a cross. Another keeps a baptismal candle in his study and lights it when the talk turns to the meaning of baptism and the promise of forgiveness. The rites set down in books, even the new ones, may feel awkward to those unaccustomed to such ritual, too formal or constrained, but one should not on that account give up on ritual expressions of forgiveness. One woman, a former Roman Catholic, was pleasantly surprised when she went to a woman pastor for private confession. Not only had the pastor typed up a possible form for them to use (they had talked about the overly hierarchical and non-inclusive character of the traditional rite); she had also set a small table for them to sit at, furnished with several appropriate symbols. There is a parable there: coming to confess and finding the table set for you. The newest and most personalized ritual acts can speak the powerful language of the church's symbolic tradition.[29]

Ramshaw's book is a careful and thoughtful consideration of the multiple ways liturgy itself attends to the ministry of pastoral care.

We have noted above, considering liturgy resources, that some of the denominational worship books include liturgy for private reconciliation. There are other resources that can be helpful in this ministry: *The Dynamics of Confession*,[30] by George Bowman; *To Declare God's Forgiveness*,[31] by Clark Hyde; *Is Human Forgiveness Possible?*[32] by John Patton; *The Ministry of Reconciliation*,[33] by Georgia Harkness; *The Forgiveness of Sin*,[34] by Tad Guzie and John McIlhon; and *Reconciled Sinners*,[35] by Bernard Cooke. These are but a few of the possibilities. Most of the many resources for pastoral care can be helpful.

Two of the best resources for a consideration of the whole matter of reconciliation in the church and in the church's worship are books one might call prolegomena to liturgy. They are both theological studies written by theologians convinced that "theology should not be an idle academic exercise

---

29. Elaine Ramshaw, *Ritual and Pastoral Care* (Philadelphia: Fortress, 1987), pp. 63f.

30. George Bowman, *The Dynamics of Confession* (Richmond: John Knox, 1969).

31. Clark Hyde, *To Declare God's Forgiveness* (Wilton, Conn.: Morehouse, 1984).

32. John Patton, *Is Human Forgiveness Possible?* (Nashville: Abingdon, 1985).

33. Georgia Harkness, *The Ministry of Reconciliation* (Nashville: Abingdon, 1971).

34. Tad Guzie and John McIlhon, *The Forgiveness of Sin* (Chicago: Thomas More Press, 1979).

35. Bernard Cooke, *Reconciled Sinners* (Mystic, Conn.: 23rd Publishers, 1986).

but must seek to be of practical service to the witness of the church."[36] *The Liturgy of Liberation*[37] by Theodore Jennings is directly an examination of reconciling aspects of liturgy itself. *Embodying Forgiveness,*[38] by L. Gregory Jones, is only tangentially about liturgy, but is a scriptural and theological consideration of forgiveness as the heart of Christian identity and mission.

36. Theodore Jennings, *The Liturgy of Liberation* (Nashville: Abingdon, 1988), preface.
37. Jennings, *The Liturgy of Liberation,* preface.
38. L. Gregory Jones, *Embodying Forgiveness* (Grand Rapids: Eerdmans, 1995).

Epilogue

M orality, justice, forgiveness, and reconciliation have always been difficult. Today they are beyond difficult; they are critical. When major
powers amass military forces and hover on the brink of what could be a nu-
clear war, ancient and local animosities become global threats capable of
dealing death to millions and radiation poisoning to millions more. Atroc-
ities of terror between Israel and Palestine, for instance, are not problems of
two small governmental entities. They are a threat to the whole Middle East
and beyond. Getting past ancient and new hatreds is a matter of survival. And
in spite of the many advances in reconciliation — one thinks thankfully of
the birth of the Economic Union in Europe as a child of the horror of World
War II — it so often seems that civilization faces an impossible challenge.

We are fully aware that there is much more to be done in lighting the
pathways ahead. We have provided some handles to get hold of in dealing
with these problems, some tools to work with, and the testimony of many
witnesses that there are pathways beyond hate and fear, and that they can be
discovered and traveled.

There is encouragement in the extent to which the concerns of this
study are advanced in academic research, the work of foundations, mediation
programs, moral education in schools and communities, and the personal
testimony of individuals who have broken through bonds of hurt and hate to
find freedom and a way forward through forgiveness and reconciliation.

Many positive resources for this crucial struggle are available to anyone
on the Internet, the World Wide Web. Sadly, also available there is an abundance of vituperation and hate. The World Wide Web is not only a hope; it is
also a dumping place for trash, at its ugliest. However, start a search for "for-

giveness and reconciliation" and hundreds of sources of help are listed, many rich in inspiration and practical guidance. Given the hurdles, discouragement and despair are inevitable. The closest cousin to idealism is cynicism, and this cousin is hard to resist. Even so, the struggle for understanding and good will against discord and enmity must be won. The commitment, energy, and hard work of individuals, nations, and collectives must stay focused, breaking down walls of fear and hate, celebrating examples of forgiveness and reconciliation.

Among these "collectives" are the world's religions, all of which in one way or another have doctrine and underlying spirituality that affirm compassion, forgiveness, and hopeful regeneration of persons and societies into love and peace. So, while one is sometimes tempted to toss religion to the winds because it is so much a root cause of our tribal animosities, religion itself has the potential to contribute much to their cure. Certainly the Christian church has an important role to play in the effort to find comity in our world. The opening words of Jesus as he begins his ministry are: "The time is fulfilled, the kingdom of God is at hand. Repent and believe in the good news" (Mark 1:15). And his initial actions are of healing and forgiving (Mark 1–3). No doubt we Christians are in something of a stasis regarding the themes of our study, but why should this be? It is time for religious leadership to step forward and articulate their life- and peace-offering message to the world. For Christians this certainly means rediscovering the faith rhythms of repentance — confession — forgiveness — reconciliation. You can't send the message if you don't get the message.

It is high time to take seriously Hans Küng's admonition that there can be no peace in our world without dialogue and peace among the world's religions. Out of such a dialogical process must come a new global ethic to guide our decisions. In this regard one has to be deeply impressed by the work of one Christian layman, Jimmy Carter. Caring and courageous, former President Carter has created and brought others into a ministry of compassion and reconciliation. Admittedly, Mr. Carter has the stature and ability to attract resources that most of us lack. Even so, he is an inspiring example of what one determined and dedicated individual can accomplish.

It is time also for Christians to turn their attention newly to issues of morality. Christian clergy and laity have been very active in the movement toward moral education in the public schools and communities. In this they have learned a lot about working with people of other faiths, and of no faith, in order to create means to speak about and teach about the moral life with young people. This movement should presage an emphasis in local congregations on issues of morality and public ministry. We will not come to full agreement among ourselves about specific issues of morality, but we can frame and communicate an idea of a Christian morality and explore ways to walk in it.

Forgiveness and reconciliation are essentially moral issues. Our decisions and efforts to understand our enemies, to take the known steps toward forgiveness and reconciliation, are of critical importance. We will do well to follow one of our most distinguished and convincing Christian moral leaders, Bishop Desmond Tutu. After the September 11, 2001, attacks Bishop Tutu admonished us to be realistic and recognize the exceedingly dangerous situation in which we find ourselves. However, he said that we must not classify people as terrorists to the point of not seeing them as human beings. Bishop Tutu called all of us ". . . to forgive one another even as God in Christ forgives us; we are in the forgiveness business whether we like it or not. And we can do this only through God's grace. It is ultimately God at work in us to make us to be like God. Yes, it is a tall order, but that is the love that changes the world, that believes an enemy is a friend waiting to be made."[1]

1. Bishop Desmond Tutu, "No Future without Forgiveness," in *From the Ashes: A Spiritual Response to the Attack on America* (New York: Rodale and Beliefnet, 2001), p. 10.

Survey of Attitudes concerning Confession, Forgiveness, and Reconciliation

Participants: Male _____   Female _____
        Ages: 20-40 _____
                40-60 _____
                over 60 _____

A: Sin

1. Sin is doing things against God's will.

   Yes _____   No _____   Not Sure _____

2. I believe in original sin which each of us experiences and cannot avoid.

   Yes _____   No _____   Not Sure _____

3. Sin is living in a self-centered way.

   Yes _____   No _____   Not Sure _____

4. Sin is failing to love God and your neighbor.

   Yes _____   No _____   Not Sure _____

5. Sin is giving money and power too much value in life.

   Yes _____   No _____   Not Sure _____

6. Is our society in deep trouble because we have forgotten and neglected the laws of God?

   Yes _____   No _____   Not Sure _____

7. Do we experience a sense of sin when we break the ethical norms of society?

   Yes _____   No _____   Not Sure _____

B. Guilt

1. Is guilt a universal human condition?

   Yes _____   No _____   Not Sure _____

2. Do the ministries of the church relieve guilt and reorient life?

   Yes _____   No _____   Not Sure _____

3. Can the church hurt people by creating in them too much of a sense of guilt?

   Yes _____   No _____   Not Sure _____

4. After believing that you have been forgiven do you still struggle with guilt?

   Yes _____   No _____   Not Sure _____

5. Does God always punish the guilty?

   Yes _____   No _____   Not Sure _____

6. Do you feel guilt because of evils in society? (poverty, war, injustice, etc.)

   Yes _____   No _____   Not Sure _____

7. Is it part of the mission of the church to make us aware of our guilt?

   Yes _____   No _____   Not Sure _____

8. Do you believe that people can have guilty feelings that are unrelated to actual guilt?

Yes _____   No _____   Not Sure _____

C. Confession

1. Is confession of sin necessary for faithful Christian living?

Yes _____   No _____   Not Sure _____

2. Is personal confession to a priest or minister necessary in order to receive God's forgiveness?

Yes _____   No _____   Not Sure _____

3. Is confession in public worship important and helpful for you?

Yes _____   No _____   Not Sure _____

4. Is confession to a person you have offended important for forgiveness and reconciliation?

Yes _____   No _____   Not Sure _____

5. Should the church provide support groups where confession and forgiveness can be shared?

Yes _____   No _____   Not Sure _____

D. Repentance

1. Is personal repentance necessary in order to be forgiven by God and others?

Yes _____   No _____   Not Sure _____

2. A most helpful form of repentance is . . .
   (Check those that apply.)

   _____ telling your pastor or priest you have offended and repenting honestly, seeking forgiveness and understanding

_____ going directly to the person you have offended and repenting honestly, seeking forgiveness and understanding

_____ doing a compensatory good deed

_____ performing penitential prayers or deeds

_____ participating in sacraments

_____ denying yourself certain pleasures and privileges

_____ seeking psychological/pastoral counseling

E. Forgiveness

1. What is the experience of forgiveness for you? (Check those that apply.)

   _____ the relief of anxiety and inner pain

   _____ feeling oneself guilt-free

   _____ better able to relate to others

   _____ a sense of joy

   _____ a sense of wholeness and relaxation

   _____ a sense of inner cleanness

   _____ a sense of peace

   _____ a sense of being grounded in God's love

   _____ a desire to share God's love with others

2. Is God forgiving by nature?

   Yes _____   No _____   Not Sure _____

3. Will God forgive any and all sin?

   Yes _____   No _____   Not Sure _____

4. Is it the role of every Christian to be a forgiver?

   Yes _____   No _____   Not Sure _____

5. Is reconciliation with the faith community an essential part of divine forgiveness?

Yes _____   No _____   Not Sure _____

6. Is divine forgiveness a process in time or an event in time?

Process _____   Event _____   Not Sure _____

F. Personal Experience

1. "I experience the need for confession and the forgiveness of God and others when I . . ."
   (Check those that apply.)

   lie

   Yes _____   No _____   Sometimes _____

   steal from others

   Yes _____   No _____   Sometimes _____

   covet the possessions of others

   Yes _____   No _____   Sometimes _____

   dishonor my parents

   Yes _____   No _____   Sometimes _____

   physically or emotionally hurt other people

   Yes _____   No _____   Sometimes _____

   worship money or power

   Yes _____   No _____   Sometimes _____

   take God's name in vain

   Yes _____   No _____   Sometimes _____

   say hurtful things about another person

   Yes _____   No _____   Sometimes _____

   envy another person

   Yes _____   No _____   Sometimes _____

overindulge (food, drink, etc.)

Yes _____   No _____   Sometimes _____

2. Should Christians work with non-Christians to strengthen the moral fiber of society?

Yes _____   No _____   Not Sure _____

G. God's Response

1. God's love for us is unconditional.

Yes _____   No _____   Not Sure _____

2. God's righteousness and love make judgment inevitable.

Yes _____   No _____   Not Sure _____

3. God judges us more by what we do than what we think.

Yes _____   No _____   Not Sure _____

4. God cannot save us or make us new if we do not repent of our sin and confess.

Repent

Yes _____   No _____   Not Sure _____

Confess

Yes _____   No _____   Not Sure _____

5. The righteous and faithful are rewarded by God with eternal life and the unrepentant are condemned by God to hell.

Yes _____   No _____   Not Sure _____

6. God forgives us when we honestly repent and are willing to change.

Yes _____   No _____   Not Sure _____

H. Liturgy

The parts of worship that help me in my need for forgiveness and reconciliation are: (Circle a number: 5 is the most helpful and 1 the least.)

prayer of confession	5	4	3	2	1
liturgy of forgiveness	5	4	3	2	1
Lord's Prayer	5	4	3	2	1
sermon	5	4	3	2	1
sacrament (Eucharist)	5	4	3	2	1
sacrament (reconciliation)	5	4	3	2	1
passing the peace	5	4	3	2	1
Scripture	5	4	3	2	1
silence and time for reflection	5	4	3	2	1
other (please indicate)					

I. Religious Education

Educational experiences that help me deal with my need for forgiveness and reconciliation are: (Circle a number: 5 is the most helpful and 1 the least.)

parent education concerning moral and spiritual development	5	4	3	2	1
resources (books, tapes, videos, etc.) for home use	5	4	3	2	1
storytelling activities (about honesty, forgiveness, etc.)	5	4	3	2	1
study of social problems where forgiveness and/or reconciliation are needed	5	4	3	2	1
training in skills of nonviolent resolution	5	4	3	2	1
preparation sessions for children and youth concerning sacramental life	5	4	3	2	1
Bible study concerning reconciliation	5	4	3	2	1

marriage and family life groups	5	4	3	2	1
small support groups where forgiveness and reconciliation can be experienced	5	4	3	2	1
church school class participation	5	4	3	2	1
youth group	5	4	3	2	1
work teams: studying and serving where conflicts exist and healing is needed	5	4	3	2	1
direct training in methods of forgiveness and reconciliation	5	4	3	2	1

other (please indicate)

J. Social/Political Issues

1. Should Christians approve President Clinton's decision to confess to the world and ask forgiveness when the government had experimented with black men having syphilis instead of treating them?

   Yes _____   No _____   Not Sure _____

2. Should Christians agree it is right for South Africa's Truth Commission to offer amnesty to persons who stepped forward to confess their crimes (even of murder) during the period of apartheid, without necessarily expressing contrition or doing anything to make amendment?

   Yes _____   No _____   Not Sure _____

3. Should the wider Christian community support the decision of the Roman Catholic Church to confess their collaboration with Nazis in the persecution of Jews, and ask for forgiveness?

   Yes _____   No _____   Not Sure _____

4. Beyond apologies and requests for forgiveness, should nations perform acts of restitution and reconciliation?

   Yes _____   No _____   Not Sure _____

Facilitator's Guide
Reconciliation Workshop*

Registration Table:

Lists of room assignments

Family name tags for check-in

Ask for volunteers for Closing Prayer Service.

Each Room:

List of families by the door

List of families on the desk and in the facilitator packet

Materials for opening activity on the assigned area for each family

Questions for video discussion in the facilitator packet

Materials for second activity in the facilitator packet

As families arrive, have music playing over the PA system.

As families arrive have them move to their assigned area where a cate-chist or aide will help them find their materials. Each family will be as-signed a grouping of desks or a place on a table, depending on the room, and at each place the materials for the opening activity will be in

*First Penance Resource Packet, Catholic Diocese of Columbus, Ohio, Department of Religious Education, 1995. Reprinted with permission.

place. Please instruct the family to have a seat and await further instruction.

Opening Activity 15-20 minutes

PURPOSE: To reinforce for the family those actions they do and can do that are reconciling and life-giving

MATERIALS: Large poster — one per family
Red construction-paper hearts — one for each member of the family
Markers, crayons, scissors, glue stick

PROCESS: Directions will be given over the PA system. Facilitators guide the families as directed by the coordinator.
Each family cuts a large heart out of the poster.
Each family puts its name on one side of the heart and begins to decorate the heart.
Each family member tells the other family members one thing he/she did to bring peace or wholeness or joy to the family.
Each person writes that positive thing on the others' hearts. In other words, each family member's heart should have as many positive things written on it as there are family members present for this activity.
When all are finished telling and writing, glue the small hearts onto the large decorated family heart poster.

FACILITATORS: Collect the scissors at the end of this activity.

FILM: The Quarreling Book

FACILITATORS: Be sure the TVs are tuned to channel 3.
When directed to do so, turn on the TV in each room and help maintain a quiet atmosphere so that all can enjoy and understand the film.

16 minutes

At the end of the film, you will be directed to distribute the questions to the families.

They are to discuss these questions *in their family group — NOT the whole room!*

1. What did you like about the video?
2. What happened to make the quarreling stop its hurtful cycle?
3. How do WE handle hurtful moments?

5-7 minutes

FAMILY ACTIVITY

FACILITATORS: Distribute large construction-paper hearts to each family along with markers or pens (whichever you have been given). Directions will be given over the PA system.

PROCESS: Each family has one red heart and writes the family name on one side.

Together, list three or four times/occasions when they remember their family at its best — most happy or loving.

Write these events around the heart.

FACILITATOR: Show the example.

5 minutes

On the other side of the heart, each family member writes one time when he/she did something knowingly that broke or hurt the family harmony as described on the other side of the heart.

5 minutes

Tear the heart into as many pieces as there are family members — tearing around each listed item or brokenness.

Each person has a piece of torn heart. These pieces will be used later in the Prayer Service.

5 minutes

Presentation of rites over the PA system

Review the form for individual confession.

Tell the number of priests who will be available.

Direct the facilitators to distribute the booklets to the family members.

Remind the volunteers to sit near the piano for the Prayer Service.

Remind families to take their poster hearts and their construction-paper heart pieces with them to Church for the Celebration of Reconciliation.

5 minutes

Move to Church for Celebration of Reconciliation.

PA announcements for Family Reconciliation Workshop

Review the form for individual confession.

Since we are beginning with the Prayer Service, all you need to do is make the sign of the cross, tell how long it's been since your last confession (as closely as you can recall), and then share the results of your examination of conscience.

Listen to the priest as he talks with you or asks you questions.

Express your sorrow: an Act of Contrition is on the booklet for your convenience, and each confessor will have one with him or her at Reconciliation.

Receive absolution. (Make the Sign of the Cross when Father blesses you.)

Say "Amen."

Return to your family's pew and pray the prayer you were asked to say or determine what you will do and when.

As a family, bring forward the pieces of your construction-paper heart and place them in the basket at the foot of the altar.

Tell the number of priests who will be available.

REMIND, BEG, DIRECT: PLEASE STAY IN THE PEWS WHILE WAITING YOUR TURN. DO NOT FORM LONG LINES AND DO NOT TALK IN CHURCH UNLESS YOU ARE ACTUALLY TALKING WITH THE PRIEST.

Direct the facilitators to distribute the booklets to the family members.

Remind the volunteers to sit near the piano for the Prayer Service.

Remind families to take their poster hearts and their construction-paper heart pieces with them to Church for the Celebration of Reconciliation.

Psychological Variables That
May Be Involved When We Forgive

Uncovering Phase

1. Examination of psychological defenses (Kiel 1986)

2. Confrontation of anger; the point is to release, not harbor, the anger (Trainer 1981)

3. Admittance of shame, when this is appropriate (Patton 1985)

4. Awareness of cathexia (Droll 1984)

5. Awareness of cognitive rehearsal of the offense (Droll 1984)

6. Insight that the injured party may be comparing self with the injurer (Kiel 1986)

7. Realization that one's self may be permanently and adversely changed by the injury (Close 1970)

8. Insight into a possibly altered "just world" view (Flanigan 1987)

Decision Phase

9. A change of heart, conversion, new insights that old resolution strategies are not working (North 1987)

10. Willingness to consider forgiveness as an option

Note: This appendix is an extension of Enright and the Human Development Study Group (1991). The references shown here at the end of each unit are prototypical examples or discussions of that unit. Reprinted with permission from p. 53 of Robert D. Enright and Joanna North, *Exploring Forgiveness.* © 1998. Reprinted by permission of The University of Wisconsin Press.

11. Commitment to forgive the offender (Neblett 1974)

Work Phase

12. Reframing, through role-taking, who the wrongdoer is by viewing him or her in context (Smith 1981)

13. Empathy toward the offender (Cunningham 1985)

14. Awareness of compassion, as it emerges, toward the offender (Droll 1984)

15. Acceptance and absorption of the pain (Bergin 1988)

Deepening Phase

16. Finding meaning for self and others in the suffering and in the forgiveness process (Frankl 1959)

17. Realization that self has needed others' forgiveness in the past (Cunningham 1985)

18. Insight that one is not alone (universality, support)

19. Realization that self may have a new purpose in life because of the injury

20. Awareness of decreased negative affect and, perhaps, increased positive affect, if this begins to emerge, toward the injurer; awareness of internal, emotional release (Smedes 1984)

Index